THE DISINHERITED

THE DISINHERITED

A Story of Love, Family and Betrayal

Robert Sackville-West

B L O O M S B U R Y

LONDON · NEW DELHI · NEW YORK · SYDNEY

First published in Great Britain 2014

Copyright © 2014 by Robert Sackville-West

The moral right of the author has been asserted

Images are from the author's personal collection except where credited otherwise

Bloomsbury Publishing Plc
50 Bedford Square
London
WC1B 3DP

www.bloomsbury.com

Bloomsbury is a trademark of Bloomsbury Publishing Plc

Bloomsbury Publishing, London, New Delhi, New York and Sydney

A CIP catalogue record for this book is available from the British Library

ISBN 978 1 4088 2482 5

10 9 8 7 6 5 4 3 2

Typeset by Hewer Text UK Ltd, Edinburgh
Printed and bound in Great Britain by CPI Group (UK) Ltd, Croydon CR0 4YY

For Freya, Arthur and Edie

THE SACKVILLES OF KNOLE

Owners of Knole are in CAPITALS

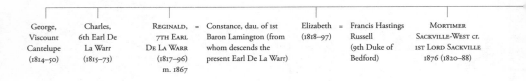

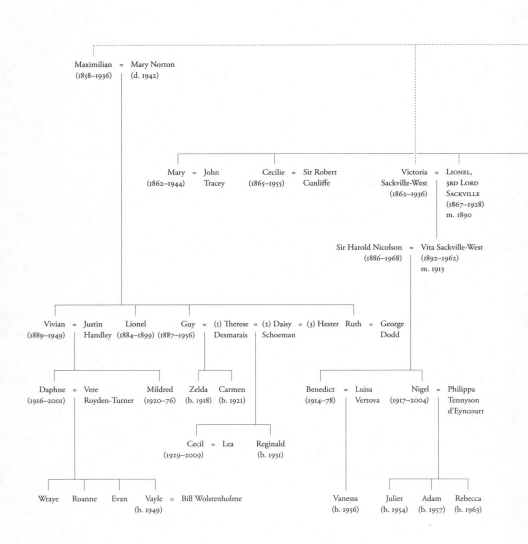

George,
Viscount
Cantelupe
(1814–50)

Charles,
6th Earl De
La Warr
(1815–73)

REGINALD,
7TH EARL
DE LA WARR
(1817–96)
m. 1867

= Constance, dau. of 1st
Baron Lamington (from
whom descends the
present Earl De La Warr)

Elizabeth
(1818–97)

= Francis Hastings
Russell
(9th Duke of
Bedford)

MORTIMER
SACKVILLE-WEST cr.
1ST LORD SACKVILLE
1876 (1820–88)

Maximilian
(1858–1936)

= Mary Norton
(d. 1942)

Mary
(1862–1944)

= John
Tracey

Cecilie
(1865–1955)

= Sir Robert
Cunliffe

Victoria
Sackville-West
(1862–1936)

= LIONEL,
3RD LORD
SACKVILLE
(1867–1928)
m. 1890

Sir Harold Nicolson
(1886–1968)

= Vita Sackville-West
(1892–1962)
m. 1913

Vivian
(1889–1949)

= Justin
Handley

Lionel
(1884–1899)

Guy
(1887–1956)

= (1) Therese
Desmarais

= (2) Daisy
Schoeman

= (3) Hester

Ruth

= George
Dodd

Daphne
(1916–2001)

= Vere
Royden-Turner

Mildred
(1920–76)

Zelda
(b. 1918)

Carmen
(b. 1921)

Benedict
(1914–78)

= Luisa
Vertova

Nigel
(1917–2004)

= Philippa
Tennyson
d'Eyncourt

Cecil
(1929–2009)

= Lea

Reginald
(b. 1931)

Wraye

Roanne

Evan

Vayle
(b. 1949)

= Bill Wolstenholme

Vanessa
(b. 1956)

Juliet
(b. 1954)

Adam
(b. 1957)

Rebecca
(b. 1963)

ELIZABETH = George West, 5th Earl De La Warr
(1795–1870) assumed name and arms of Sackville-West 1843
m. 1813 (1791–1869)

Mary = (1) James = (2) Edward   Col. Hon. William = Georgina, dau. of
(1824–1900)   Gascoyne-Cecil   Stanley (15th   Edward Sackville-   George Dodwell
              (2nd Marquess   Earl of Derby)   West (1830–1905)   m. 1860
              of Salisbury)

                        LIONEL, – Josefa Duran = Juan Antonio   Arabella = Sir Alexander
                        2ND LORD   (Pepita)   de Oliva   (1835–69)   Bannerman
                        SACKVILLE (1830–71)   (1831–88)
                        (1827–1908)

Gabriel = Flora   Amalia = (Richard)   Henry = Emélie
Salanson   (1866–c. 1925)   (1868–1945)   William Martin   (1869–1914)   Alexandre
(d. 1935)   (d. 1914)

      Lionel = Odette   Elie
      (1890–1954)   Derminot   (b. 1895)

Maud, dau. of (1) = MAJ.-GEN. SIR CHARLES = (2) Anne, widow of   Hon. Bertrand = Eva, dau. of
Capt. Matthew Bell   SACKVILLE-WEST, 4TH LORD   Stephen Bigelow   Sackville-West   Maj.-Gen. Inigo
(d. 1920)   SACKVILLE (1870–1962)   (1872–1959)   Richmond Jones

      Edward, 5th Lord Sackville   Diana
      (1901–65)   (1906–75)

Elizabeth = Thomas   Jacobine, dau. of (1) = Lionel, 6th = (3) Jean, widow of   Hugh = Bridget, dau. of
(1911–88)   Barlow   J. R. Menzies-   Lord Sackville   Sir Edward Imbert-   Sackville-West   Capt. Robert
                            Wilson (d. 1971)   (1913–2004)   Terry (d. 2009)   (1919–2001)   Cunliffe, RN

Henry   Anna
(b. 1944)   (b. 1949)

            Teresa   Catherine   Sophia   Victoria   Sarah
            (b. 1954) (b. 1956) (b. 1957) (b. 1959) (b. 1960)

Jane, dau. of = Robert, 7th Lord Sackville   Mary   Elizabeth   Jane   William
Mark MacAndrew   (b. 1958)   (b. 1960)   (b. 1962)   (b. 1964)   (b. 1967)

Freya (b. 1998)   Arthur (b. 2000)   Edie (b. 2003)

Contents

Introduction   1

1   The Villa Pepa   23
2   Lost in Translation   48
3   Continental Drift   68
4   The Surprise Inheritance   90
5   Sibling Rivalry   113
6   Laying Claim to Knole   129
7   Parallel Lives   160
8   Skulduggery in Spain   172
9   A Death in the Family   192
10   In the High Court   210
11   'Sackville Tragedy in Paris Flat'   226
12   Victims of Circumstance   237
13   Slaving Away at Knole for Nothing   259

Notes   281
Select Bibliography   287
Acknowledgements   293
Index   299

Introduction

One evening in October 1852, my great-grandfather, William Edward Sackville-West, accompanied his older brother Lionel to the theatre in Paris. Lionel pointed out to him a very pretty young woman sitting on the other side of the hall, and expressed the wish that he would meet her soon, as he knew her only by sight. His wish was soon to be granted. Just over a week before Lionel was due to return to Stuttgart, where he had been posted by the Foreign Office, Sir Frederick Arthur, an older friend of his, and man of the world, took him to the Hôtel de Bade on the Boulevard des Italiens and introduced him to the pretty young woman, who had taken rooms there. She was a dancer, generally known as Pepita de Oliva, and was en route from Madrid to Germany to fulfil a series of professional engagements.

Many years later, those who had met Pepita in her twenties would still remember her beauty, and the airy and graceful way she walked: '*muy airoso*', they would say as they recalled the young woman who had caught their attention as she swayed down the street. Hers were the sort of striking features that 'would remain impressed on one's memory': her olive complexion, her tiny waist, her large, dark, almond-shaped eyes, the gentle smile that always played on her lips. But it was the extraordinary luxuriance of her hair that was her crowning glory: black, shiny, and naturally waved, without the aid of curling irons. Those who had had the good fortune to see her hair down, as she combed it, always commented that it reached below her knees. On occasion, she even let it down on stage to prove to the audience that it was real. In all portraits of Pepita, a lock of this fine hair forms a kiss-curl, or *sortijilla*, on each temple, licking the tip of her ear.

Pepita as a young woman in the 1850s

My great-great-uncle Lionel later recalled how Sir Frederick and he 'treated her as a respectable danseuse, with respect and propriety, for aught I know she was at that time living a perfectly respectable life'. Nevertheless, his 'intimacy', as he described it, with Pepita started soon after his introduction to her, and at her initiative: 'She first suggested this condition of things to me on the occasion of my second or third visit to her. I seriously say this. I visited her partly with the intention of its leading up to that object, the actual fact came about at her solicitation.'

For his last week in Paris, he visited her every day, and although he did not reside at the hotel, he 'lived in adultery with her'.

Lionel was the fifth son of the 5th Earl De La Warr and his wife Elizabeth, who, as it happens, were in Paris at the same time as their sons, but unaware of Lionel's romantic adventures. He had entered the diplomatic service at the age of eighteen, as one of the few career options considered suitable for Victorian gentlemen. His older brothers had already chosen the others – Charles the Army, Reginald the Church, and Mortimer the Court – and so it was that, in February 1852, at the age of twenty-four, Lionel had been appointed to his first salaried posting, as attaché in Stuttgart. As a fifth son, he had, or so it appeared, very little prospect of succeeding to either of his family's two inheritances: Buckhurst Park, a comfortable house and estate in Sussex, or Knole in Kent, a stately home (where I now live) with its legendary 365 rooms, fifty-two staircases and seven courtyards. Lionel's father had been Lord Chamberlain to the Royal Household in the 1840s, and his mother was a close friend of Queen Victoria, who was a regular visitor to Buckhurst.

Pepita's origins could not have been more different to her lover's. She had been born in the backstreets of Málaga in southern Spain in 1830. 'Oh such a slum it is,' her granddaughter Vita Sackville-West wrote, when she was taken by the poet Muñoz Rojas to Pepita's birthplace in 1949 on a lecture tour for the British Council; 'very narrow, you could almost shake hands from one little balcony to the other overhead, crowded with people and children, but there can be no doubt at all that it was exactly the same when Pepita was a little girl'.

Pepita's father, Pedro Duran, was a barber by trade, who died when Pepita was about six. Accounts vary as to the cause of his death, from being accidentally shot in the finger during a festival to expiring from a bad cough. After Pedro's death, Pepita's mother, Catalina, who had grown up helping her own father make canvas sandals, moved house to the Calle de la Puente, where she took in washing for about a year, before starting to sell clothes door-to-door. It was not long before Catalina's lover, Manuel Lopez, a shoe-maker, moved in with them, bringing with him his daughter Lola.

Pepita's older brother Diego was always rather wild – or 'harum scarum' as people described him – and generally eluded his mother's control, and so Catalina channelled her energies into her daughter. She was very ambitious for Pepita, paying for her to go to school, and then to dancing lessons, and for the silk dresses that she had to wear for those lessons. But her efforts were not wasted. By her late teens, Pepita was dancing in the Theatre Principal in Málaga, where a cousin of Catalina recalled her first night: 'She was the best dancer . . . She was just like a bird in the air, she danced so well.'

In January 1849, Catalina and Manuel moved to Madrid to seek their fortune, and in the autumn took Pepita for an audition with Antonio Ruiz, director of the ballet at the Teatro del Principe (or Teatro Español). Ruiz arranged for her to have lessons in Spanish dancing with a member of his company, but another dancer, a twenty-year-old called Juan Antonio de Oliva had seen Pepita and fallen in love with her at first sight, and managed to replace him as Pepita's teacher. Within a few months of their first lesson, Pepita and Oliva were engaged.

They were married on 10 January 1851 in the parish church of San Millán, where Oliva had been baptised. Pepita was 'dressed in black and wore a black lace mantilla but no veil', causing Oliva's Madrilenian sister to remark – with some regional snobbery – that 'she looked like an Andalusian going to a bullfight'. The ceremony was followed by a wedding breakfast at the Café Suizo, and then dinner at the Fonde de Europa, with dancing afterwards in a hall hired for the occasion. The couple lived at first with Catalina and Manuel at

Pepita's husband, Juan Antonio de Oliva

15 Calle de la Encomienda, travelling around Spain on dancing engagements, to Toledo, and then to Valencia, where they separated in the spring of 1851. The causes of the split are unclear. According to his sister, Isabel, Oliva himself was 'always very reticent in the family circle as to the relations between himself and Pepita' but 'stated that the causes of the separation were not honourable to Pepita, and that there were some things which he could not tolerate and that he blamed mostly her mother'. Some people said that Oliva was a spendthrift and a gambler, while others felt that Oliva was holding Pepita back in a career that was just beginning to take off. In October 1851, Pepita danced in the Grand Theatre in Bordeaux, and the following May at Her Majesty's Theatre in London. *The Times* 'respectfully' announced 'the first appearance of the Spanish dancer Dona Pepita Oliva' in a divertissement following a production of Bellini's celebrated opera *Norma*.

The fact that Pepita was already married when Lionel first met her in October 1852 – a fact that was later to have significant consequences for all the characters in this story – made him think that 'it was a wrong thing to have this liaison with her'. But it did little to deter him. Over the course of an on-off relationship that lasted until her death in 1871, Pepita was to have seven 'illegitimate' children, five of whom survived into adulthood. The second of these children was called Victoria, and was the mother of the writer Vita Sackville-West.

In 1936, Vita came across a trunk of unpublished documents as she was clearing out her mother's house near Brighton, shortly after Victoria's death. The papers included witness statements taken in Spain and France fifty years before, in preparation for a high-profile succession case, and they helped Vita to clarify a number of family myths that had grown up around her mother's heritage: for example, that Pepita was *not* the illegitimate daughter of a gypsy acrobat and the Spanish Duke of Osuna. Vita took the papers back to Sissinghurst, and began to research and write *Pepita*, the double portrait of her mother, Victoria, and her grandmother, Pepita. It was published to great acclaim and commercial success in October 1937 (it sold 10,000 copies in the first two months) and was to be perhaps the most personal, warm and appealing of all Vita's books.

Vita used *Pepita* to explore the duality in her own nature: her mixture of conventionality and unconventionality, the English and the Spanish, the grandee and the gypsy. In her attempts to describe her relationship with her mother, Vita emphasised Victoria's 'Spanish' characteristics. 'Although on one side of her lineage,' she wrote, Victoria 'had the opulent Sackvilles aligned behind her, on the other she had all that rapscallion Spanish background.'

I remember reading *Pepita* as a teenager. Like many others, I was captivated by its deeply romantic account of the affair of an Andalusian dancer with an English lord. I had been brought up on the staider, more conventional side of the Sackville family, a side apparently unstirred by passionate Spanish blood. And so I was thrilled by this washing of the family's dirty linen in public, just as I was thrilled by *Portrait of a Marriage*, which I read around the same time. *Portrait*, an account by Pepita's great-grandson, Nigel Nicolson, of the unconventional marriage of his parents, both of whom were homosexual, divided opinion within the family, just as *Pepita* had done. For me, it came as a rather delicious revelation that life at Knole could ever have been quite so rackety and louche. It also highlighted a difference in temperament between two branches of the family: the Sackvilles, who have always been a reserved and reticent family, keeping their secrets safely guarded; and the Nicolsons, who have always lived their lives more publicly. At the time, Vita's uncle Charlie wrote to her to say that he was 'cross' and upset by the way the Sackville men were portrayed in *Pepita*, just as a generation later my uncle Lionel was furious with Nigel at his revelations in *Portrait of a Marriage*.

Many years later, I was researching *Inheritance*, my book about Knole and the Sackville family, who have lived there for the past 400 years, and was beginning to worry that it might become simply the story of one damned duke (and his dancing girl) after another (for Pepita was by no means the first foreign dancer in the family). And then it dawned on me that the book was really about the power of a place. For hundreds of years, Knole has pulled generations of Sackvilles in and then pushed them away with an energy and character far more intense than that of any of the individuals who have lived there. This power was felt particularly by those members of the family who never had a hope of inheriting – the daughters, the younger sons, the widows. But what about the bastards, the doubly disinherited? One of these illegitimate children, Victoria, was the subject of the second half of *Pepita* and featured prominently in *Inheritance*. I have spent many days in her mercurial company, in the improbably bucolic setting of the University of Indiana in Bloomington, immersed in her detailed personal diaries that now reside there. But Victoria had four equally illegitimate siblings – Max, Flora, Amalia and Henry – and it is their story, too, that I set out to tell here.

In the family albums in the Library at Knole there are photographs, as you would expect, of all the 'official' Sackvilles: of elderly dowagers plodding around the gardens at Buckhurst; of my great-grandfather William Edward; of Mortimer looking saturnine, a pair of mutton-chop whiskers almost meeting at his chin; of Lionel as a foppish young man, around the time he met Pepita, lounging against a pillar, his hands stuffed into the tops of his trousers and his hat at a jaunty angle. There are pictures of him as an older man as well, with those heavy-lidded Sackville eyes and a lugubrious, hangdog expression. But what came as more of a surprise was the inclusion in these albums of the 'unofficial' Sackvilles, of children with swarthier, Spanish looks.

As I was writing *Inheritance*, I was continually sidetracked by photos of these very different-looking children, many of them taken in photographers' studios in France in the 1870s. There is Flora, with her luxuriant hair, in peasant costume; Amalia, a young girl in a smock with a lace collar; Henry, heavy-set and glaring at the photographer, as he sits on a barrel in a sailor's suit against the painted backdrop of a storm-tossed sea. There are photos of Flora on a steamship to America, and of Amalia as a young woman at Knole and in Cannes, with her cinched-in waist and her bird-like features. The children's guardians are there too: Count Henri de Béon, looking dashing as a young man, and later, as he leans against a haystack in a makeshift agricultural setting, very much the gentleman of property, his waistcoat beginning to strain at the paunch; the Count's mother is there, and so is Lionel's friend Marion Mulhall. And who on earth is that frightful bounder in a monocle and bowler hat, with his wing collar and waxed moustache?

Lionel (*far left*), lounging against a pillar in the Stone Court at Knole, with his brothers and sisters

After his first week in Paris with Pepita, Lionel returned to Stuttgart in November 1852, and used his influence with the manager of the theatre there to get his new lover a dancing engagement. Pepita performed in Stuttgart for three weeks before moving on to other theatres in Germany. Once Lionel had been appointed first attaché in Berlin in June 1853, where he was to remain for the next five years, it was easy for him to visit Pepita in the towns in which she was dancing: Hamburg, Breslau, Frankfurt, Mannheim, Cologne, Bremen, Heidelberg. Pepita always stayed in what Lionel referred to as 'first-rate hotels', and he would join her there: at the Marquardt in Stuttgart, the Bade in Paris, the Trombetta in Turin. And, in this way, what he described, rather forensically, as the 'immoral intercourse' between himself and Pepita continued over the years and across the capitals of Europe. There were the occasional separations, for example when Lionel heard that Pepita was living with a Prince Youssoupoff in Munich in 1855, and felt obliged to write to her 'expostulating with her on her conduct'.

Pepita was always more celebrated abroad than in the land of her birth. She was one of several Spanish dancers who found fame and fortune in Europe in the mid-nineteenth century, dancing traditional dances from their native country: La Madrilena, La Aragonesa, El Jaleo de Jerez, and her favourite, El Ole, a dance from Andalusia. Spain was seen at the time as rather exotic, and these dances captured some of the passion and pride, sensuality and raw energy popularly associated with the country. The rattling of the castanets, the clicking of the fingers, the swaying of the body, the flashing of the eyes, and the stamping of the feet were far from the orthodoxies of classical, French-Italian ballet, the pirouettes and entrechats. At the height of her career in 1854–5, Pepita would be filling theatres night after night, for three to four weeks running in a major city, before moving on – generally by train – to the next venue on her European tour. She usually topped the bill in the large commercial theatres, where she performed in Berlin, Vienna, Budapest, Prague, Copenhagen, coming on solo for half an hour at the beginning and end of a show, which might also include a play or another variety act. It was very hard work, and the only real time off was the summer months when the theatres were closed.

There was undoubtedly an erotic, as well as exotic, draw to her performance. By the standards of the time, she was scantily dressed: her bodice tight, to draw attention to her bust, and her skirts short and often swirled into the air with flamenco

© Nicolson family

Pepita, dancing *La Aragonesa*

abandon to reveal her legs. Commercially produced lithograph portraits of Pepita appeared in the cities in which she was performing. These draw attention to her tiny waist, lovely eyes and heavy, winged eyebrows, her thick wavy hair parted at the centre, and the kiss-curl at each temple. In some of the portraits she is dancing, her arms arched above her head, her fingers clasping castanets. Vita had a portrait of her grandmother dancing La Aragonesa, which conveyed a great 'impression of energy and vitality'.

The short ballet skirt of rose red silk is flounced with white and blue. She wears a tight bodice of white satin with panels of dark blue velvet. Her throat and shoulders are bare, but for the narrow shoulder straps provocatively slipping. She is lightly poised on one toe, her tiny foot pointed in a pink satin slipper. Two pink roses lie dropped on the ground beside her; a third one nestles in her dark hair behind her ear. A heavy gold bangle encircles one wrist; the castanets are lightly held. Her eyes flash, and her lips are parted in a smile.

Another portrait in Vita's possession was of Pepita dancing El Ole, in which 'she is wearing a tight bodice and short flounced skirt, also a wide sash with long heavily embroidered ends. In her ear is the brilliant ear-ring; her hair floats loosely far below her waist. Again, as in the other picture, her lips are parted, but this time she is not smiling.' Contemporary cartoons, meanwhile, show gentlemen plucking the flowers from their wives' hairdos to throw at Pepita's feet on the stage. There were several precedents for liaisons between these Spanish dancers of the demi-monde and European aristocrats – notably, that of the Irish-born Spanish dancer Lola Montez with King Ludwig of Bavaria in the late 1840s.

I could not help noticing an echo of a previous passage in Knole's history. During my researches into *Inheritance,* I was increasingly struck by a number of recurring themes: how Knole was built and then furnished on the profits of public office; how the family fortunes reflected those of the English aristocracy in general; how depression afflicted generation after generation of Sackvilles, prompting their gradual withdrawal and the withdrawal of their house from the world; how they tended to take Italian or Spanish dancers as mistresses. In the late eighteenth century, John Frederick Sackville, 3rd Duke of Dorset, installed his mistress, the Italian ballet dancer, Giovanna Baccelli, at Knole, and commissioned the painter Thomas Gainsborough to produce a full-length portrait of her. He captured Baccelli mid-movement, in a moment of perfect equilibrium. You cannot help feeling that the work of these commercial artists in the mid-nineteenth century presents a rather cheaper, cut-price version of Pepita the dancer.

Pepita returned regularly from northern Europe to visit her friends and family in Spain, and sometimes her mother and

Manuel would follow her to Germany. Each year, Pepita appeared more prosperous than the year before. On one of her trips home in the early 1850s, she was staying at the Peninsulares in Madrid, one of the splendid hotels to which she had grown accustomed, and arranged to meet Manuel Guerrero y Casares, director of ballet at the Teatro Real. Although Manuel never thought much of her dancing, he did note the magnificence of her jewellery, in particular a heart-shaped gold pendant hanging from her neck with a large emerald in its centre and a surround of diamonds. A cousin of Catalina's, who earned his living selling fruit off the back of a donkey, was struck by a very similar piece of jewellery when he had lunch with Pepita and her mother in Málaga, on their brief return to the city of her birth. 'They seemed much better off – they were all dressed like gentle-people,' he observed.

By the mid-1850s, Pepita was at the height of her career, and a wealthy woman. When, a couple of years after their meeting in Madrid, she bumped into Manuel Guerrero again, this time in Vienna, she was dressed as splendidly as before, with the same superb jewellery, but this time she also had 'a magnificent carriage with a splendid pair of horses, coachman and footman and everything of the first order'. He could not help noticing that, however polished and refined Pepita had become, there was still 'something in the carriage of her body which stamped her as not being a lady of birth'. Manuel Guerrero saw her once more in 1858 in Copenhagen, where Pepita was performing her trademark El Ole at the Casino Theatre. She was staying at one of the most expensive hotels in the city, probably the Hotel d'Angleterre, 'in great style and ostentatious luxury'. And yet again, he had something slightly sniffy to say about Pepita – perhaps due to some professional rivalry with his own wife, the Spanish dancer Petra Camara. When shown a portrait of Pepita he recalled that this was 'exactly the posture in which she used to place herself though I do not consider it artistic'.

By now Catalina and Manuel had settled in Granada, at No. 8 Calle de las Arandas. The lawyer who lived opposite remembered Pepita visiting, and their talking several times across the street from their respective balconies. Pepita was 'beautiful and sympathetic and of pleasant conversation'. She was, he continued, 'in the habit of going to and coming from foreign countries where she performed, gaining a lot of money, with which she supported her mother's house, which always displayed excessive luxury . . . It was said that she had relations or an engagement with some foreign personage of importance, very rich and who gave her heaps of money.'

In the summer of 1855, however, Catalina and Manuel were driven out of Granada by an outbreak of cholera, and escaped to the small town of Albolote, four miles away. Here they bought the Casa Blanca, a house in the main square, which they refurbished extensively. 'It was handsomely furnished for people in that class of life,' noted the local priest. They had a four-wheeled carriage with a cover over the top, and two carriage horses called Malagueño and Garbozo – all in all, a very 'stylish turn out'. In addition, Manuel had a saddle horse, a dark chestnut named Esmeralda, and there was a horse for Pepita to ride when she visited, a piebald called La Preciosa. The garrulous Catalina would boast about her daughter, 'The Star of Andalusia', *La Estrella de Andalusia*, as she was known abroad, and describe the exalted company she kept in Germany, including veiled references to some Bavarian prince. Catalina told everyone that it was Pepita's money that kept them in such style, a fact confirmed by her next-door neighbour who observed that Catalina and Manuel certainly did nothing themselves to earn a living – 'all they did was to spend their daughter's money'.

Some of their new neighbours were snobbish about Manuel and Catalina. Goggle-eyed, and short and stout of stature, an 'insignificant, common-looking chap', Manuel swiftly became a figure of fun, 'like a workman dressed as a gentleman', wearing a gold chain and rings. He 'seemed to be the sort of man who might have risen from the position of artisan and had suddenly become better off', claimed the village priest; 'Catalina looked very well when dressed, but when one entered into conversation with her – one plainly saw traces of an inferior origin.' She and Manuel were said to quarrel frequently, 'and she had been heard to tell him during these quarrels, that she would kick him out and send him back to his trade'.

The couple gave themselves a great many airs and graces. For example, they would have their servants carry up to four luxurious armchairs from the Casa Blanca to church every Sunday – one for Catalina, one for Manuel, and one each for Pepita and Lola if they were there. These would then be placed prominently facing the High Altar, in front of the congregation. One villager overheard the priest telling Catalina that the 'Church was not a Theatre and the chairs must be taken away'. 'So far as I know,' he continued, 'they did not attend Mass again.'

In the summer of 1856, Pepita came from Germany to stay with her mother at the Casa Blanca, accompanied by Manuel's daughter Lola, a couple of servants, and two black dogs with long woolly coats called Prinnie and Charlie. The party alighted from the stagecoach at the point where the road to Albolote leaves the main road from Granada to Jaen, and was met by Pepita's family in their carriage, who took them back to the house. A day or two later, Catalina held a party for Pepita at the Casa Blanca, to which she invited the local magistrate and the entire town council. A brass band from the neighbouring village of Atarfe was hired to serenade her, and there was dancing into the small hours, as chocolates, sweets and liqueurs were handed round. Pepita, who was wearing 'a rose-coloured silk skirt with flounces, and very good jewellery', greeted everyone and went out onto the balcony to salute the people in the square below. 'It was a regular fete,' recalled Micaela Gonzalez

Molina, the wife of a local cattle-dealer and Catalina's next-door neighbour.

Pepita stayed for almost two months. Villagers remembered her many years later, strolling in the street, or chatting from the balcony of the house. She dazzled the local landowners' sons with her striking looks. José Ramirez Galan was one of those who, as a teenager, serenaded Pepita soon after her arrival, and then became a regular visitor to Catalina's evening receptions where there was music, dancing and light refreshments. 'I remember Pepita teaching me to waltz – she wore slippers of gold-brocaded velvet. I thought I should have died of ecstasy – she was so charming and handsome . . . Her face and figure remain engraved upon my memory, notwithstanding the lapse of time.' After Pepita had left Albolote, Catalina gave him a portrait of her daughter as a souvenir, which he kept in a drawer with his papers. Every now and then he would take it out to look at, for 'she was worthy of being remembered' – until, five years later, he got married, and his new wife made sure that it was tidied away for good. José's older brother, Francisco Ramirez Galan, used to go to the evening parties at the Casa Blanca, too, and remembered Pepita as 'very attractive, dangerously so. I was a young man at the time and she made a great impression on me.' The other members of the family were less impressive, however: 'Pepita appeared to be superior to the others; but the rest were inferior. Lopez used to dress up and show off on horseback . . . He was just the sort of man to get up on the box and take the reins.'

As well as Pepita's looks, it was her finery that was much remarked upon: the dresses, the silver salvers she had brought from abroad, and the jewellery that was remembered in great detail years later, not just the heart-shaped gold pendant, but also a brooch shaped like a lizard and 'set with streaks of gold and emeralds alternately', a gold brooch in the shape of a frog with blue stones, and 'a great number of bracelets, including one shaped like a snake'.

Pepita paid a second visit to Albolote in the summer of 1857, but there was far less stir this time and she only stayed three weeks. By now Catalina had bought a new house, the Caseria Buena Vista, sometimes known as La Caseria de los Pavos Reales (The House of the Peacocks), on the outskirts of Granada. There was a garden, a kitchen garden, an orchard, a meadow and some arable land, plus a couple of small vine-yards, where Don Manuel would spend his time 'giving directions to the men' – when he was not 'shooting rabbits, or any birds he could see'.

Before they left Albolote, Catalina and Manuel stripped and gutted the Casa Blanca, removing many of its architectural features: the ornamental iron bars that framed the windows, the marble sinks, mantelpieces and fireplaces, windows, balconies, an iron gate, indeed anything else that might come in handy as they renovated Buena Vista. Pride of place went to a bronze statuette of Pepita dancing El Ole, which they placed in the basin of a fountain in the courtyard at Buena Vista. From then on, the house was often known as the Caseria de la Bailarina.

Pepita visited Buena Vista in the spring of 1858 – the year emblazoned on a large new entrance gateway to the property. This time she was pregnant, and she stayed for six months or so. Occasionally she was spotted strolling in the vineyard, and at least one labourer recollected 'with admiration' her 'large dark eyes [and] long arched eyebrows. She was a very hand-some woman.'

At around midday on 20 May, Pepita gave birth to a boy. When Pepita had trouble suckling the child, Catalina engaged a wet-nurse called Ana, who was herself the veteran of ten chil-dren (and two miscarriages). The baby, who eventually came to be known as Max, was baptised three days later in the parish church of San Ildefonso, as the legitimate son of Don Juan

Antonio Gabriel de la Oliva and Dona Josefa Dominga Duran (although the couple had lived apart for more than six years). His names, in full, were Maximiliano Leon José Manuele Enrique Bernardino: the first was seen as confirmation by some that his real father was Duke Maximilian Joseph in Bavaria, one of the godparents; the second was the Spanish equivalent of Lionel, another contender for paternity. The Duke, or Max in Bayern as he was often known, was a member of the Bavarian royal family, but a free spirit, nevertheless, with a passion for folk music, and in particular for playing the zither. In summer he could be seen hiking around the forests near his home at Possenhofen castle in peasant dress, but he was equally at home in the concert halls and theatres of Germany and Austria, which is where he probably met Pepita.

After the christening, a crowd of people, mostly boys, followed Pepita's carriage with its escort of two mounted Civil Guards, the mile or so from the church to the house. As they went, they picked up the silver coins thrown to them from a straw basket by the coachman, in a traditional gesture of largesse.

Several months later, Pepita returned to Germany with Max and a nurse, to a house she had bought in Heidelberg. Lionel stayed with them in 1859, paying some of the household expenses and 'an occasional wine bill or something of that sort'. That spring, Pepita's aunt Micaela and her husband, who was going blind, came to Heidelberg for medical treatment, which Pepita paid for. They stayed in lodgings nearby, also at Pepita's expense, and Micaela saw Pepita almost every day. On a couple of occasions she remembered meeting a foreign gentleman, who appeared to take particular notice of the child: 'I heard from Pepita that he was a personage. He had all the appearance of being wealthy. He was rather tall, fair, good-looking and handsome, of a distinguished appearance . . . I think I heard that his house was somewhere in or about London . . . He appeared to be in the prime of life.'

Lionel continued to visit Pepita as much as his official duties and her professional engagements would allow. He was now secretary at the legation in Turin, and in the summer of 1860 he took to renting villas for Pepita and Max for a few weeks at a time in northern Italy. The first of these was on the outskirts of Turin. A colleague from the legation, Dudley Saurin, would later recall accompanying Lionel on his walk from work at the end of the day to within a short distance of the villa, 'and then I went to the right and he to the left'. For it was understood that Lionel would never introduce his mistress to his colleagues or take her out into 'Society', like other members of the legation. After Turin, there were villas in Como, Arona (on Lake Maggiore) and Genoa. While Pepita stayed in Italy that summer, under his 'protection', as Lionel described it, 'the intercourse continued'.

In 1861, Pepita returned to Germany, to a house she had bought in Hakenfelde on the outskirts of Berlin. Lionel stayed with her there for two months in the winter of 1861–2 – 'the longest time I had ever stayed with her up to that time' – and it was presumably then that Pepita's second child, Victoria, was conceived. Catalina was staying there too for some of the time, and it was possibly from her, via her son Diego, that news filtered back to Oliva that Pepita had a child. Although Oliva never saw the son whose baptism certificate proclaimed he was his, he told people that everyone said the boy looked 'very handsome, quite a jewel' and just like him.

Victoria was born at apartments Lionel had taken for Pepita at 4 Avenue de l'Impératrice (now Avenue Foch) in Paris on 23 September 1862. In contrast to Max's papers, Victoria's certificate of baptism described her as the daughter of Josephine Duran and of a *'père inconnu'*, 'father unknown'. Lionel was there for the birth, as were Catalina and Manuel. But soon after, Lionel and Pepita appear to have separated. It was only when Lionel received a telegram in Turin two years later, saying that Pepita was very ill, that he hastened to Baden

Baden, where she was with Max and Victoria. Pepita confessed
that she had just had a miscarriage, and had been living with
someone else, 'but who he was', claimed Lionel, 'I never could
find out'. Their reconciliation marked a turning-point in their
relationship.

Pepita's career had, in any case, begun to peter out, and she
gave up dancing. Their life together became more domestic.
Whether Lionel's lack of commitment had contributed to their
separation or not, it was certainly the case that Pepita had been
seeking a greater sense of legitimacy. Lionel later described how,
after Victoria's birth, Pepita begged him that if she had any other
children by him, he would have them registered in his name. 'I
always resented this idea,' he complained, 'and objected as long
as I could. Ultimately I was prevailed upon as will afterwards
appear.' As it happened, all Pepita's children after Victoria were
to be registered rather differently from her first two.

Pepita made her last visit to Buena Vista probably in 1863. A
lawyer, acting for the family in a dispute concerning a right of
way through the property, particularly remembered her little
boy being fond of some lozenges the lawyer was taking for a
throat infection. Pepita told him that she was a dancer, 'living
under the protection of an English gentleman, to whom she
was not married'. She had, however, 'sufficient money to overcome the well-known scruples of the Granadinos on such
subjects, and the best society in Granada went to her house'.

In 1864, there was a sale at Buena Vista 'of everything in the
house'. Rafaela Moreno Pinel, who lived nearby, remembered
how the sale was superintended by Catalina. 'Now and then
Manuel Lopez tried to intervene, but she turned him away
saying "You don't know how to manage these things." She
drove a hard bargain, but he was more indulgent.' Rafaela
bought a good many things: a glass toilet bottle engraved
'Pepita de Oliva'; plated forks and spoons engraved 'C.O.' for
Catalina Ortega; and a dining table (although she had to wait

till some time afterwards for one of its leaves to be delivered, since Catalina and Manuel carried on using it as a table top, supported on packing cases, until they actually left the house).

It is possible that Oliva and Pepita continued to have a certain affection for each other – some people even said that tears would form in Pepita's eyes whenever his name was mentioned. Lionel, too, acknowledged that she was 'continually in communication' with Oliva by letter, and 'used to send him money to keep him quiet as she always dreaded his claiming some rights over her or the children'. Perhaps this explains Oliva's arrival in Albolote in 1867 to take possession, as the legitimate husband of Pepita, of the Casa Blanca.

That summer, Oliva was performing at the Teatro Isabel la Católica in Granada. Every morning, when rehearsals were over at about eleven, he would leave on horseback for Albolote and spend the day there supervising the workmen dismantling the house, before returning for the evening show at half past seven. He became a standing joke, as he regaled his fellow dancers with his sales of the day: a doorway, a window frame, 'so many cartloads of bricks', and so on. Over the course of a fortnight he salvaged lintels, tiles, wooden beams, fireplaces, and sold them on the spot until pretty much all that remained of the house were some of the external walls. Eventually, the town council gave Oliva notice not to pull anything more down, as the house adjoined a public place and was becoming dangerous. Under a power of attorney that he claimed had been given to him by Pepita, he then sold the Casa Blanca to the Gonzalez family next door. One of his colleagues later recalled being told by Oliva in 1867 that 'he was getting some money from a house which belonged to his wife Pepita Oliva, the famous dancer . . . He said that there had been a son born, to which his name had been given, that he had intended taking judicial proceedings, and that in order to stop his mouth the family had given him something.'

It was not the last that anyone would hear of Oliva. Lionel

himself noticed his name on a playbill in Madrid in 1867, and went to watch him dance. By then Oliva was a little stouter, as photographs of him in his dancing clothes show, looking like a portly bullfighter. Catalina too was spotted many years later, by one of her former neighbours from Albolote, in a secondhand shop in Málaga. 'There was a great difference in her appearance and apparel from what I remembered her,' he noted. 'She seemed crestfallen and in straitened circumstances – she seemed decayed. I just bowed to her.' And Pepita, the inspiration for Vita's book and the starting point of this one, settled in south-west France, where she was to assume a new role as a mother and home-maker.

Such was the fate of some of the key characters described in the witness statements which Vita discovered in the trunk in her mother's house. Those documents offer a window into another world – the teeming backstreets of Málaga in the mid-nineteenth century, with its cast of actors, barbers, chambermaids, door-to-door saleswomen – that is such a contrast to the broad ancestral acres of Knole, with its leisured elegance. It is a parallel world in another sense, too. For whereas Vita, in *Pepita*, focused on a single line of mother-daughter relationships, I wanted to find out more about the parallel, but very different, lives of the characters who were gradually erased from the record in Vita's account: Max, Flora, Amalia and Henry. 'Of no interest to me' Vita scrawled in red crayon across one of the documents in the trunk, dismissing it as 'The case from Henry's point of view'. Like generations of illegitimate children before them (including the son of La Baccelli and the 3rd Duke), these children were thus consigned to the roll of the disinherited at Knole.

I

The Villa Pepa

As you wander along the Boulevard de la Plage in Arcachon, in south-west France, today, there are few traces of the town's former elegance. The summer smell of sunblock and *frites* hangs in the air; shops selling beach mats, balls and fishing equipment alternate, on one side of the boulevard, with cafés providing *pizzas à emporter*. There, on the other side, between the blocks of holiday apartments, is a row of ornate railings shielding one of these modern residences from the street, with an entrance gate in the middle, surmounted by the scrolling letters 'SW' and a baronial coronet.

This is all that now remains of one of Arcachon's exclusive nineteenth-century villas, the Villa Pepa. The initials, which stood for the name Sackville West,* had been commissioned by the mistress of the house, a woman styling herself the 'Countess West'. Her real name, however, was Josefa Duran, and she was most certainly not a countess. Indeed, the question as to whether Pepita, as she was known to friends and family, had ever been married to Lionel Sackville-West would come to dominate the lives of the characters in this book.

---

* I have followed the style, adopted in documents of the time, of referring to the 'illegitimate' branch of the family as Sackville West, without the hyphen, and the 'legitimate' branch as Sackville-West.

In the summer of 1866, Lionel, who was then a secretary at the British embassy in Madrid, brought Pepita, the mistress with whom he had been enjoying an on-off relationship for the previous fourteen years, to Arcachon. Their relationship had been interrupted by Pepita's performances as a dancer, by Lionel's postings, and by Pepita's other affairs. But it was now time, they felt, for her to move from temporary accommodation in a honey-coloured, neoclassical sandstone house, overlooking the Jardin Public in Bordeaux, into something more permanent.

Lionel bought a house at 167 Boulevard de la Plage from a Captain Cutler for 100,000 francs, and there he installed Pepita and her two children, Max and Victoria. Arcachon was exactly the sort of discreet, slightly out-of-the-way resort where you might install a mistress, as the Duke of Saxe-Coburg had done in the nearby Villa Fougas. The town was within a day or so's travelling distance of Lionel's postings, at first in Madrid and then in Paris, with the intention that he could visit for holidays. The price included 8,000 francs for the furniture and contents: the pepper-grinders and the *poissonière* in the kitchen, the armchairs in the vestibule, the eleven beds and six commodes, the coffee cups, crockery, chandeliers and so on. Here, Pepita, with the help of six servants, including a gardener and a cook, would be able to bring up her growing family, screened from prying eyes by the villa's fretted balconies and shuttered windows.

The Villa Cutler, as it was originally known, was a fine building wrapped all the way round by a veranda. Pepita had it extended by a local builder, Auguste Desombre, who put up the front wall, the railings and the gate in 1866, added another floor, and crowned the building with a belvedere. He gave an exotic lilt to the villa so that the roofs curved up at the eaves to make it look a little like a Chinese pagoda. In the grounds, he built stables and a gardener's house, two jaunty bathing pavilions in the Chinese style at the waterfront, and a couple of years later a small chapel. The gardens ran around the house from the Boulevard to the sea, catching the west winds which blow gently across the Bassin, an immense salt-water lake separating Arcachon from the Atlantic Ocean. It is these water-laden breezes that moderate the climate here, and make it more temperate, without losing the warmth of the Midi.

The Villa Pepa, seen from the beach at Arcachon

By the time the Villa Pepa was put up for sale in 1876, it had been transformed into a substantial nine-bedroomed property. This time, it was sold with 27,300 francs' worth of Lionel and Pepita's furniture: in the anteroom, for example, two chairs of old carved oak covered in green leather, with blue cretonne covers, a large armchair covered in garnet velvet, a brass suspension lamp, a card table in old oak, a Medallion mirror with a frame of old carved oak. The dark woods and heavy fabrics of the interiors, so typical of the seaside villas of the Second Empire, flattened the light flooding in from the Bassin.

The town that Lionel and Pepita chose for their young family was relatively new. Before the railway from Bordeaux reached the neighbouring village of La Teste in the 1840s, hardly anyone

visited what is now Arcachon. The journey from Bordeaux would
have taken three days in an ox-cart across some of France's most
desolate and depressing moors: Les Landes, which stretched flat
and featureless as far as the eye could see, a wasteland scorched in
summer and waterlogged in winter. In 1857, however, the railway
line – that great moving force in France's colonisation of its own
country – was extended to Arcachon, and the town could now
be reached in just over an hour from Bordeaux. Through the
carriage window you might still glimpse the outlandish sight of
a few shepherds, cloaked in sheep's fleeces and perched on stilts
so that they could better survey their flocks, poised, floating,
between the earth and the vast sky.

Gradually, a seasonal, transient population of holiday-
makers joined the hamlet's original inhabitants of oyster
farmers and fishermen. A guide to *The Health Resorts of the
South of France* by Dr Edwin Lee, published in 1865, a year
before Lionel's purchase of the Villa Pepa, included a chapter
on Arcachon, 'with remarks on the chief causes of pulmonary
consumption and on the influence of climate on that disease'.
It described a town of very recent creation: Arcachon had only
become a separate municipality in 1857; its *mairie* was built in
1858, and the following year, the Emperor Napoleon III and his
wife visited the town for the first time. In 1860 this freshly
minted town acquired a coat of arms and a motto that reflected
its rate of growth and its aspirations – '*Heri solitudo, hodie vicus,
cras civitas*' (Yesterday solitude, today a town, tomorrow a city).

Arcachon was a town '*fondée sur la maladie*', and in particular on the hope that its climate would cure, or at least relieve
the symptoms of, that great nineteenth-century killer, tuberculosis. In 1835, Dr Jean Hameau had been an early pioneer of the
benefits of sea-bathing and Arcachon had at first developed as
a *station balnéaire*. The bathing resort was concentrated around
the Ville d'Eté, strung out along the Boulevard de la Plage,
with the little fishing port at one end, and the church of Notre

Arcachon en 1866

The view from the Ville d'Hiver towards the Ville d'Eté,
in the year the Sackville Wests moved to Arcachon

Dame and the gateway leading to the grounds of Monsieur Pereire, one of the principal founders and proprietors of Arcachon, at the other. In between were a striking series of villas, including the Chateau Deganne at No. 163, which was 'said to be a good imitation of Chambord'; Mr Johnston's villa at No. 165; the beachfront Grand Hotel which opened in 1866, the year the Sackville Wests came to Arcachon, with 150 rooms and *cabinets de toilette*, and offering '*bains et services de balnothérapie*'; and, of course, the Villa Pepa at No. 167.

As its appeal as a health resort broadened, Arcachon became a town of two halves. In the Ville d'Eté, the doctors promoted the therapeutic benefits of sea-bathing in summer, while in the other half, the Ville d'Hiver, they extolled the soothing effects of a soft 'balsamic' climate in winter. Dr Gustave Hameau, Dr Jean's son and for many years the Médécin Inspecteur at Arcachon as well as family doctor to the Sackville Wests, noted the Ville d'Hiver's excellent location. It was close to the sea, but screened from it by dunes covered with pine forest. These pines had been planted from the late eighteenth century onwards by the French government in order to bind the shifting sands of the shore and stop them turning the land into a desert. The trees broke the force of the Atlantic winds and imparted to them, once they had passed, moisture-laden over the great expanse of the Bassin, the 'resinous emanations', which were considered so 'sedative to the nervous system'.

The pine-scented air was supposed to work wonders for those suffering from asthma, bronchitis and consumption. 'The whole air is perceptibly impregnated with the balsamic odour of turpentine,' wrote Hameau, 'and we know that the balsams and turpentines in vapour are remedial agents of much power in bronchial affections. This impregnation arises not merely from the presence of pine forests on a great scale, but from the gathering of turpentine or resin from the live trees.' This gathering was done by the indigenous population of *résiniers* who scraped away areas of bark from the trees, and tapped the resin which oozed from the trunk into wooden vessels. The obvious good health of the *résinier* himself – and an apparent absence of any pulmonary complaints, particularly consumption – seemed evidence in itself of the healing powers of the atmosphere.

Hameau was a member of an unofficial alliance of doctors, property developers and railway entrepreneurs, who helped create an artificial town in the middle of a wilderness. He was one of those who encouraged the Société Immobilière d'Arcachon, headed by Emile Pereire, to buy up land in what became the Ville d'Hiver. There, they carved a great park from the forest, on an incline facing south, and laid it out with promenades and *allées*, linking scores of isolated Swiss-style villas, which preserve to this day traces of the town's former elegance. All of these villas were built to a different design but had a common feature: a veranda running all the way around the ground floor. Planted with magnolia, bougainvillea, olean-der and orange trees, and palm trees as well as the pine, the entire Ville d'Hiver was a lush, large-scale, open sanatorium, with a climate 'very favourable for invalids of a nervous and excitable constitution, for consumptive patients liable to haem-orrhage, or exhausted by copious muco-purulent expectoration'. One of these invalids was Charles-N. Faduilhe who, in the preface to his doctoral thesis in medicine in 1866 (the year Lionel and Pepita acquired the Villa Pepa), described his own return to health in Arcachon from consumption: 'It was there, abandoned, and condemned to death by all the doctors who had seen me that I found some relief to my sufferings, and the hope of a cure. In Arcachon I found the courage to undergo all the trials and tribulations I had to endure over three long and deadly years.'

Life in Arcachon could be a trifle dull, but as Dr Lee noted, this was no bad thing: 'Too often invalids complain of the absence of the diversions (distractions) of a town, and of having always before their eyes a monotonous verdure. This, however, is an essential condition of their amelioration. The calmness of the atmosphere, the silence of the forest, a certain isolation of the inhabitants, a great mass of verdure, and the resinous emanations from the fir trees, constitute a combination of sedative conditions of which not one is superfluous.' This plea for a peaceful life was echoed by Dr Roth in another guide, published in 1879: 'In other places pleasures have, it may be, their utility; but here, for natures which must be tranquillised at any price – which must be guarded against every drain on the nervous system – the quiet amusements, which will spring up naturally among acquaintances, as the colony of strangers augments, will always be sufficient.'

People could walk and ride in the sand dunes and forest; dine at the four-storey Railway Buffet, which was built and decorated in the Chinese style and struck new arrivals to Arcachon with its architectural audacity the moment they stepped off the train; read *The Times* in the reading room of the

Grand Hotel the day after publication; or meet in the Casino, 'an extensive building in the mauresque style, situated on an eminence with a terrace in front, commanding a pleasing prospect, and comprising a tastefully decorated hall and concert room'. 'Bathed in the perfume of exotic flowers,' in the words of one guidebook, and 'hanging like the [Babylonian] gardens of Semiramis,' the Casino opened in 1863 and evoked 'the dreamy fantasy of the Orient'. Its architect, who also designed the Grand Hotel, the Railway Buffet, and several of the first villas in the Ville d'Hiver, was Paul Régnauld, 'a great magician', according to *Le Journal d'Arcachon*, 'who has managed to transport the Alhambra into our desert'.

———

So this was the strange, almost fantastic, world into which Lionel and Pepita introduced their new family: a resort in which invalids drifted between life and death in their forest villas; a small town that was growing fast, from around 400 resident inhabitants in 1857 to 3,000 in 1871, with as many as 300,000 visitors a year; a place where social boundaries were shifting like the shoreline, but never fast enough to disguise the exclusion of Pepita and her family.

Victoria came to Arcachon at the age of four, and her earliest memories are of living at the Villa Pepa with her mother, a beautiful woman, by all accounts, with luxuriant hair and a love-curl licking each cheek – although photographs cannot disguise her double chin and the fact that, by this time, Pepita was becoming a little stout. She had tiny dancer's feet that could be seen peeping out from beneath the dresses which she wore very short at the front but longer at the back – one with a train several yards long. Several times a year, 'Papa' would come to visit – 'a great event', celebrated with much fanfare – and stay for a fortnight or two.

© Nicolson family

Pepita with her eldest daughter, Victoria, the future Lady Sackville

Victoria spent most of her time in her mother's company, sitting with her as she did her needlework, speaking in French (as her mother knew no English), and sleeping in her bed. As a treat, Pepita would take out her castanets and dance for the children's entertainment in a dress covered with black lace, her thick hair let down in two long plaits below her knees. Of an afternoon Victoria might drive out with her mother in a horse-drawn carriage to visit the poor (a nice, sentimental touch, that) or to the magistrates' court in the neighbouring village of La Teste to deal with 'troubles about the servants', for Pepita enjoyed relations with her servants as volatile as Victoria's were later to be. Court records from the late 1860s describe a string of cases in which the 'Countess West', or sometimes 'la Comtesse d'Houesse', is sued by servants and tradespeople – chambermaids and coachmen, butchers, midwives, gardeners and nurses – for non-payment of laundry bills, wages or summary dismissal. According to a housemaid, who had served at the Villa Pepa for a few months, Pepita was a very 'change-able' person, with quite a temper, and her washerwoman confirmed that she used to send servants away 'for the slightest thing – she was most particular'.

Victoria also remembered the slights and social exclusions of life in Arcachon. The Sackville Wests lived next door to the Johnstons, Bordeaux-based wine merchants who had been one of the first families to build a summerhouse on the shore of the Bassin. The Johnstons' Villa Mogador was separated from the Villa Pepa by a low wall, but Victoria and her siblings saw the little Johnston girls, Minna and Bella, only 'very rarely, and then always surreptitiously, because they were forbidden by their parents to associate with us'. Similarly, when the young Sackville Wests went to a children's ball at the Casino, no one danced, or even spoke, with them. Being left out in this way made such an impression on Victoria that she burst into tears, but it was only much later that it became clear to her that it was because of her 'mother's position that people objected to their children associating with us'.

When the Sackville Wests stayed in Paris for a couple of months each winter, at first in a house that Lionel had bought in the Avenue d'Eylau and then from 1869 in the Rue de la Faisanderie, their life was just as solitary. Victoria was told not to play with other children in the Champs Elysées, and always turned back at a particular point, ten minutes from the embassy, when she accompanied her father on his walk to work. Once there was a fête in the Tuileries, she recalled, to which her father went officially. 'My mother cried bitterly because she could not go with him. I did not then know the reason of this but I conclude it was on account of her not being recognised in society.' This impression was confirmed by Lionel's Foreign Office colleagues. When asked many years later to recall his years, 1868–71, as an attaché at the embassy in Paris, Baron Saumarez described how, although he was 'on quite intimate terms with Lord Sackville [as Lionel later became], he never mentioned to me the fact that he had children. I have heard the name of a lady who was known as "Pepita", I was told she was a Spanish Danseuse. Lord Sackville never mentioned to me his relations with that lady – he never introduced her to me nor as far as I know to any of my colleagues – I never heard of Lord Sackville or saw him going out into Society with that lady.'

According to Victoria, her mother never visited Arcachon's main church, the church of Notre Dame, but went occasionally instead to the chapel at Le Moulleau to pray – although never for confession or communion, 'in consequence', as Victoria later realised, 'of her living in adultery'. What might, therefore, have been for Pepita the setting for an idyllic family life – an imposing beachfront property, a delightful climate – was spoiled by being excluded from society, cut off from the company of other families and children, from the consolations of the Church, and from her husband's colleagues. Victoria suffered these hurts too, and would bear an impression of them for the rest of her life. The reasons for them would only become clear much later, casting a pall of shame that she never quite succeeded in shaking off.

It is easy to see how the confusion arose: a muddle entirely of his own making. Lionel accepted the fact that Pepita was always known in Arcachon as Countess West, even calling her 'Madame West' himself, and addressing her in letters as 'my little wife'. And yet, on the other hand, he strenuously denied that 'he ever got married or went through a form of marriage with Pepita during the residence at Arcachon . . . the idea of a marriage between us was never for a moment discussed. We both of us knew that she was legally married with a husband living and that therefore we should be committing bigamy if we went through a form of marriage.'

A similar contradiction extended to the registration of his children's births during the Arcachon years. Flora was born on 11 November 1866 at the Villa Pepa, and registered the following day as 'of father and mother not named'. The following year, however, Pepita put pressure on Lionel to recognise Flora as their legitimate child. 'I was very strongly opposed to this and for a long time absolutely refused to be party to such a proceeding,' Lionel later claimed, 'but was ultimately prevailed upon to do so chiefly with the object of shielding Pepita's reputation. She said she was very anxious that the children should bear my name and that was the only way of accomplishing this object.' Amalia was born in Paris on 16 February 1868, and was the first of the children to be described at once in the register as the legitimate daughter of Lionel and 'his wife'. Yet again Lionel later had 'no recollection of signing the register of the birth although the official copy obtained states that I did so sign'.

The fifth surviving child, Henry, was born at Arcachon on 24 June 1869 and, given the fact that both his birth and baptismal certificates describe him as the legitimate child of the Hon. Lionel Sackville-West and of Dona Josefa Duran, his wife, it is no wonder that he was to have some expectations of his legitimacy. Despite physical evidence to the contrary, Lionel was later to deny any memory of signing the register. The Mayor of Arcachon was present at the registration, however, and, though nursing his own private doubts, assumed that the 'Count and Countess West' must have been lawfully married 'because I could not believe that Count West being a gentleman of honour would deceive the State and I did not believe that he would come and make a false registration'. The 'gentleman of honour' in question was the future British Minister (the equivalent of ambassador) to the United States.

The question of whether Lionel and Pepita were ever married was the subject, decades later, of a celebrated court case, in which the domestic arrangements of the Villa Pepa were to help decide the inheritance of Knole, the largest stately home in England. In the process, evidence was taken from people very different from those who stalked the galleries of Knole: station masters and cemetery keepers, washerwomen and wine merchants, coachmen and concierges, house painters and shoemakers – indeed, a cast of characters straight out of a novel by Balzac. From their accounts emerges an intimate picture of life in a seaside resort in south-west France in the 1860s, a study in small-town snobbery, and a household rather more rackety than that described by Pepita's daughter Victoria and, later, her granddaughter Vita. Victoria presented a curiously sentimental version of a happy and rela-tively well-ordered childhood, while Vita played up the romantic aspects of the story: the love affair between her glamorous grand-mother, Pepita, and her grandfather, Lionel, the distinguished diplomat. The tale of the crotchety courtesan and the perjurious peer would have reflected the more prosaic reality.

Among those who were asked for their views on whether the 'Count and Countess' were ever seen together 'in Society' – because that would have been a sure sign they were married – were several of the people who played a prominent part in the development of Arcachon: Dr Gustave Hameau, the Reverend Samuel Radcliff and Harry Scott Johnston, a director of Pereire's Société Immobilière and the father of Minna and Bella. Johnston, for example, claimed that although he knew Pepita by sight, he never had any closer acquaintance – 'on the contrary that was to be avoided', as it was generally believed she was Mr West's mistress. Johnston and his wife 'mixed in the best society in Arcachon', and it was inconceivable that they should meet 'the Countess' there. 'It was notorious she had been a dancer,' he continued. 'The Countess had not a very good reputation in Arcachon. I have seen people dining at her house but I never saw any ladies there – small dinner parties consisting only of men [in particular, a Comte Auguste de Clouet, a dentist from Bordeaux]. Her mixing with these fast young men and living alone . . . gave me the impression she led a fast life.'

Lionel may have been hoping to find in Arcachon a bucolic backwater where his growing family could lead a life free of censure. But he had failed, perhaps, to appreciate the size of the English colony there; a community large enough to support its own Anglican church, to give its name to the Promenade des Anglais, and to cherish the snobberies and social conventions that they had brought from home. There was no escape after all.

The Reverend Samuel Radcliff, the British chaplain, had come to Arcachon in 1866 for the sake of his health, and was to spend the rest of his life there. He found the resort very 'rustic' at first, but threw himself wholeheartedly into the life of the town, organising paper-chases on horseback in the woods, translating into English Gustave Hameau's book on the climate of Arcachon, tending to his flock, playing golf. Between 1867 and 1871 he lived opposite the Villa Pepa on the Boulevard de la Plage. Pepita, he recalled, 'was what would be called a fine woman', in whom 'one could see the remains of former beauty, but she was at that time stout and rather coarse-looking'. He confirmed Johnston's impression of her social exclusion: 'She was not regarded as a desirable acquaintance. She was not in any way received or recognised in Arcachon society. It was rumoured that she drank freely . . . The general reputation was, I believe, that they [Lionel and Pepita] were not married. Their connection was looked upon as a very shady affair.' Such suspicions, or concerns, did not impress the patrician Lionel who was later, as Lord Sackville, to claim that there was in any case 'no society in Arcachon which I in my position in life would have cared to mix with'.

These sentiments would certainly have extended to his French neighbours. Louisa Dignac lived at No. 220 Boulevard de la Plage and, as Pepita's laundress, visited the Villa Pepa almost every day, seeing 'the Countess every time . . . in the drawing-room, in her bedroom – everywhere'. Louisa noted how opinion in Arcachon was divided as to whether Pepita was Lionel's wife or mistress, but she added a further twist to the complicated domestic arrangements by reporting the 'general opinion that the Count de Béon was her [Pepita's] sweetheart'. In this version, the eldest son, Max, was the son of the Prince of Bavaria (of whom there was said to be a portrait photograph in the drawing room), Victoria was Lionel's daughter, and Béon was the father of the last two children, Amalia and Henry.

Photographs from the family albums at Knole: *left*, Pepita's oldest son, Max; *right*, family friend, Henri de Béon

Henri de Béon, the assistant station master at Bordeaux's main railway station, is a slightly elusive figure, and it is unclear where he first met Pepita and whether it was Lionel himself who had introduced them. In a witness statement taken in 1897, the builder Desombre described how Pepita had sent him to Bordeaux to invite Béon to dinner, in order to thank him for helping them all so graciously into a railway carriage. Béon accepted the invitation and, according to Desombre, 'the following day I saw him at the Villa, so he must have stayed all night'.

In any case, by 1868, when he was in his late twenties – ten years younger than Pepita – Béon had left his job in Bordeaux, and Pepita, who was forever worried that people were cheating her, had appointed him her 'superintendent'. He was living at the villa, sometimes accompanied by his mother, and sleeping in a bedroom that 'communicated' with the Countess's room. It was Béon who would pay Louisa for the laundry, who managed all of Pepita's affairs, and who generally seemed, Louisa said, 'on very familiar terms with her', to such an extent that 'I used to say to myself "Yes, you are the superintendent and something more".' Sometimes she would spot them drinking together – Pepita 'used to be always drinking champagne'. A shoemaker called André Fay lived just opposite the Villa Pepa and he, too, often caught sight of Béon coming and going. He could never understand why 'Count West, a very good man, amiable and kind-hearted', tolerated Béon, who was generally thought to be Pepita's lover. 'People used to say that they were surprised at Count West allowing Count de Béon to be in the house, and that he ought to have sent him into the Bay. He looked to be a lazy fellow. But the Countess seemed to be master, and it appeared that she could make Count West do anything she liked.'

Whether or not Pepita had behaved in a 'respectable' sort of way while in Arcachon would later become a matter of some significance, from which it could be inferred whether she was more likely to have been Lionel's mistress or wife. The fact that she wandered around the garden *en négligée*, with her beautiful black hair hanging loose, was remarked upon, although the house painter Georges Tregan admitted that he never saw her do anything in the garden 'to give rise to scandal or comment'. It was testimony such as this, taken a quarter of a century after Pepita's death, gleaned through glimpses over a garden wall, or from a veranda, that give us this insight into the domestic life of Arcachon in the dying days of the Second Empire. Just as boundaries between land and sea were blurred, so were the social barriers, the shifting small-town snobberies, and the nuanced line between truths and half-truths. When Desombre boasted that he used to smoke a daily cigar with Count West, or that he generally declined the Wests' frequent invitations to dinner, his neighbours pooh-poohed his statements on the basis that, as a member of a completely different social class, Desombre was very unlikely to have been invited to dinner in the first place.

———

Pepita died at home on 11 March 1871, aged forty, a few days after giving birth to a short-lived son, Frédéric. Béon was the only person living in the Villa Pepa at the time, besides the children and the servants. Lionel was in Paris, where he had been sent as chargé d'affaires, but applied for a week's compassionate leave from his boss, Lord Lyons, the British ambassador to France. In *Pepita*, Vita described how her mother Victoria remembered the moment when Lionel arrived at the Villa Pepa:

> She was in the room, a frightened and heartbroken child of nine [sic], praying beside the bed on which lay the still body of

Pepita, a crucifix clasped between her stiffened fingers, the lighted candles burning steadily over the unearthly beauty of the pallor of death. Beside her lay the tiny figure of the dead baby who had cost her her life. As my grandfather reached the room, he stopped for a moment at the threshold, then ran forward and threw himself on his knees beside the bed, sobbing out that it was he who had killed her. It was in vain that they tried to comfort him by telling him that she had died with his name, 'Lionel', upon her lips.

Vita's description captures the melodrama of the deathbed scene, and the romance of her grandparents' love. Even though the children were very young when their mother died – Victoria was only eight years old, and Henry not yet two – they each of them treasured their very different, and possibly unreliable, memories of her for the rest of their lives, jealously guarding them from their siblings.

Lionel entrusted Béon with all the arrangements. Frédéric was registered as the legitimate son of Lionel and 'his wife', and on Pepita's own death certificate, she was registered as Lionel's 'wife'. Béon organised the funeral, too, with Lionel conceding that the arrangements be 'made as for a lady who enjoyed the position of my wife'. There were notices in the local paper and lithographed invitations to the funeral signed by Lionel, which described the deceased as his wife (indeed, in one handwritten letter, he informed a friend, Colonel Fritz Holst, of the death of '*ma pauvre femme*'). Opinion was, nevertheless, still divided over whether they had been married. 'It is not an uncommon thing, especially in Arcachon for persons to speak of themselves as married when they are not so,' observed the chemist who helped Dr Hameau embalm Pepita's body so that 'Count West' might see it in all its ethereal beauty when he arrived from Paris.

It was snowing – an extraordinary event for that part of France – on the day that Pepita's coffin was taken from the church of Notre Dame, from which she had been excluded in life, for burial in the windswept municipal cemetery above the town. Although no handsome monument was erected to her memory, there is no question that she was buried here as Lionel's wife. The municipal authorities had previously refused permission for her to be buried, as she had wished, beneath the little chapel that she had had built in the garden of the Villa Pepa.

Lionel also asked Béon to take care of the children, which he did with the help of his mother, first at the Villa Pepa, then at Mme de Béon's house in Bordeaux, and from 1873 in Paris. In the first few years after Pepita's death, Lionel often wrote to Béon, expressing his great gratitude to his 'dear friend' for all that he had been doing on his behalf. It was only many years later, when Lionel believed that Béon had 'behaved very dishonestly about money matters' during this period, that they were to fall out.

After Pepita's death, Lionel – with five children to support – was in desperate financial straits. He turned to his younger brother, William Edward, appointing him as his man of affairs. William Edward, or 'Gummer' as he was known within the family, was persuaded to lend him £4,500: if not, he would be 'up a tree'. Security consisted of a life insurance policy, some silver plate, and jewellery, which Lionel himself was going to have valued in Paris and included a fan set with emeralds and a diamond tiara. In return, Gummer was to receive interest at five per cent. Lionel was now in a position to issue letters of instruction to Gummer on where to make the payments

– mostly into Béon's account in a bank in Bordeaux. These letters were also interspersed with gossip – a dinner last night at Versailles with Adolphe Thiers, the French head of state; riding a *vélocipède* for the first time and grazing his face against a wall; and news of heavy fighting in Paris during the popular uprising of 1871. Lionel was at the same time angling for a posting to Rio de Janeiro (at £6,000 a year) or, failing that, to Buenos Aires (at just over '£3,000 a year and yellow fever'), which he eventually accepted in September.

Despite the loan, Lionel was further in debt. 'You will be surprised at all this paper,' he wrote to Gummer, 'you are however the only person who can help me out of a hole into which I am put by a lawsuit here and which has rendered me liable immediately for this amount.' He was being taken to court by his creditors and was unable to leave Paris to take up his new appointment to the Argentine Republic until they were paid. 'Under these circumstances,' he wrote once again to Gummer, 'I hope you will assist me and prevent by so doing most disagreeable consequences.'

Lionel's sisters were helping him out as well. Two of them had married very successfully into that small group of super-rich landed families with incomes of over £75,000 a year. Elizabeth's husband was the Duke of Bedford, and Mary had married first the Marquis of Salisbury, and second the Earl of Derby. As a result, the repercussions from Arcachon spread to some of the greatest stately homes in England. In January 1873, Elizabeth, writing from Woburn, sent an order to her bank for £2,000 to be remitted to William Edward on behalf of Lionel, to enable him to leave Paris, although she feared that his debts were 'more than we as yet know'. Her husband Hastings, the Duke of Bedford, was less sympathetic, forbidding her to do any more to help her brother and advising William Edward that it was his duty to his own wife and children not to help the feckless Lionel any further.

Elizabeth hoped that her sister Mary might get at the truth, for 'it is too serious an affair to go on making mysteries . . . I can't say how much I am distressed at all this, & I see nothing but misery to come.' Just as Lionel had always been deliberately unclear in Arcachon about his status as a father and a husband, he was equally vague about the scale of his financial mess – with bills appearing here, there and everywhere. In March 1873, Mary joined the correspondence from Knowsley, agreeing to lend Lionel £1,000 and expressing to William Edward the hope that Lionel would now confide in him the state of his affairs. Her husband Edward, the 15th Earl of Derby, had recently become aware that 'the beginning of the mischief was a connection of many years standing with a Spanish woman, I believe, originally a dancer, by whom he has a family left on his hands to maintain. She died last year. It is an awkward business altogether.' Lionel had hinted to him that he was 'likely to marry a young Jewish lady with a fortune believed to be £200,000', which would pay off the loans made by his sisters. 'But it does not seem clear,' Edward noted in his diary, 'that there is any certainty of the event coming off.'

By 17 March, Lionel was back in London, and Mary was worrying that he had not disclosed to his brother and sisters the full scale of his borrowings, that the money they were lending him was simply being used to service his other debts: 'If this be so, the sums with which we have assisted him are only so much thrown into the fire just to enable him to get off now.' Two days later, Lionel assured her that this was not the case; but, as Mary wrote to William Edward, 'when people are in money difficulties I have but little confidence in statements. He said he was waiting for information about what sum was to come from what you term "the other way out of his difficulties". He said he must be assured it would be £200,000. I doubt this being likely.'

Lionel's siblings had every reason to distrust him. When Mary had the jewels, on which the security for the loan was based, assessed in England, their value was 'miserably low' – and far less than the valuation Lionel had had done in Paris. His siblings insisted that, as a condition of a new loan to him of £5,000 from the North British Insurance Company (to be repaid out of his salary), the jewels and the plate, which he had offered as security for previous loans from family members, must now be turned into hard cash. The silver that Lionel would need for his embassy in South America would have to be electroplate. Writing to William Edward in May, Mary quite understood Lionel's 'feelings of parting with the plate & jewels (those that belonged to Mama) but after all, she would have wished to leave them for such an emergency'. Mary went on to explain how her 'great object in getting the plate disposed of out of your hands & his, is simply in plain words this – As long as there is anything to raise money upon, depend upon it, it will be raised. In these matters it has been so since the world began.' The sisters and their husbands were not only much richer than Lionel, but also more worldly wise, alert to the way in which funds could be raised several times over on the same security.

Lionel himself was obtuse about the arrangements that were being made on his behalf, feigning ignorance of what was being done, or blaming the family solicitors for any delays. He was enjoying life in Argentina, writing to William Edward from Buenos Aires on 5 September 1873: 'There is everything to be had. Riding, Shooting, Boating, Clubs & Theatres, & a splendid Climate . . . I have two gunboats.' But he was running into further financial difficulties, and there were repeated requests from his bankers, Maynard, Harris & Crice, for further funds to cover the bills he was forwarding them from Argentina. Lionel promised to live more cheaply next year, by giving up his house and his cook, and even suggested to William Edward that the plate and jewels should be sold to 'square' Maynard – conveniently forgetting that these already formed the security for previous loans from his brother. Mary hoped that 'he might have found a nice person with some money whom he might have married out there, but this does not seem likely I fear'.

Instead, she and her husband continued to bail Lionel out, sending the bank £300 in October 1874, when 'the last grain of sand' threatened to 'break Messrs. Maynards' back for Lionel'. She was endlessly forgiving of her feckless brother. 'I really do not think he has recklessly run into difficulties again,' she wrote to William Edward, 'but it was absolutely impossible for him to live upon £1,000 at B. Ayres' and to support the children. 'Lionel's letter to you confirms my belief that he never understands a word of business. And strengthens my wish and Lord Derby's to exhort you to sell the plate and get your £1,000 back safely.' Predictably, the plate had been revalued in London at two-thirds of the value on which the security had been raised. 'How wonderful is Lionel's inaccuracy & forgetfulness about money! I cannot the least see what is to come & what is to be the end, except that Bessie & I shall have to go on paying! Some people say it is better thus than that things should get into a muddle again. Perhaps it is, but anyhow it is inconvenient.'

―――――――

There was, of course, the house in Arcachon. The Earl of Derby had located the Villa Pepa on a trip to France in November 1873, but a year later it was still unlet and therefore providing no income towards the £1,000 annual cost of bringing up the five children. There was also some doubt as to who actually owned the house. It was hard to get a straight answer from Lionel, so in November 1874, the Derbys started making enquiries. Mary wrote to Béon asking whether the French property belonged to Lionel or the children, and also tried to find out what the situation was under French inheritance laws. 'If Lionel is so muddle-headed about the plate and jewels,' she wrote, 'he is probably ten times more ignorant about French law & c. I hope a crash may be averted meanwhile, but I do not see very clearly how.'

The reason for the confusion was that, by a deed of gift in 1868, Lionel had made the Villa Pepa over to Pepita. On her death, therefore, it belonged to her estate, rather than to Lionel, and thereby to her estranged husband, Juan Antonio de Oliva. In the sort of conundrum that would be played out in the courts decades later, Lionel could not have it both ways: if he had married Pepita some time in the mid-1860s, Henry was his eldest legitimate son; if he had not married Pepita, the villa belonged to Oliva.

Oliva was discouraged initially from taking his claim further by the strength of the forces ranged against him: the Derbys and the Bedfords, two of the wealthiest families in England. In August 1876, however, the state-appointed trustees of Pepita's estate sold the Villa Pepa to a Monsieur Lesca for 100,050 francs and, three months later, Oliva, backed speculatively by a firm of Bordeaux wine merchants, claimed the whole of his late wife's estate, including the Villa Pepa, for himself and his son Max. A tribunal in Bordeaux decided, in 1879, that Oliva, as Pepita's lawful husband, was entitled to an account of her estate from the state-appointed trustees, subject to any liabilities. As it happened, these liabilities, including court costs, were to absorb the assets, and Oliva was never to receive anything from the proceedings. But the judgement did have the significant effect of establishing in a French court that Pepita and Oliva had stayed married.

There was a grisly postscript to the story of the Arcachon years. In September 1896, a quarter of a century after Pepita's death, her youngest son Henry visited the town with his brother-in-law, Gabriel Salanson. They were there to collect evidence in support of Henry's claim to legitimacy, and needed to establish that Pepita had been a woman of 'good repute', whom people believed at the time had been married to Lionel. First, however, they needed to confirm that the woman buried in the cemetery that freezing March day had indeed been Pepita, and to this end they arranged to have her body exhumed. It took some time for the cemetery keeper, accompanying the Chief of Police and Dr Hameau (who had been the Sackville Wests' doctor while they were in Arcachon and whose wife Marie had been a pall-bearer at Pepita's funeral) to find the grave because there was no headstone. But eventually they found the site, and three or four workmen, plus a carpenter, Monsieur Comdom, opened the grave and took the coffin out. According to the cemetery keeper, 'the body was quite life-like and as if she would speak' (it had been embalmed) and Pepita was identified; 'Mr. Henry West appeared to be very much upset and grieved, and he cried on the occasion of the opening of the coffin'. The coffin was then closed up and placed in the depository, awaiting further instructions from Henry and Gabriel who intended to have the body re-interred and a monument erected. Months passed without instruction, and there the body remained.

For the rest of her life, the middle child, Amalia, cherished the memory of her mother. In 1900, she applied from England for a six-metre square plot in the cemetery at Arcachon, and Pepita's body was taken out of the depository and laid to rest again, joining in the heathland above Arcachon the servants with whom she had squabbled, the neighbours who had spied on her, and some of the founding fathers of what was now a very prosperous town. It was Amalia who renewed the concession for the plot when it expired in 1915, and again in 1927, a full fifty-six years after her mother's death. Finally, in 1971 – by coincidence, a century after Pepita's death – when there was no one left to renew the concession, Pepita's body was taken out of the ground for a second time and her bones consigned to a communal ossuary on the outskirts of the town.

Lost in Translation

After Pepita's death in 1871, the children remained in the care of their mother's friends, the Béons. Max was sent to school in Bordeaux, while the others stayed on initially at the Villa Pepa in Arcachon. Here they continued their secluded existence, shuttered from the world. Their father, on the other hand, as his granddaughter Vita later observed, was not the sort of 'man ever to enjoy dealing with a difficult situation', and having escaped to Buenos Aires as British Minister to the Argentine Republic in 1873 (or more properly, Envoy Extraordinary and Minister Plenipotentiary), he stayed in the post until 1878, when he was transferred to Madrid.

There is an account of what it was like to arrive in the Argentinian capital at the time. Marion Mulhall, who was later to play a significant role in the lives of the Sackville West children, had accompanied her husband to Argentina, where he edited the first English-language newspaper in South America. In *Between the Amazon and the Andes, or Ten Years of a Lady's Travels*, Mrs Mulhall described her first impressions of the place as 'unfavourable, owing to the difficulties that attended our landing'. As she made her way ashore, 'along the slippery planks, through a drizzling rain, we had to be very careful of the numerous holes that occurred at intervals, for [these] had already put so many people hors-de-combat that the municipality had set apart a special ward in the hospital for the victims of this "bridge of sighs"'. The rains lasted three days, leaving more than a dozen dead horses floating in the flooded streets, and in one place a shattered brougham, whose driver had been drowned. 'Storms of this kind occur generally in March and September,' she reported, 'very often preceded by extraordinary signs, such as a shower of beetles, dead mice, or fish. The beetles fall almost as thick as snowflakes; the fish rise in waterspouts in front of the city, and are then blown inland over the houses; and as for the mice, it is supposed they come from Patagonia.' She went on to describe an outbreak in early 1871 of a plague, with symptoms similar to yellow fever, in which 26,000 people died. These included 270 members, or about a sixth, of the British community.

Lionel's account of Argentina on arrival was more favourable. He wrote to Victoria, in French, about all the 'pretty flowers and birds', and about his journeys on horseback to the mountains of the interior, where he had seen lions and tigers, and he promised to teach his oldest daughter to ride on his return. During the five years he was in South America, Lionel wrote to Victoria occasionally, but never to his other children – encouraging the belief that she was to hold for the rest of her life that 'she was always his favourite, as I had been my mother's'. He was, as he told Béon from Buenos Aires, 'so busy and bothered that it is impossible for me to gather my thoughts', or to answer letters from Flora or Max. There was also the distraction of the 'fearful', suffocating heat, and so, half-heartedly, he simply asked Béon to pass on a 'thousand kisses' to his children.

Before leaving for Argentina, Lionel had made an agreement with Béon, which was to be the source of much future argument. Béon was to accept charge of the children and an apartment in Paris, where he and his mother were to live with the children and for which Lionel was to pay the rent. The signed agreement contained a schedule of the articles of furniture in the apartment, and between 1873 and the summer of 1876, when Lionel returned on a visit to Europe, Béon was reduced to selling many of these, as he later claimed, to defray expenses.

In 1874, Lionel authorised Béon to act as his agent in the sale of the Villa Pepa and the house at 200 Avenue d'Eylau in Paris. He was in debt again, but reassured Béon that he would do everything he could to keep him out of trouble: 'You do not know how I suffer. It seems as if I was destined to be always in a sad position and what affects me the most is that I place you in the same . . . It is a consolation to have a friend such as you, and one who has done for me what no one else would have done.' As Béon's goodwill towards the family began to leave him out of pocket, he became increasingly keen for Lionel to return to France to settle his account and pay for the expense of bringing up the children.

While her younger siblings moved in with the Béons, Victoria was sent to board at a convent run by the Sisters of St Joseph de Belley, at 17 Rue de Monceau in the newly fashionable 8th arrondissement (on the site of a school, the Cours Saint Louis, later attended by former President Nicolas Sarkozy). The area had been developed during the Second Empire by the same Pereire brothers who had transformed Arcachon, and had largely escaped the devastation suffered in other parts of Paris just a couple of years previously. The banks of the Seine still bore the scars of the uprising in 1871, when symbols of imperial power from the Palais de Justice to the Tuileries had been turned to rubble and ash by insurgents. Further damage – and the loss of tens of thousands of lives – had been caused two months later, when government troops retook the capital from the Communards.

The Rue de Monceau itself consisted largely of grand 'hôtels particuliers' built for the big Jewish financial families. The Camondos lived at No. 61, the Rothschilds at No. 43–7, and the Ephrussis at No. 81. It was here that the young collector

Charles Ephrussi displayed Impressionist paintings by Berthe Morisot, Manet, Monet, Pissarro and Renoir, and assembled his collection of Japanese netsuke. And it was down the Rue de Monceau that Charles would stroll in his top hat and black frock coat, on his way to the offices of the *Gazette des Beaux-Arts* for which he contributed articles.

Madeleine Lemaire was another familiar sight in the Rue de Monceau, as she took her afternoon walk surrounded by a flock of dogs. Mme Lemaire lived at No. 31, and painted flowers in a large glass pavilion in her garden; from April onwards, the scent of her lilac trees wafted into the street, causing passers-by to stop. Her speciality was roses (of which one lover claimed she had created more than anyone except God), but she was equally cele-brated as a Society hostess, a 'strangely powerful person', whom Marcel Proust used as one of several models for Mme Verdurin in *A la Recherche du Temps Perdu*. Crowds of artists, musicians, poets, playwrights and clubmen thronged to her salon, spilling on summer evenings out of the studio into the garden itself, while their carriages waited outside and clogged the street.

Victoria's life at No. 17 was very different. Conditions at the boarding school, which had been founded by the Sisters of St Joseph in 1851, were spartan but, as the prospectus insisted, salu-brious. For fees of 1,000 francs per annum, parents could park their daughters there for most of the year. The girls were only allowed out one day a month, and, in addition to the summer vacation, for two brief holidays at the New Year and at Easter, and even those could be spent with the nuns, for a supplement of 150 francs.

Photographs and illustrations of the time show a large institu-tion, arranged around two courtyards. The classrooms, dormitories and an infirmary overlook a large walled garden, where girls ranging in age from five to eighteen play or simply sit under the trees. The school's regime, the prospectus continued, was '*maternel*', with the nuns participating in all aspects of the lives of the girls in their care, eating with them and sleeping in the same dormitories. It was hoped that, this way, the *Réligieuses* would instil in their pupils '*une piété solide*', good judgement and feelings of respect, gratitude and love for their parents – the last a rather tall order in the case of the Sackville West girls.

Victoria would probably have started in the *deuxième classe*, with a curriculum that included religious instruction, arithmetic, geography, ancient history, French history and English. But she would have had some catching up to do because she was, at eleven on entry, barely able to read and write, never having had lessons before. Victoria was miserable at what she described as her 'inhuman Convent', although she did manage to recall it later with some humorous detachment. 'Just think!' she wrote to Vita. 'Fifty years ago, a little girl of 12, all dressed in white and wearing a long tulle veil, was kneeling trembling at the altar in the Convent Chapel, for her "First Communion" and hoped she would become the Bride of Christ, who filled all her dreams of Love in those days. And that little girl is your broad-minded old Mama who, fortunately for her, did not become the Bride of Christ and does not sing any more ridiculous cantiques [hymns] such as this one she sang softly that memorable day . . .'

The little girl disliked the cold (the rooms, the prospectus claimed, were all '*parfaitement aérés*'), the discomfort and the discipline, and resented the fact that she was no longer Mademoiselle Pepita, as she had been known by her family in Arcachon, but 'Mademoiselle quarante-deux'. This was the number marked on all the clothes that comprised her regulation *trousseau*: the eighteen handkerchiefs, eight nightcaps, six petticoats, eight pairs of stockings, three dresses – all black, for '*L'uniforme est noir; il est de rigueur dans la maison.*'

Victoria's father was uneasy about her status, too, but for other reasons. When the mothers of schoolfriends asked Victoria to stay with them, Lionel was unsure how he and the Béons should respond, for he wanted to protect her from the possibility, through such encounters, of learning the painful truth about her past. The sense of social exclusion that had started across the garden wall separating the Villa Pepa from the Johnstons' villa in Arcachon continued, as the secrets and lies surrounding her status compromised her capacity to have friends.

Victoria rarely visited the Béons, and when she did she was instructed, like the other children, to keep away from the drawing room or any other room where there might be visitors to the house. At first they were told by Béon that this was because a man called Oliva was out to kidnap Henry and his sisters (it was around 1876 that Pepita's husband Oliva had reappeared to insti-tute legal proceedings in Bordeaux, and Lionel had asked Béon to do whatever was 'needful' to conduct proceedings on his behalf). But the reasons for keeping the children out of the reception rooms also included the fact that the Count felt it inappropriate to introduce illegitimate children to his friends.

With Max away at boarding school in Bordeaux, the roles within the family were soon established. Encouraged by her father at a distance, Victoria assumed the role of responsible older sister and dutiful daughter. Lionel counted on Victoria to be '*sage et obéissante*', particularly to Madame de Béon, and to take good care of the family, and he promised to make it up to her on his return. He was particularly keen that Victoria should look after Flora when she joined her older sister at the convent. Victoria, in turn, relished the power her role conferred, and found the memory of it too delicious ever to relinquish in later life.

Although the close-knit world of the Sackville West children had begun to pull apart after the death of Pepita, the charming, childish letters they wrote to each other during the 1870s suggest a great affection between the siblings – in marked contrast to their later correspondence. In a letter crammed with spelling mistakes, Henry tells how he cried when Victoria left for the convent, begs her to write him a longer letter than her last one and, on no account, to forget to enclose a picture of herself. In August 1878, he describes, in a letter from the lycée at Vanves

(now the Lycée Michelet), on the south-western outskirts of
Paris, a visit to Buttes Chaumont, the park established ten years
before in the north of Paris. He had just seen the lions, tigers,
jaguars, hippopotamuses and an elephant in the zoo when, after
lunch and a boat ride, he and his friends encountered a party of
'deaf-and-dumb children' who he feared were going to attack
them. The same month, Amalia writes to Victoria, hoping for
good weather in Berck-sur-Mer, a resort on the northern coast
where Victoria was on holiday with the nuns. There is a letter
from Flora too, in which she imagines all the things her sister
must have been doing at Berck – travelling there in the *wagon lit*
with her chums, fishing for shrimps, riding donkeys on the vast
white sands, swimming in the sea – and she asks Victoria to
bring back some shells for her little sisters, as she had done the
year before. Scrawled at the end of the letter is a hasty note from
Béon: *'deux mots seulement ma chère Pepita, pour te dire tout le
plaisir que m'a fait ta charmante petite lettre'.*

In the ten years following Pepita's death, the children saw
their father, on leave from Buenos Aires, for one brief period in
1876 and once again in 1880. While he was in Europe on the
first of these visits, Lionel stayed for a few days with the Béons
in Paris, visited Victoria in Berck and Boulogne in August, and
took Max out of school in Bordeaux. In September, he saw
Max off by steamer from Southampton to South Africa, where
it was hoped he would make a life for himself. He lodged at
first on a series of farms as he learned about agriculture. It must
have been hard for an eighteen-year-old Catholic boy speaking
very little English to be transported from south-west France to
these hard-scrabble, pioneer farms on the other side of the
world. Lionel was at first unimpressed by accounts of Max: 'It
seems that he has a very difficult disposition and he is very
obstinate but I hope to succeed with him.' Gradually, however,
as the truth surrounding Max's circumstances emerged, he
became more sympathetic.

Amalia (*left*) and Flora (*centre*) in 1881. Is the stormy background to Henry's photograph (*right*) a sign of things to come?

In March 1878, Max wrote to Lionel in French from a farm belonging to the Norton family at Greenwich, Umvoti. As he recovered from an acute inflammation of the bowels, which had kept him up for six nights on end vomiting blood, Max described how he had been treated on the various farms where he had been sent to work. A Mr Shepstone had put him out to a Mr Woodroffe, whom he believed at first to be 'a perfect gentleman' but who soon revealed himself to be 'so harsh to me, making me work like a Kaffir'. He was made to wait at table and generally treated as a servant. When Max fell ill, Mr Woodroffe simply laughed at his condition, and sent him out to work, precipitating the violent inflammation that had 'nearly carried [him] off'. What particularly distressed him was the lack of respect with which he had been treated, and he was pleased when his father eventually wrote to these farmers to let them know who he was. 'I have some pride Father,' Max wrote, 'and I do not like to be taken for a vagabond as they previously believed me to be.'

Max did not feel, however, that his time had been wasted: he now spoke good English, could tell a good animal from a bad one, and had learned to ride. 'I wish to be useful to you and to show you that you have in me a sensible and grateful son,' he wrote to his father, but could not see how he could help him so long as he remained in Natal. Ideally, he would like to leave Natal but, at the very least, he hoped that his father would procure some more suitable career for him.

Through the good offices of Lady Derby, Max was taken on to the staff of Sir Bartle Frere, who had been appointed two years earlier as High Commissioner (the equivalent of Governor-General) for Southern Africa. 'If he does not make his way now it will be his fault,' wrote Lionel.

From September 1878 to March 1879, Frere was in Pietermaritzburg, where he had been directed by the Colonial Office to deal with the escalating unrest. He was living in the English-style villa residence of the Governor of Natal Sir Henry Bulwer, and it is likely that this is where Max lived and worked too. That summer in the dusty capital of Natal was a time of increased tension. Frere's attempts to create a confederation in the region were being resisted by the states of Southern Africa, including the Afrikaners of the recently annexed Transvaal and the various Black African states. In Natal, where the British were outnumbered twenty to one, there were frequent cases of cattle-rustling and attacks by King Cetewayo's Zulu warriors on Christian missionaries and their converts. As he tried to convince his political bosses in London of the seriousness of the threat posed by 'the demon king', Frere complained of leading 'a very dreary life . . . grumbling at deficiencies I cannot supply & delays I am powerless to shorten'. He had little support, no civil service, and communications across the vast expanses of mostly virgin land – Pietermaritzburg was 1,000 miles from Cape Town – were very slow.

'The continued preservation of peace depends,' he continued, 'on the caprice of an ignorant and blood-thirsty despot, with a most overweening idea of his own importance and prowess, and an organised force of at least 40,000 armed men at his absolute command, ready and eager at any moment to execute, in their ancient fashion of extermination, whatever the caprice or anger of the despot may dictate.' When Cetewayo ignored an ultimatum by Frere, British troops were ordered into Zululand. In January 1879, one of the columns was massacred at Isandlwana – with more than 800 British troops killed (the equivalent of an entire regiment). Many of the families in Pietermaritzburg lost a member. The Anglo-Zulu War had begun, and Pietermaritzburg itself was only seventy miles from the front.

Max's time on Frere's staff, therefore, came at a crucial moment in South Africa's history. The dispatches he was clerking dealt with the consequences of Isandlwana, which included the censure and eventual recall of his boss. Yet he never took to the task. The news his father received about Max had started to put him out 'greatly'. 'He tells me that he does not find himself at ease with the Governor. He does not like to copy despatches, that the work was bad for his health [one of the first of many references in the correspondence to Max's health]. He has changed his ideas and believes that farming will suit him better, and has returned to his old friend Mr Norton . . . It is impossible to do more than I have done for him and he was in a position to make a fortune. Now it is necessary to begin again.' In short, Lionel was 'very discontented with his conduct'. He had himself been 'writing out despatches for 20 years', he complained to Béon, 'but young men nowadays have other ideas', and, by the way, could Béon 'get [him] more of this Champagne?'

———

Life for the children changed on Mme de Béon's death in November 1879. 'I feel very much for all you have gone through,' Lionel wrote in commiseration to Béon on the nineteenth, 'I also do not wish to speak of arrangements that have to be made for my children before knowing what you would think of doing yourself. In all cases your interests are mine and you can rely on my devotedness.' In the event, Flora and Amalia went to join Victoria in the convent and, according to what Victoria told her father, were pleased with the arrangement.

Despite Lionel's promise to Victoria not to leave the girls in the convent for long, a year passed before he arranged for them to be removed. He engaged the help of Mrs Mulhall, since she was 'the only Catholic lady of [his] acquaintance', and he needed advice about educating them as Roman Catholics. Lionel had got to know the author of *Between the Amazon and the Andes* in Buenos Aires, where she and her husband 'moved in the best Spanish and English Society'. Indeed, Lionel himself featured in the book, as a member of a shooting party she had encountered in Paraguay consisting of British and French diplomats. 'It was curious to hear the different opinions on the expedition,' she wrote. 'The Frenchmen complained bitterly about the mosquitoes and the rough life, which the Englishmen, on the contrary, enjoyed, as they had capital sport, having killed three tigers, a quantity of *patos reales*, and other birds, besides capturing a live alligator . . . I am indebted to the Hon. Lionel Sackville-West for the following notes on sport, which I give with his permission.' There followed some detailed recommendations from Lionel about the different guns required: a breech-loading and a muzzle-loading gun, as well as a short Snider rifle for shooting deer, and an 'Express' rifle for shooting jaguars on the rivershore from a boat.

Mrs Mulhall was 'only too happy to do anything for them when she went over to England', and in the summer of 1880 she and her husband accompanied Lionel on a visit to his daughters in Berck-sur-Mer. Soon after that, the intrepid Mrs Mulhall, whom the preface to her book described as 'the first Englishwoman to penetrate the heart of South America, travelling for thousands of miles through untrodden forests', escorted them to England. On the Channel crossing, Mrs Mulhall told Victoria that her parents had never been married (a delicate task which Lionel later claimed he had never specifically commissioned her to carry out). 'This was a great shock and surprise to me, but I naturally did not at first realise the consequences,' Victoria later recalled.

Marion Mulhall, breaker of shocking news

On arrival in England, Mrs Mulhall took the children to Grasslands, her house in Balcombe, Sussex, for a few months.

From here, Victoria wrote an affectionate letter to Béon in November, acknowledging the kindness and care they had received from his late mother, and asking him to send her a photo of himself, and if he had one of her own mother, too (even if she had to return it, having gazed at it). She asked after Henry, or 'Bébé' as he was known in the family, who had stayed behind in France at school and had developed a 'quinsy' (abscess) on his eye. 'Goodbye dear Béon,' she ended her letter, 'I kiss you from all my heart, Your little friend Pepita.' It was as if the Béons were as much a part of the family as her father and his distant relations. But all this was to change. Towards the end of the year, Mrs Mulhall took them to the Convent of the Sacred Heart in the Highgate Road in London, where they stayed until July 1881.

In March 1881, Victoria confided to Béon that she had been informed by Mrs Mulhall 'as delicately as possible' of 'certain little family matters that you know about papa and mama'. It had been Aunt Mary, Lady Derby, who had thought it time for Victoria to learn the truth, so that she would not be 'vexed' at the 'differences that are made for us'. Aunt Mary, 'who seems the best disposed towards us of the world', had also thought it a good idea if they were to be known from now on as West rather than Sackville West, a name 'which is so well known here'. Victoria was already so well schooled in the dark arts of secrecy and discretion that she asked Béon not to write to her on this subject at the convent, 'where they do not know anything', and where the nuns were inclined to open and read her mail. He was to send all letters via her father, whose correspondence she always received under seal.

The new nomenclature extended to their first names, too. As a young girl, Victoria, whose full name was Victoria Josephine Dolores Catherine, had sometimes been known as 'Lolo' (short for Dolores) and sometimes, like her mother, by the pet name of Pepita (a diminutive of Josefa or Josephine).

Indeed, her father and sisters called her Pepita throughout the 1870s, and it was as Pepita Sackville West that she had been enrolled in the convent school run by the Sisters of St Joseph. Her aunt Mary now insisted she be called Victoria; and that 'Fleur de Marie', as she was originally named, should be called Flora.

Why, at just the moment when Lionel's children were moving to England and meeting for the first time some of their wealthy and aristocratic relations, were they being asked to change their names? Was it simply for form's sake that they were being asked to call themselves plain West rather than Sackville West? Or was there a more strategic reason? In September 1881, Lionel was encouraged by his sister Mary, Lady Derby, to sign a memorandum declaring that 'my adopted children, Max, Henry, Josephine, Flora and Amalia, are not legitimate, nor in succession to family property'. The memorandum was sent to William Edward, my great-grandfather, who acted as his older brother's agent, paying for the maintenance of the children out of money set aside for this purpose by Lionel.

William Edward and his sister Mary had discussed the problem of Pepita in the 1860s, and 'the awkwardness of [Lionel's] position in the diplomatic service arising from his connection with her as his mistress'. Then, in the 1870s, after the death of Pepita, their discussions had focused more on the financial mess that Lionel had created for himself, and the obligation to maintain the daughters. Now more than a career or money was at stake. There was the succession to Knole itself.

It would be hard to imagine something more settled than Knole. In *Knole and the Sackvilles*, Vita Sackville-West's love letter to the house in which she had been born and grown up, and which was to exercise a hold on her greater than any human being, she captured the spirit of the place:

It has all the quality of peace and permanence; of mellow age; of stateliness and tradition . . . It has the deep inward gaiety of some very old woman who has always been beautiful, who has had many lovers and seen many generations come and go, smiled over their sorrows and their joys, and learnt an imperishable secret of tolerance and humour. It is, above all, an English house. It has the tone of England; it melts into the green of the garden turf, into the tawnier green of the park beyond, into the blue of the pale English sky; it settles down into its hollow amongst the cushioned tops of the trees; the brown-red of those roofs is the brown-red of the roofs of humble farms and pointed oast-houses, such as stain over a wide landscape of England the quilt-like pattern of the fields.

In parallel with this settled, rooted place was the shiftless exist-ence of Victoria and her siblings. During the years since they had left the provincial backwaters of Arcachon, they had effectively been orphans, leading hand-to-mouth lives in the charge of a series of guardians. As they moved from the houses of friends to rented seaside villas, from Catholic boarding schools to London lodgings, their names changed too – in contrast to their legiti-mate uncles, aunt and cousins, for whom the principle of preserving an association between the family name, Sackville, and the family place, Knole, remained paramount.

As a fifth son, Lionel had had, at birth, very little prospect of succeeding. But, due to a combination of unlikely family circumstances and legal complications, he was by the late 1870s heir to the title and to Knole. The oldest son, George, had died in his thirties in 1850. The second son, Charles, a soldier, had always hated the idea of being 'thrust forward to fill the gap' created by the death of his adored elder brother, and, in 1873, he eventually committed suicide by drowning (the last time that he was seen alive was crossing the road to the towpath along the River Cam). The third son, Reginald, a clergyman,

had then succeeded to the senior of the two family inheritances
– as Earl De La Warr and owner of Buckhurst in Sussex. There
was a provision, however, in the family settlements, known as
the 'shifting clause', which precluded him, as Earl De La Warr,
from inheriting Knole as well; and so, after a bitter court battle,
it was the fourth son, Mortimer, a courtier, who assumed
ownership of Knole in 1873. In 1881, Mortimer, who had by
now been created Baron Sackville of Knole in his own right,
was in his sixties, married and childless. Lionel was next in line,
and Lionel's younger brother, William Edward, the only
brother with legitimate children after that. The question of the
legitimacy, or otherwise, of Lionel's children was becoming
ever more pressing.

Lady Derby was the family member most insistent on establishing some clarity. She was probably the most powerful and
meddlesome of that generation of siblings, and brought to
family politics the same energy and control (not to mention
capacity for intrigue) that she had brought to her proxy political career. In the 1860s she had attempted to establish her first
husband, the Marquess of Salisbury's, country seat Hatfield as
a powerhouse for aspiring Tory politicians, and in the 1870s,
she had promoted, behind the scenes, the interests of her
second husband, the Earl of Derby.

Aunt Mary visited the girls at the convent, as did their
grandmother, the Dowager Lady De La Warr. Whenever they
went to Derby House, however, they would be turned out of
the drawing room – 'banished', as Victoria later described it –
to prevent them meeting any visitors. Those visitors included
another of their aunts, the Duchess of Bedford, who used to
visit her sister at six o'clock every evening, but steadfastly
refused to see her nieces and actively disapproved of the help
Lady Derby gave them. 'To this day,' Victoria claimed in 1897
(the year of the Duchess's death), 'I have never seen her.' This
may not have been a great loss since, according to Georgiana

The children's Aunt Bessie, Duchess of Bedford

Blakiston, the author of a book on Woburn and the Russells and a great-niece of Elizabeth's husband, 'the unimaginative and ponderous temperament of the Duchess of Bedford was not capable of raising the cloud of gloom that encompassed their family life [her husband eventually shot himself]'. Their uncle Mortimer, Lord Sackville, refused to see any of his nephews and nieces, too.

Another of their rare visitors at the convent in Highgate that summer was Eugénie Louet. Bonny, as she was known in the family, was then governess to Lady De La Warr's family, and she brought with her the two De La Warr girls, first cousins of the young Sackville Wests. It was the first time that Victoria, Amalia and Flora had met Bonny (she was later to become Victoria's lady-companion and trusted confidante), and they plied her with questions about their history. Later that year, Bonny accompanied the girls to Buckhurst for the day.

Victoria left the convent in July 1881 with nothing but a certificate enabling her to seek employment as a governess. She later showed the certificate to Vita, describing how at that time in her life there seemed no other path open to her. 'I must say,' Vita wrote in *Pepita*, 'that I smile to think how she would have turned any employer's house upside-down within a week. Anyone less adapted to the position of a governess I can scarcely imagine.' The girls spent the summer holidays in lodgings in Eastbourne, where Henry, who had been escorted back from Paris by Mr Mulhall, joined them. It was then off to new lodgings with another governess, Miss Hillier, in Denbigh Street, Pimlico.

Victoria did not tell her sisters the shocking truth about their illegitimacy, but passed the news on to Henry, before he was taken by his father in October 1881 to board at Stonyhurst, the Jesuit college in Lancashire. She thought it better that Henry should learn of his illegitimacy from her, rather than from the other boys at school. But she told him to keep it a secret, 'as it was a dreadful thing. He seemed to be astonished but probably did not realise what it meant.' His schoolfellows inevitably did find out, and made his life a misery as a result. Despite Aunt Mary's efforts to change the family name that Lionel's children went by, Lionel had enrolled Henry at Stonyhurst as his son, and in the name of Sackville West – in a vain attempt to spare him any unpleasantness.

'There was something awesome, too, in the great stone-flagged corridors, the huge rooms, rude desks etc., and the stray glimpses of the inhabitants . . . Nothing since has ever approached that sense of despairing desolation and abandonment. He felt that there was no friend here for him, not a soul to whom he could turn, or who would not laugh, or at least smile, at his sorrows.' This is how the author Percy Hetherington

Fitzgerald described his first term at Stonyhurst in the late 1840s. But the first impressions for Henry, who spoke very little English on arrival, who was used to the company of women, and who felt lost in his translation to the cold, damp slopes of Longridge Fell, must have been even more miserable.

Henry attended Stonyhurst for five years, and he did not distinguish himself, moving slowly and anonymously up the school through the years, or 'schools', named after the components of a classical education: Elements, Figures, Rudiments, Grammar, Syntax . . . The intellectual subtlety and sophistication of the Jesuit education (at a time when academic standards under Father John Gerard were improving) were wasted on poor Henry. It was a communal life, the day starting with prayers and Mass in chapel, followed by an hour's study at 7 a.m., breakfast at 8 a.m., and ending at 7.30 p.m. with dinner at refectory tables in the dining hall, beneath the stags' heads and portraits of distinguished former pupils on the walls. Everything was on the grand scale: a Renaissance-style mansion, with marble floors, great oak staircases, fine plasterwork ceilings and a study place with 200 seats. While Henry was there, a vast new 560-foot south front was being built, with dormitories covering an area of 2,000 square yards on the upper floor. These developments expressed the driving vision of Stonyhurst's creators, but Henry himself was left behind by education on such a grand, almost industrial, scale.

———

While the girls were in Denbigh Street, plans were made and permission sought for Victoria to join her father, who had in 1881 been appointed British Minister to the United States in Washington, as his hostess and the mistress of his house. Aunt Mary was warm-hearted as well as meddlesome. She had noticed that her illegitimate niece, however insecure and ill-educated, had a certain style, and persuaded the Foreign Secretary, Lord Granville, that it would be a good idea to send Victoria to Washington. Queen Victoria gave her consent, on condition that Washington's notoriously snobbish and exclusive society agreed. A committee, consisting of Mrs Garfield, the wife of the American President (who was assassinated that year), Mrs James Blaine, the wife of the Secretary of State, Mrs Bancroft Davis, the wife of the Assistant Secretary of State, and Mrs Donald Cameron, the wife of a leading Republican senator from Pennsylvania, was formed – and approved the proposal.

Many years later, when the question arose of whether Victoria and her sisters were generally considered legitimate during their years in America, Maria Stockton Cheston (née Howell), the daughter of a US admiral who had come to live in Washington, recalled 'a discussion amongst the leading ladies of Washington Society'. They had debated 'whether she [Victoria] should be received in Society . . . on the ground of her illegitimacy' and 'decided that she should be received – it was absolutely accepted in Society in Washington that she was illegitimate . . . The same opinion was held all the time she was there without exception.'

As in so many aspects of his life, Lionel later claimed to have been completely ignorant of all these machinations: 'When I was at Washington, Victoria came to me first and then my other daughters joined me. I did not make any application personally for leave for my daughters to be allowed to come out to me – I believe Lady Derby made the application, I have no personal knowledge on the subject, I say it from what I have heard. I do not know that any consent was obtained from any authority at Washington for my daughters to join me.' Lionel also continued to be economical with the truth about his daughters' illegitimacy. It is hardly surprising that, as a result of such connivances, all of the children would be so confused about their names and identities for the rest of their lives.

3

Continental Drift

In December 1881, Victoria set sail for the United States on the Cunard Line's RMS *Bothnia*. She was accompanied by John Sturgis, an American acquaintance of her aunt Mary, and his daughter. Mr Sturgis thanked Lady Derby 'for giving my daughter so sweet a sister & myself a companion so charming . . . I quite envy her father the possession of a child at once so docile & of so good a disposition. You must not consider my expression extravagant but must remember that 12 days' intimate association on board ship is equal to an equal number of years of acquaintance on land.'

Victoria joined her father in Washington, moving into the British legation, a recently built, red-brick mansion in the seventeenth-century-French style, on the corner of Connecticut Avenue and North Street, about fifteen minutes' walk northwest of the White House. A *porte cochère* at the front of the mansion carried the royal court of arms, and from there a flight of stone steps led up to the front door and a hall dominated by a portrait of Queen Victoria in her coronation robes, hanging at the head of the grand staircase.

The surrounding area preserved a surprisingly rural air for a national capital. The novelist Henry James captured Washington's appeal at this moment when the United States was poised to

Lionel Sackville-West (*centre*) on the steps of the British Legation in Washington

usurp Great Britain's industrial leadership of the world: 'It is very queer and yet extremely pleasant: informal, familiar, hetero-geneous, good-natured, essentially social and conversational, enormously big and yet extremely provincial, indefinably ridicu-lous and yet eminently agreeable. It is the only place in America where there is no business, where an air of leisure hangs over the enormous streets, where everyone walks slowly and doesn't look keen and preoccupied. The sky is blue, the sun is warm, the women are charming, and at dinners the talk is always general.' At one of these dinners, Henry James was particularly taken with Victoria, the Minister's 'most attractive little ingénue of a daugh-ter, the *bâtarde* of a Spanish ballerina'.

Victoria's role was to act as social hostess for the British Minister and to manage his household – a role requiring some skill, since her father's disposition did not incline to the soci-able, and his means, as a younger son, were limited. Mrs Blaine, the wife of the recently replaced Secretary of State, particularly noted the rather derelict air of the legation before Victoria's arrival and the poor quality of the food.

Victoria was a little lonely at first – 'I so much regret that my little sisters are not here with me,' she wrote to Béon – but despite her shyness and her broken English, she was soon managing the legation 'with a knowledge that is not to be believed', as her father reported. She generally made a very favourable impression. Mrs Blaine, whom she visited the day after her arrival in Washington, found her charming. Mrs Henry Adams, the Society hostess, thought Minister West's 'convent-fledged daughter' elegant and loved her 'charming foreign accent'. 'It's a curious position for a girl of eighteen to be put at the head of a big establishment like the British lega-tion,' Mrs Adams wrote to her father. 'She is delighted with her first week here. As I can't endure English misses, it's a great relief to have this pretty girl after Lady Thornton [the previous Minister's wife] with her neuralgia and sharp tongue . . . a funny little church mouse in contrast with the sharp-clawed grimalkin who preceded her.' She was certainly an asset to her father, 'the quiet, sad-eyed British plenipotentiary'. He, on the other hand, 'does not improve on further acquaintance; is *very* dull – no conversation – and it seems to me a nullity'.

Lionel's professional style, as one of his colleagues in London later recalled, was as laconic as his personal style. When Minister West sent a letter from Washington reporting on the impact of the Irish Question on relations between Britain and the United States, it arrived 'looking very pregnant in a big envelope'. All it contained was an extract from a newspaper on the subject. His boss at the Foreign Office simply lifted his eyebrows, and held out the document at arm's length, observing, ironically: 'This is a satisfactory elucidation of this important question and shows conclusively the advantage of a well-informed diplo-matic agent.' Lionel's former colleague went on to describe the diplomatic agent in question, Minister West, as:

a curious person. His conversation is just like his correspondence – when it exists at all. At first sight you would think he was about as bad a man as you could have here. But I can't think he is at all a bad man. The Americans thoroughly understand him and tell him all sorts of things they don't to anyone else. They have a common taste for whiskey, poker and business, and a common hatred for female society. He never humbugs anyone, and never makes any bones over what he wants, and he always gets it. To our Government unfortunately he is so hopelessly reserved that unless he is directly asked for anything he never gives anything at all.

By contrast, Victoria took to her role instinctively: she was a natural hostess, organising dinners, dances and paper-chases, and participating in the established Washington social rituals of afternoon calls and ladies' lunches. As she did so, she grew from a shy, inexperienced convent girl into a popular and confident young woman and, in the process, as her friend Mrs Elizabeth Cameron later observed, she raised 'the whole status of the Legation'.

Victoria was beautiful at this stage of her life. To her mother she owed her Mediterranean looks, her dancer's figure and tiny waist, the lustrous dark hair that hung to her hips, long eyelashes, and olive skin so fine (and unlined into old age) that she would never in her life wear make-up. Arched eyebrows framed her expressive dark blue eyes, and particularly in profile – with her classic nose and her long neck – she exuded a delicate grace. She was to become a spectacular social success. The press was enthusiastic – the scrapbook she kept of her cuttings extolled the 'sweet and winning charm of her manners'. 'She is not yet nineteen years old,' raved one correspondent, and yet she combined 'the dignity of a woman with the unconscious sprightliness of a child. Her style of beauty is more Castilian than Anglo-Saxon.'

Victoria brushes her luxuriant hair in the Legation

No wonder, then, that she attracted so many suitors. In the 'Book of Reminiscences' she wrote in 1922, she listed those who had proposed to her, including, so she claimed, the President himself, the widower Chester Arthur. 'It was the second proposal I had at Washington,' she wrote, 'I burst out laughing in his face and said: "Mr. President, you have a son older than me and you are as old as my father."' Throughout her life, Victoria was attracted to rich and powerful men older than herself. But her conquests also included two young men on her father's staff: Charles Hardinge, a future head of the Foreign Office, and Cecil Spring-Rice, who joined the legation as Hardinge left it, and was himself to become Ambassador to the United States during the First World War. Her favourite, though, was probably Baron Carl Bildt, the chargé d'affaires at the Swedish legation. Every year, for the next half century, Victoria was to mark in her diary the anniversary of the day, 8 May, that 'Buggy' Bildt, who used to drive her out in his buggy 'with great dash and speed and *chic* along the flowering avenues of Washington', first proposed.

Victoria declined all of her suitors. She was still unmarried after six years in Washington and although she was regularly described by columnists as 'the reigning belle', and 'the most beautiful woman in diplomatic circles', she was no longer 'a bud'. This was partly, as she explained in a letter to her brother Max in South Africa, because 'I am so happy with Papa and help him in so many ways that I prefer to stay with him and take care of him', and partly because 'I can't make up my mind to marry any man because I can't trust any man enough. They are all so spoiled by Society and club life.' There was another reason, however. Victoria was always ambivalent about sex. And when Bonny, the French lady-companion she had brought to Washington, explained the 'facts of life' to her, she went right off the idea of marriage, and turned Buggy down without giving any reason. '*Ce pauvre Buggy!*' she later told Vita.

Victoria was joined in Washington in December 1883 by Flora, seventeen, and Amalia, fifteen – a development which, as Mrs Elizabeth Cameron recalled years later, 'Washington thought . . . rather too much' on account of their illegitimacy. The junior sisters were at first too young to enter Society, attending the legation ball of January 1884, in 'simple dresses of white nun's veiling and lace and corsage bouquets of apple blossoms', according to the *New York Times*, and sitting in the drawing room on either side of a governess. But in January 1885, Victoria organised a magnificent coming-out ball for Flora (with Scottish dancing), and a couple of years later Amalia came out at another big ball. From then on, the Misses West were publicly inseparable and fully received in Washington society. Amalia was sometimes described as the clever one, Victoria as the beauty, and Flora as shy and reticent. According to one American newspaper, 'Miss West [Victoria], who has scores of admirers in New York City, has

been a most painstaking mother to her younger sisters.' As
her father became more and more dependent on Victoria, the
sisters were subtly nudged into the shade from which they
never really emerged.

The three sisters on the transatlantic crossing

In the summer of 1886, the Misses West were escorted by
Bonny on a short visit to England – they tended to travel to
Europe in the summer as life was cheaper there, returning to
Washington in the autumn. It was the first time that Victoria
had seen her younger brother, Henry, since he had been packed
off to Stonyhurst in 1881. He was now going out to South Africa
to join Max, and she took him to the stores in London to buy
his outfits. Henry confided to her that he was very glad to be
going away because 'the boys at Stonyhurst had found out
about his birth and he could not stand it'. Victoria suggested
that, from now on, 'he drop the name of Sackville in order not
to identify himself and have unpleasant questions asked'.

During her years in Washington, Victoria worried not just about her illegitimacy, but also about money: the cost of running, and entertaining at, the legation, and the future of the family finances in general. The market-trader spirit that was later to inspire her interior decorating shop, Speall's, was already in evidence, as she tried to persuade Béon to send her tapestries for her to sell on at a profit to American buyers. 'It is quite natural,' she wrote in November 1887, 'that I like to make a little money, because if Papa was to die we would be very poor.' The same month she wrote to her brother Max, bemoaning the fact that their father had been taken in and fleeced by their former butler, Wills, and that as a result 'we have got to get square now . . . When Papa has to retire in ten years, his pension being only 13 hundred pounds a year, he will not be able to give us any allowance, we shall have barely enough to dress on and to live . . . If he were to die, what should we do? It makes me shiver to think of it. Let us hope, dear brother, that he may live long; he is so good and kind.' She also hoped, as she wrote to Max in January 1888, that their uncle Mortimer, the current Lord Sackville, would live a long time too (in fact, he was to die later that year). She did not like the idea of the Sackville title and Knole bypassing Max, as they inevitably would on account of his illegitimacy, and wished to defer that moment for as long as possible – in any case, 'the money would not benefit us much, as it is all employed to keep the house in good order, so it is much better that Papa should never be Lord Sackville, don't you think so?'

Max had learnt of his illegitimacy in the most brutal fashion in 1882. After six years in South Africa, Max had written to his father saying that he wished to get married to Mary Norton, the daughter of the farmer who had taken him in during his illness, and he was hoping to find out what his father could do for him 'in the way of settlements', as he imagined himself to be his heir. Max came to London to press for an answer, and was delighted to see his 'little sisters', Flora and Amalia, again, and to visit Henry, who had just broken his collarbone, at Stonyhurst. Lionel's younger brother, my great-grandfather William Edward, was deputed, 'much against [his] inclination', at Lady Derby's request, to tell Max the truth. Mrs Mulhall had already been asked, but refused to carry out the task.

On 9 March 1882, he met Max at 17 Upper Grosvenor Street and told him that Lionel and Pepita had never been married. 'He seemed utterly astonished and was much overcome,' recalled William Edward, 'but did not doubt my word. I had never seen him before and have never seen him since.' His only contact over the next few years was to make payments quarterly, at his brother's request, to Max and then Henry in South Africa through his Bankers Messrs Cox & Co.

On the other side of the Atlantic, in Washington, Lionel broached one evening with Victoria the fact that he and her mother had never been married – for the simple reason that Pepita already had a husband. He told her that he had loved Pepita, and would have been 'only too happy to marry her' if Oliva had died; the discussion in no way altered Victoria's 'personal feelings' towards her mother, whom she had always looked upon 'as a saint'.

Other members of the extended Sackville family were also being made aware for the first time of the family secrets. In the summer of 1882, Max's fourteen-year-old first cousin, William Edward's son, Lionel, a future Lord Sackville and husband of Victoria, was staying with his mother in the spa town of Homburg, where she had gone to take the waters for the disease that would kill her the following year. She told him that his 'uncle had lived for several years with a Spanish "actress" and had had children by her', that 'she had always heard that the mother was a very good woman' and that it was his 'grand-mother, Lady De La Warr's wish that the family should be kind to the children'. A couple of months later, Lionel met his young cousin, Lady Edeline Sackville, at Buckhurst, who told him that she was going to see 'our cousins, Uncle Lionel's children' (Flora and Amalia had stayed on in England after Victoria had left for America). Lionel did not think, however, that Edeline would be aware the cousins were illegitimate, as she was younger than he was, and 'would hardly have been told'.

Max was stunned by the news that his father and mother had never been married. He had recently got back in touch with Béon after a long silence, for which he apologised profusely, blaming his 'incurable laziness'. Béon had been like 'a second father' to him, wrote Max: 'I know how you love us and what a good heart you have or I should be afraid to address myself to you after so many years.' And it was to Béon that he confided his great unhappiness: 'They have told me the secrets of our births, secrets I had not the slightest knowledge of which has nearly sent me mad. Oh, if Father had told me sooner. When one is of my age and about to commence life a thing like this is sufficient to make you despair concerning everything.' He was particularly worried how these revelations would affect his engagement to Mary Norton. How could he 'return to her and tell her the truth!' The fear of losing her oppressed him even more than the English climate ('one never sees the sun'), as he counted the hours until his return to Natal. He did not have a single regret nor a bitter thought, he claimed, for any worldly possessions he may have lost, 'I who fancied myself the heir of my Father since childhood.' He was now beginning to ask himself how he could have been so blind. 'The blow has been the more rude as I was not prepared for it. Oh how could my father allow me to pass all these years in ignorance . . . What an injustice that the children must suffer for the faults of their parents.'

Mary did not reject him on his return, however, and accepted him for what he was. 'All the rest seems indifferent to me now, and how little importance do I attach to what I have lost, position and title in one day. I never valued all of this very much and now that all my wishes are fulfilled in spite of all, what do I care! I am very happy.' Max was aware of the sacrifices Captain and Mrs Norton were making on his behalf and 'although Mr Norton has been very kind and spoken to me with plenty of regard', he did impose some conditions. For a start, he decided that his daughter needed time – a year's engagement – to reflect on the changed circumstances: a year which Max was confident would pass quickly as he worked 'like a negro' on the farm he was about to purchase, and the house he would build on it, 'all for her sake'.

Captain Norton also wanted Max to get hold of his birth certificate, to establish exactly who he was, and to make this a further condition of his consent to the marriage. In July 1882, the Sackville family solicitor wrote to the Attorney General of Natal asking whether this was strictly necessary, since 'there would be considerable trouble and expense in obtaining it from Spain'. In a second letter, he explained how Max's father had proposed giving him £1,500, and his aunt had proposed settling on him a further £1,500, to purchase and stock a farm. Surely, the solicitor argued, a letter from his firm remitting the £1,500 and forwarding the settlement of a further £1,500 would be accepted 'as sufficient evidence of identity without a certificate of Baptism from Spain'. In the light of all this, the Attorney General concluded that he did not believe a birth certificate was absolutely necessary.

Despite these reassurances, Captain Norton was still demanding the production of Max's birth or baptism certificate the following year. Lushington Phillips, an agent acting for the Sackville family, argued that even if such a certificate could now be obtained, 'it would give you no further information as to his status [beyond the fact that he is the avowed son of Lionel Sackville-West] which would interest or affect you or yours beyond what you now know'. The request would be distressing to Lionel, and serve only 'to raise the ghosts of a buried past and supply matter for gossip'. There was an implication that Captain Norton and Max were pursuing this line of inquiry purely out of curiosity. 'I am sorry West has made the request; it cannot be complied with and has caused useless pain,' Phillips concluded in a letter to the Sackville solicitor, 'for I am pretty confident the want of a Baptismal Certificate or information on it will not delay the marriage a single day'. But was Max's curiosity really so unreasonable? The twenty-five-year-old had only just learnt that he was illegitimate, and there were further revelations about his paternity to come.

The taint of illegitimacy would torture Max for the rest of his life. Why, he asked, in all the various legal documents produced by the Sackville solicitors at the time of this settlement, was he called simple Max West rather than his 'full name of Sackville West . . . Mr Norton and I noticed this difference and were puzzled. We could not help noticing it as it was so plainly marked. What is the object of this?' The object was clear: to erase him from the family record.

Max was staying with his future in-laws, the Nortons, on their farm, Greenwich, near Riet Vlei, as he scoured the country for a farm to purchase. It took time, and the frustration is apparent in his letters. In the autumn of 1882, he eventually bought a 2,500-acre farm called Dartington, on a tributary of the Mooi River, in Natal, for £1,200 from a Mr Studdy.

British immigrants had started to settle the Mooi River in the 1850s (Mooi means 'beautiful' in Afrikaans, which is exactly what the area is). At first, these pioneers farmed sheep, shearing them once a year and transporting the wool by wagon to the local capital, Pietermaritzburg. It was a hard, hand-to-mouth existence, constantly under threat from stock diseases and from packs of wild dogs and warthogs that came down from the Drakensberg Mountains to roam the grasslands. In the 1880s, however, the railway was extended from Durban on the coast to Johannesburg in the interior, passing through the Mooi River district, and the face of farming was transformed. Farmers could now produce more than they needed, and use the railway to market the surplus farther afield. Towards the end of the century, progressive farmers began to import pedigree stock from Britain, and in particular Shorthorn cattle. Max was a founding member of the Mooi River Farmers' Association, which was formed in 1893 to promote the market for sheep and cattle. As a result of all this, the Mooi River became, by the time of the Boer War, a prosperous stock-raising and horse-breeding area.

The money for Dartington came from the £1,500 settled on Max by his father, but in order to stock it he needed the further £1,500 given to him by his aunt Mary. This sum was to come partly from the sale of a family-owned farm, called Aberfeldy, in Griqualand – a fact that Max chose not to appreciate, preferring instant cash (which he believed he had originally been promised) rather than deferred money from the sale of Aberfeldy. On 4 October 1882, he wrote to Lushington Phillips about the problem: 'Expecting to receive the full amount in money as stated, I laid my plans accordingly, and now everything is upset. Do not think I grumble, I am thankful that at last I can start and work, but if the thing could be managed, if Lady Derby would give me the £630 and keep the farm I should like it much better . . . Do try, dear Judge Phillips, to change this.' He went on to beg another favour: could he pay a London saddler out of the balance of the £1,500 for a lady's saddle and bridle he had ordered? 'It is for Miss Norton and I would not disappoint her for anything.'

Next, there was the problem of a sitting tenant, Mr Ford, on the Dartington farm, with about six months of his lease left to run. Max had not previously been aware of this, and was desperate to get on to the property. 'How I shall manage I don't know,' he wrote to Phillips:

> for God's sake let us have no more delay; let's have everything settled once for all . . . I really despair sometimes at the time that is flying away. Five months gone now and I might have had my house built and all this time I have been doing nothing, living a wretched life at the Nortons expecting to hear every day that all was settled. There seems to be always something springing up in the way . . . The Nortons are as anxious as I am that I should go, how can I live so in their house in idleness when I expected to be off.

At least, the saddle had been sent out from London to his wife. 'It's a great weight off my mind,' wrote Max and he thanked Phillips for his help.

———

In 1885, Henry was still at Stonyhurst, and his father was wondering what to do with him. 'He is lazy . . . and the education at Stonyhurst is not practical, and he has not the qualities for business here,' Lionel complained. He was rather put out that 'those people there had the idea of making a priest of him'. And so it was decided, in 1886, that Henry should be sent to South Africa too. He stayed with his older brother at first, their father advising Max 'to keep him well in hand'. Victoria, too, encouraged Max to look after Henry, pointing out that while she helped their father by taking care of his household 'and managing everything', Max should help by taking care of Henry. 'Henry is not a bad child, he is still a mere child, I am sure – "*et ne se rend compte de rien*". He is not careful of his clothes or of anything, as he does not understand yet the value of money. I am sorry for you dearest Max, that he wears out his shoes and clothes so quickly. I will try to reason with him and make him understand to be more economical.' In letters to Max's wife, Victoria asked Mary to put up with him in their home, even if he was sometimes 'tiresome', but then, as she observed, life was not always '*couleur de rose*'.

Henry appreciated the fact that his older brother was 'very kind' to him: Max paid him pocket money to help him plant the orchard at Dartington, and taught him some of the rudiments of farming. Henry was happy at first, and wrote to his father that he could not think of 'any other life but farming [that] would have suited [him] so well'. But the brothers soon quarrelled, with Henry claiming that Max had stolen his best cow. Henry had to leave Max's farm, and was put under a Mr Nourse Varty at Stag Stones, on the Mooi River, to learn more about farming.

Victoria was 'very sorry' about the quarrel, as she wrote to Max in December 1889: 'Poor Papa has already so much worry and anxiety from many sources and he was in hopes his sons would give him satisfaction. Let us hope that at last, as you don't live with Henry any longer, you will kindly remain good friends. It is so sad that you two should be almost like enemies. Do be kind to him, dear Max and forgive him once more, make up with him.'

Mr Varty gave Henry a certain amount of responsibility, and in 1891, Lionel proposed to provide his younger son with a total of around £3,500 to purchase and stock three small farms, Farleigh, Hall Cross and Burgundy, with a total of just over two thousand acres. Henry was initially grateful – 'greatly indebted' – to his father for his kindness, 'and in return I shall try to do my best to get on well to please you'. Henry kept his father closely informed about progress. 'I have made a very good start . . . You cannot imagine how careful I have been with money,' he wrote in April 1892, getting Farleigh in order, ploughing forty acres of land, planting five acres of wattle for shelter and firewood, fencing in paddocks with two and a half miles of wire, and supervising the six men who worked for him.

––––––––

Outside the family circle, the muddle over his children's legitimacy persisted, with Lionel claiming that 'when my daughters stayed in Washington, they passed as my legitimate children, but everybody knew they were illegitimate'. The girls went by the name of West, and Victoria's official visiting cards were printed 'West' rather than Sackville West. These fine distinctions, with all that they meant for the sisters' sense of self and status at the time, were to become particularly significant twenty years later.

Victoria and Amalia in a carriage in the Massachusetts countryside

On the grounds of their illegitimacy, the girls were not, for example, presented at the Queen's Drawing Room, on returning to London on leave, as would have been the daughters of other British ambassadors. (Victoria, in fact, was not to be received at Court until after her marriage.) Cecil Spring-Rice, when secretary at the legation, hoped that favourable reports of Victoria being well received in London by visiting Americans would filter back to Washington, as 'it would do her and our poor Legation here a great deal of good'.

Matters came to a head with Flora's engagement. Flora became engaged to Gabriel Salanson, a third secretary at the French legation in Washington, at a ball in February 1888. Flora was at the time 'the most English-looking of the three sisters, who are Parisian to the tips of their toes', according to one newspaper report. 'She is medium in stature, has an elegant figure, blue eyes, blonde hair, and the tiniest hands and feet to be seen upon a mortal. She carries herself like a young princess, dances like a fairy, is vivacious and witty, has a sweet disposition and a cordial manner, and is greatly admired and beloved in her circle here.' Gabriel Salanson was 'a Society favourite', too, according to another newspaper report: '[he] is short and stout of figure and has a handsome, florid face. He comes of a good French family, is twenty-eight years old and is immensely rich.' This last claim was not true, as would later become clear.

Neither of them had consulted their families beforehand, and Gabriel was never to raise the subject of the engagement directly with his future father-in-law. It was Victoria who heard the news first – from Flora on the way back from the ball as they clattered through the streets in a brougham. 'I remonstrated with her,' Victoria recalled later, with a degree of social confidence that she can hardly have felt at the time, 'on the ground that he would not make a suitable match – his social position not being as good as ours'. And it was Victoria who first told her father of the engagement. 'I never cared about Salanson,' Lionel claimed, 'I took no active part with reference to the engagement or the marriage. I simply held aloof and let them manage their own affairs. I never even asked Salanson as to his means.' Nor, amazingly, or so he later claimed, did he have anything to do with the financial settlement made on Flora's marriage, which was left entirely to Béon and Gabriel.

Gabriel's superiors certainly approved of his marriage to the well-connected Flora. Lady Derby made 'numerous' enquiries about the young man, and found them quite satisfactory. Victoria, too, eventually came round to the idea, writing to Max, 'I think they will be quite happy together. What a pity you can't assist at the ceremony. Flora will be a pretty bride, her features are not very good, but her skin and her figure are lovely . . . I rather dread going to London, *où on a toujours l'air de me regarder avec pitié*, I feel it so' – this yet another reference to her illegitimacy.

'You know all about my father and mother?' Victoria had asked Gabriel, in her sitting room at the British legation, the day after his engagement to Flora. 'Of course I do,' he replied (although he was later to claim that he was unaware of the fact), 'all Washington knows it, and it makes no difference to me.' But whereas Gabriel knew that Flora was illegitimate, his recently bereaved father Louis, a former Counsellor General of Aisne in Picardy, did not (Gabriel's mother had died while he was at sea, travelling to France to tell his parents of his engagement). Nor did his uncle Charles, a general and Grand Officier de la Légion d'Honneur. Any suspicion of Flora's illegitimacy needed, therefore, to be kept from Gabriel's father, who was unwell at the time and who, it was thought, would never give his consent to the marriage if he knew the truth.

In April, a couple of months before the wedding, Victoria and her two sisters, accompanied by Bonny, were seen off at the railway station in Washington by the legation staff. They were bound for France, to buy Flora's trousseau and to prepare for the wedding. Lionel was due to join them in Paris just a few days before the ceremony, once all the arrangements had been made. Amalia was particularly worried by how much she would miss Flora after her marriage; as she confided to her Washington friend, Amy Heard, whose father was to become the American Minister to Korea, she found it much more fun being 'chaperoned' by the easy-going Flora than by her more censorious and bossy eldest sister. In any case, there was no hope of marriage for herself, 'poor little Malia', at the moment, as 'all of those who have given me a bit of heart this winter are so poor'.

There were lengthy discussions at the Hôtel de l'Empire, where the wedding party was staying, about how to keep the older Salansons in the dark. Béon proposed to get hold of Flora's birth and baptism certificates, in which Lionel had attested years before that Flora was his 'legitimate' daughter. Knowing that the claim was fraudulent and had been made only to spare Pepita's feelings, Victoria and her father, when he arrived in Paris, became increasingly nervous about '*les papiers*' – as the certificates were always referred to by the conspirators. They attempted to distance themselves from the elaborate deception. Lionel, in particular, as the original perpetrator of the falsehood, was sure that 'he and all of them would get into a bother over the business', but was persuaded by Béon and Salanson to go along with the story. As Lionel later confessed, he colluded in Béon's plan 'in order to hoodwink M. Salanson Père and the other guests at the ceremony'. When pressed as to why he had signed the marriage register acknowledging Flora as his 'legitimate daughter', he simply reverted to the familiar excuse that 'I did not read what I signed before I signed it'.

Béon and Gabriel also needed to spare the public embarrassment of Lord Lytton who, like Lionel's other diplomatic colleagues, knew that Flora was illegitimate. And so, when the word '*légitime*' was pronounced by the Maire at the civil marriage ceremony in Paris on 16 June 1888, half a dozen of the forty or fifty guests, led by Béon and Gabriel, coughed exaggeratedly and in unison to drown out the obvious lie. Victoria 'did object inwardly, but I made no objection. I had nothing to do with it.' This was the first of many little conspiracies, orchestrated by Béon and Gabriel but in which the Sackvilles were complicit, that were to come back to haunt the family. Gabriel and Béon laughed and congratulated themselves afterwards on the success of their trick as they repaired to the Hôtel de l'Empire.

The religious ceremony, a couple of days later, was conducted by the Bishop of Soissons, from the Salansons' native Picardy, who, according to *Le Gaulois*, gave a most elevated address on the institution of Christian marriage. It took place in the English Roman Catholic church of St Joseph, in the Avenue Hoche, not far from the convent school the girls had attended a decade before. Flora – as her future brother-in-law, the young Lionel, read in a newspaper cutting shown him by an Oxford contemporary – wore a white silk dress with a flowing veil and sprays of orange blossom. '*Toutes les notabilités de la colonie anglaise et les membres de l'ambassade assistaient à cette cérémonie*,' continued *Le Gaulois*. Victoria agreed that 'the whole ceremony was one of a lady of high position being married to a French gentleman' – although not one, she added, of particularly high standing.

Lionel and his two unmarried daughters returned via London, where they spent a few days, to the United States and rented a holiday home for the summer in Beverly, Massachusetts. One rainy day, while Victoria was away, her father was drawn, through sheer boredom, into the indiscretion that was to cost him his diplomatic career: an indiscretion that was particularly uncharacteristic for someone who so rarely, as his colleagues observed, put pen to paper.

Lionel had been tricked into answering a letter from a 'Mr Murchison', a former British subject now naturalised in the US, in which he was asked for his opinion as to which of the candidates in the forthcoming presidential election would be most favourable to Britain's interests. Flouting all protocol, Lionel replied, suggesting the Democrat candidate, the incumbent president Grover Cleveland, and in October, the Republicans (who had posed the trick question) had Lionel's unwise response published in the *New York Tribune*. There was an outcry, with popular indignation mounting as the date of the election approached. 'It was ironical,' someone later remarked to Vita, 'that your grandfather of all people, the most taciturn of men, should have been sacked for expressing himself too freely.'

Victoria and Amalia were staying with the Trevor family at Glenview, their late-Victorian country mansion overlooking the Hudson River, when, according to one of the Trevors, 'the ground was blown from under the feet of Sackville-West by the exposure of his foolish letter . . . Victoria was terribly upset and bemoaned the fact because she said that her father never would have answered that letter if she had been with him. I think Victoria was clever enough really to have kept her father on the rails.'

Lionel was recalled from Washington in disgrace. Before they left, the Sackvilles held, as was the custom, a sale of their personal effects at the legation, a sort of upmarket yard sale: from bric à brac, including brass hot-water kettles and old parasols, to items of far greater value, such as the brougham, the buggy, and the landau and Victoria carriages. The sale was a great success, with any objects bearing the Sackville family monogram and crest fetching particularly high prices.

The Washington *Evening Star* recorded the final days in the city of Victoria, the young woman who 'has never made a mistake in all the delicate social duties that she has been required to perform in seven years at the British legation'. Victoria and her father spent their last evening with Mrs Whitney in her box at Albaugh's theatre, but the exact hour of their departure from Washington 'was kept within the circle of their intimate friends, as Lord Sackville [as he now was] feared an unkind demonstration at the station'. The following day, 23 November, Lionel and his daughters left Washington by train.

As the train rounded the curve, they waved the bouquets of yellow roses they were carrying from the vestibule of the front car until they passed out of sight.

There was, however, one consolation for Lionel's recall in disgrace from Washington. On 1 October, Lionel's older brother Mortimer had died childless at the age of sixty-eight, and unexpectedly Lionel had inherited Knole and the Sackville title. From now on, the Misses West started to call themselves Sackville West again.

4

The Surprise Inheritance

'I am so worried about the future,' Victoria wrote in her diary towards the end of 1888, after a particularly rough Atlantic crossing. On their return to England from America after the Murchison Affair, the future was uncertain. Despite the hundreds of letters of support he received from friends, former colleagues and members of the American public, and despite his own best efforts to defend his actions (which he later published privately in *My Mission to the United States*), Lionel had left his job in disgrace. He was still on full pay but, as he told Victoria, he could not 'count on its continuance if nothing turns up', and it looked increasingly unlikely that he would get another post (he was to be retired on a pension in April 1889). Most worrying of all, Knole itself, which he had inherited so unexpectedly, was encumbered with problems.

Like all landowners, the Sackvilles had been hit by the agricultural depression of the 1870s and 1880s, in which land rents fell by around fifty per cent. In any case, the Sackville estates were already far too small to support Knole, one of the largest private houses in the country. In 1883 these estates consisted of a total of 8,551 acres, yielding £11,250 a year, a pittance compared with those commanded by Lionel's sisters, the Duchess of Bedford and the Countess of Derby.

The Sackvilles' immediate problems included the succession duties that had to be paid on Mortimer's death, and the complication of Mortimer's will itself. Mortimer had become increasingly deranged in his dotage, claiming that his servants were plotting to poison him, and falling out with all the members of his family except his wife. In his will, he left much of his personal estate to Queen Victoria's four Maids of Honour (he was only a life tenant of Knole itself, so he could not leave that as well). Whether this was to spite his relatives or whether, as Vita suggested, 'he had private reasons for wishing to benefit one of them, and hit on the method of doing it without singling her out into scandalous publicity', the Sackvilles contested the will. They believed that the Maids of Honour would not dare to come to court and face the scandal, and would settle out of court instead – which they did. In the meantime, however, as Victoria wrote to Max, there was 'no money whatever to be paid to Papa for at least two years . . . We are in a bad fix for the present, as Knole is so expensive to keep up.'

Knole itself had begun to look a bit shabby. A book of photographs, presented as a memento to Queen Victoria in 1881, celebrated the ancient magnificence of the house and its treasures: the tapestries, and the paintings by Reynolds and Gainsborough, which the family's advisers were now looking to sell (and several of which were soon to find their way to the sale rooms). But there is plenty of evidence, too, of a general neglect and decrepitude. Ivy clings to the walls, winding itself through cracks in the leaded windows, and giving the house an overgrown and forlorn feel. The glowing green-and-gold tapestries that swathe the walls may look magnificent in Mortimer's book of photographs, but they were a little threadbare; the russet velvets that covered the chairs of state were frayed; the silver furniture was tarnished; and, here and there, the portraits of ancient Sackvilles sprouted a fungal bloom after centuries of exposure to the damp. In the attic galleries, which had been used for hundreds of years as store rooms, priceless chairs, chests and table tops were arrayed along the walls, the marquetry slowly flaking to the floor with the mounds of frass left by the woodworm. Then as now, leaks developed at points in the several acres of roof, with the water dripping into buckets strategically placed on the floor, or onto the objects themselves, and the lath and plaster hanging in festoons from the ceiling. Accounts of the time describe fires periodically breaking out in the chimneys of this labyrinthine mansion, the smoke billowing out through the wood panelling, and the sound of rats scuttling and scratching behind the wainscots.

For the truth is that Sackvilles have never been quite rich enough for the size of their house. Thomas Sackville, Earl of Dorset, who took possession of Knole in 1604, may have turned a draughty and ramshackle medieval mansion into a Renaissance palace – a great show house to celebrate his success as Lord Treasurer to King James I – but within a generation, the house that Thomas had remodelled was too big. Built to accommodate a household of more than a hundred people, Knole's exceptional size was already an anachronism.

The general gloom had been intensified by the gradual withdrawal of Knole from the outside world, as Mortimer descended into his private hell. Mortimer had become irritated by the popularity of the park, complaining about people 'galloping promiscuously about', and in 1883 he had posts placed across the main gate to prevent horses, and even prams, from entering. There was a public outcry. On the night of 18 June 1884, 1,500 people from Sevenoaks broke down the posts across the entrance and, singing 'Britons never never shall be slaves', marched on the house where they deposited the posts at the main door, smashed a few windows, and shouted abuse at Lord Sackville. Mortimer felt so threatened that he soon left Knole, to live for a time in the Grand Hotel at Scarborough.

On the morning of 11 August 1887, while Mortimer and his

wife were still in Scarborough, a fire broke out in the corner of the Great Barn at Knole, setting light to 300 tons of hay. Although the fire was under control by mid-afternoon, it did £3,000 worth of damage and could so easily have spread through the stables to the North Wing, with devastating consequences. Crowds of people flocked to Knole to watch the spectacle, and to help. The irony was not lost in one contemporary account: 'Although Lord Sackville has been wont rigidly to exclude the public of late years from Knole, on Tuesday last the people literally saved his mansion by ignoring his exclusiveness and flocking at the first sound of alarm in hundreds to the place, where they manned the hand-engines and assisted in other ways to subdue the flames.'

Local residents watch the great fire of 1887 in the Barn at Knole

It was also ironic, perhaps, given the possessiveness the place was to inspire in several of his children, that Lionel himself was not keen at first to live at Knole. Victoria thought he preferred Wildernesse – the nearby home of his friends, the Hillingdons, where he spent a lot of time – a hundred times more than the house he had just inherited. 'Knole is a regular white elephant,' he wrote to Max from Cannes in February 1889, enclosing an advance of £100 on his allowance, 'and I do not expect to get much benefit out of it.' This was confirmed by Victoria in a letter to her brother in which she claimed that her father had had to borrow the money to send his son. 'You have no idea how much he must borrow to keep up Knole. All that is very unfair and trying.' She went on to advise Max with all her heart not to 'have any more children, as you say they cost such a lot to bring up' (Max and Mary were to go on to have four) and enclosed some photographs of herself – 'My photos don't give you an idea of what I am like, as I always look so cross in them, and yet I never feel cross! People tell me right and left that I am very pretty but please, dearest Max, don't think for a minute that it makes me vain; my head has never been turned by success or compliments.'

As worrying to Victoria as the family's financial future was her precarious position as an illegitimate child; Victoria was always acutely conscious of this 'stain', as she described it, that went beyond the merely social to the very heart of her identity. In *Pepita*, Vita explained her mother's later materialism and cynicism in the light of her illegitimacy: 'I see now that owing to the difficult beginnings of her life, and to the stigma which had lain over her birth, making everything delicate and doubtful, she had unconsciously absorbed the idea that the world was a hard place where one must fight one's own battle for one's own best advantage.' She noted a change around the time of her mother's departure for Washington: 'Then everything had been startlingly reversed. Instead of anxiety, there was security; instead of being the unwanted little foreigner, hustled away at a stranger's approach, she had become the spoilt young hostess at Washington, the autocratic young mistress of Knole . . . Yet none of this, I think, ever succeeded in obliterating those early impressions: life had treated her harshly once, and might at any moment do so again; therefore one must make the most of the opportunity when it offered, and one must, in fairness, teach one's child the same lesson as a possible safeguard when needed.'

For centuries, under English common law, any child born outside matrimony was considered to be 'nobody's child', and therefore unable to inherit family titles or land. This law was pilloried in one Victorian novel, in particular. In *No Name* by Wilkie Collins, the Vanstone sisters are cruelly disinherited when it transpires that – for perfectly good reasons – their parents had never married, and that they are therefore bastards. 'Mr Vanstone's daughters are Nobody's Children,' explains one of the lawyers in the novel, 'and the law leaves them helpless . . . I am far from defending the law of England, as it affects illegitimate offspring. On the contrary, I think it a disgrace to the nation. It visits the sins of the parents on the children.' One of the daughters goes a stage further in describing her position (in the third person): 'She is a nameless, homeless, friendless wretch. The law which takes care of you, the law which takes care of all legitimate children, casts her like carrion to the winds. It is your law – not hers. She only knows it as the instrument of a vile oppression, an insufferable wrong.' Collins himself had fathered three illegitimate children and wrote about the predicament with great passion, tackling not just the legal context but broader questions of name and identity. The sensational twists and turns of his novel would be echoed in some of the later episodes of the increasingly Gothic Sackville saga.

While waiting for Mortimer's will to be settled before moving into Knole, Lionel spent the winter in Cannes with his two unmarried daughters. Socially they were a great success, 'dining with the greatest personages'; they were pretty, accomplished, and Amalia, at least, was a competent pianist and enjoyed performing in 'private theatricals' in people's villas. As Victoria wrote to Max in February 1889: 'I am glad to see that "*le monde*" and society are friendly disposed towards us, in spite of the blot on our name. Everybody knows of it, but no one says the least thing which can make me feel it . . . But you have no idea, dear Max, how much I feel my position, and I am often very nervous and unhappy about it . . . I quite agree with you that it would be better if we had never been born.'

It was not long before Victoria caught the eye of the Prince of Wales – an interest on his part that she was to swear in a letter to Béon was 'altogether paternal'. She had met the Prince for the first time on 19 February, at a dinner given by the de Falbes. She was '*terriblement intimidée*', and took another guest, Miss Stonor, with her as chaperone when the Prince asked her to accompany him to the smoking room after dinner. He agreed to sign her *carte de dîner* on condition that she send him a photograph of herself. A week later, she was dancing the *quadrille d'honneur* with the Prince at a ball ('he was searching me out everywhere'), and the following day travelled with him on the train to Nice for the 'Bataille des Fleurs et des Confetti'. Amalia often accompanied them, and for the rest of 1889, the letters Victoria received from the Prince of Wales usually referred to Amalia as well, and ended with greetings to both her father and her sister.

It was a heady time for Victoria. At dinner with the Goldsmids in early February, she met the fabulously wealthy Marquis de Löys Chandieu – 'L.C.', as she referred to him in her diary. After a whirlwind courtship conducted at dinners, balls and a day trip to Monte Carlo, where they watched the clay pigeon shooting, and played roulette, L.C. proposed. By the end of the month, Victoria had been introduced to his mother and sister, and he had written to Cardinal de Hohenlohe in Rome seeking a dispensation for a mixed marriage – for Victoria was Catholic while the Marquis was Protestant. The Cardinal advised that there was a canton in Switzerland where the permission they sought might be granted, but Victoria already sensed that the religious obstacles were insurmountable. She had several 'stormy interviews' with L.C. on the subject, and it soon became clear that the Marquis's mother strongly opposed mixed marriages. Victoria's friends, on the other hand, advised her that there could be no harm in her raising any children of the marriage as Protestants, if that were to be a condition.

At the same time as Victoria was failing to make any firm resolutions about the engagement – persuading herself one day that she should marry L.C. and the next that she should give him up – she was also doing her best to marry Amalia off. Although the sisters were, in many ways, equals, going to the same picnics and so on, Victoria's six years of seniority, and her years of acting as confidante to her father, encouraged her to assume responsibility. Whether it was a question of finding suitors for Amalia, getting her invited to parties, or simply arranging her accommodation, Victoria had views. Should Amalia return to England or, if some remuneration could be agreed (and Gabriel was always quite demanding on this point, eventually agreeing a sum of 600 francs a month), could she live with the newlywed Flora and Gabriel Salanson in Paris? When Amalia sought permission and money to return to Cannes later that year, it was Victoria who was inclined to say no: she was conscious of the reputation of her sisters and, by extension, herself – a sensitivity heightened by the stain of her illegitimacy. Miss Hillier, their former governess, also thought that Amalia was far too independent. Their father, on the other hand, agreed to Amalia's request on condition that Amalia never went out alone and did not act in plays. Nevertheless, the following year, Amalia asked her father's permission to act in a play, and Victoria telegraphed back: 'No' – 'It's much better if she doesn't expose herself to malicious gossip.'

On 3 July 1889, Victoria visited Knole for the first time. She travelled down from London with Maria Cheston, her friend from Washington, and lunched at the Royal Crown Hotel in Sevenoaks. At the house she met the housekeeper Mrs Knox 'who seems nice and obliging; I was particularly struck by the paintings and the tapestries; and the order which reigns throughout the house and gardens is remarkable . . . The house is absolutely vast.' So immense, in fact, that you could easily get lost in it, she continued. Later in July, she was back at Knole with her father and L.C., before finally moving in on 24 August. '*Cela me semble drôle* to keep house,' she wrote in her diary; 'I don't particularly enjoy it, but it's a big distraction; and I need things to distract me from an *idée fixe* which obsesses me.'

The nature of this '*idée fixe*' is not completely clear, although it may have had something to do with the fact that, less than a month before, while staying with family friends on the south coast, she had met her cousin Lionel, William Edward's oldest son, my great-uncle. Over the course of the summer, she was to meet Lionel at other house parties, including one at Buckhurst with the De La Warrs. 'Lionel', she wrote, 'is as kind as could be', and he appeared equally taken with his older cousin. He was also, in the likely event of Victoria's father failing to produce any legitimate sons, the ultimate heir to the Sackville title and to Knole. Although L.C. had visited Knole with Victoria and her father on 23 July, it looked as if this relationship was floundering and the engagement off.

Just as she was getting to know her first cousin, Victoria was also discovering the Knole estate, picking fruit in the kitchen garden, exploring the 1,000-acre deer park, and immersing herself in the fabric of the house and its contents. From the day she arrived, she slept in what had been Archbishop Thomas Cranmer's Room in the sixteenth century, when Knole had been the private residence of the Archbishops of Canterbury. She tried on jewels from the safe which, she claimed, pleased her Papa, spent an afternoon admiring the magnificent silver in the Plate Room, and helped Mrs Knox look for china in the cupboards. Every evening she discussed the following day's menu with the chef. Within her first week there, she had read the diary of Lady Anne Clifford, a previous châtelaine of Knole. Lady Anne's account of daily life and domestic drama in the house in the early seventeenth century, it later transpired, was to prefigure Victoria's own diary, with its feelings of bitterness and betrayal, of disappointment and disinheritance. But, for now, there was a sense of settling down after all the years of wandering – and a serenity in the photographs for which Victoria posed for the local photographer Charles Essenhigh Corke. In scenes of a touching domesticity, staged in the midst of Knole's ancient show rooms, she sits at a spinning wheel, her hair falling to the ground, or works on her embroidery, or affects to read. She looks wistful at times, her face in profile displaying the fineness of its features, although from some angles there is a heavier set to her jaw that would become more pronounced with age.

In August, the Prince of Wales wrote to Victoria from Homburg that he was very sorry not to see her there, 'but quite understand the reason & am so glad that you and your Father are residing at Knole – which is one of the finest & almost unique place [sic] in England. Nothing would give us greater pleasure than visiting it next year as it is many years since we were there.'

Victoria was learning to love the deference that her new position demanded. '*Le mot "Sackville" a un effet magique ici,*' she noted approvingly in her diary, and the 'bowing and scraping' (one of only a few English expressions in her predominantly French prose), and the way the servants queued to see her as she went out to dinner in a 'ravishing dress of pink *crêpe de chine* trimmed with white ribbons'. She liked visiting 'the wives of the Estate staff in their little cottages', and the novelty of arriving at the annual hunt ball at the Royal Crown Hotel, with the crowd shouting three cheers for Lord Sackville: 'Hip, hip, hurrah!' How, she asked herself, would she ever be able to accustom herself now to '*une existence pauvre*'?

Victoria poses for Charles Essenhigh Corke at Knole

Young Lionel had been aware of the circumstances surrounding his cousin's birth since his mother had told him in Homburg in 1882, and was very sensitive to Victoria's predicament. 'Lionel knows how much I have suffered on account of my birth,' wrote Victoria, 'and he has told me that he would be only too happy to give up Knole if that made any difference. He is so good & so kind.' On 6 September (just over a month after they had first met), Lionel declared his love for Victoria in the King's Room, and explained to her the following day the means by which 'Vicky's house [as he described Knole] could always be her house.'

An idea was beginning to form: an idea planted by Lionel

himself, but nurtured by the hints of neighbours and other suitors. The young diplomat Cecil Spring-Rice, who was hopelessly in love with Victoria, realised that she would never be as happy as at Knole and told her, unwittingly, that she should therefore marry Lionel. Similarly, several of Victoria's visitors told her what a pity it would be if she did not stay at Knole for the rest of her life. 'Ah! If only they knew how easy that would be for me,' she confided slyly to her diary. How '*Providentiel*' it would be if she were to marry her first cousin.

Victoria was torn once again by the visit of L.C. to Knole for three days at the beginning of October. They drove over to Ightham Mote and Chevening, and walked in the park at Knole, admiring the view of the house from afar: from the north, in particular, Knole looks immense, with its outbuildings – a barn, an old brewhouse, a granary, and workshops for carpenters, bricklayers and painters – clustering higgledy-piggledy beneath the Clock Tower, like the yards and farm buildings of a medieval village.

'Here I am torn between Lionel & Löys', she wrote; 'both of them know how they stand *vis à vis* each other, because I have always been *très loyale* towards them both. "I will either be a marchioness or a peeress"; I know which I'd prefer . . . Löys begs me not to abandon him, although he knows what it would mean for me to keep my beautiful chateau. I understand him so well; he has been so unselfish. I've come to believe that he loves me *tout son coeur*.' Poor Lionel wrote to Victoria regularly from Erfurt, where he was learning German for his Foreign Office exams, his tone becoming increasingly desperate as he realised that the Marquis was staying at Knole: '*Je te trouve parfaite ma chérie*, in every possible way. Physically you are perfectly lovely and morally you are the most noble, pure-minded person I could ever have imagined possibly could exist. You are my very idea of what a woman ought to be and my only ambition is to make myself a little more worthy of you . . .

but my own darling, try and arrange everything *loyalement* with Abroad [which is how he referred to L.C.] and make me happy for ever.'

Gradually, Victoria was won over by Lionel and his attentions, and by the more practical considerations. Whatever wealth L.C. could bring to a marriage (and he became even richer on the death of his uncle), Victoria did not want to give up Knole; and, as she argued, 'happiness has to come before ambition'. Lionel acknowledged that he was, from a worldly point of view, nothing compared to the Marquis: 'My darling I know you are not a bit worldly or ambitious but he can give you everything to make you happy and comfortable and you would be able to do so much for your sisters and brothers and I can give you nothing – not even a home.' But he could, eventually, give her Knole. On 11 December, Lionel took her up to see the King's Room by moonlight, and on the way down proposed formally. Victoria accepted. '*Jour de ma vie*,' she wrote in her diary, echoing the Sackville-West family motto. These were the words, it was said, uttered in 1356 by one of the West ancestors on being knighted after the Battle of Poitiers for his part in the capture of the French King. Across the centuries, the motto still had a celebratory, seize-the-moment resonance for a generation of Sackvilles, whose present was as yet not overwhelmed by the past.

L.C. was due to arrive at Knole a couple of days later, and when she told him that she had accepted Lionel, he would not believe her. 'You can't have, I can't give you up. You are mine,' he sobbed. To console him, she told him that her decision was not just for her own '*bonheur*', but for that of her family too. It was a means, '*providentiellement*', of caring for her father, guaranteeing the future of her brothers, and legitimising her own name. Towards the end of his visit, Victoria concluded that 'L. and L.C. are both very honourable men and love me so truly and unselfishly; they just want me to be happy.' She asked herself whether she was marrying for love. '*Par amour? Je n'en sais rien* . . . I am so tired of the struggle my life has become and wonder what the future holds.'

It was not just L.C. who was in '*un état de prostration complète*' when he left Knole. A year of stress was beginning to have its effect on Victoria too, and she left for Christmas with her aunt Mary at Knowsley utterly exhausted. Aunt Mary knew nothing yet of Victoria's secret engagement to Lionel, but she certainly approved of her having turned down L.C. in order to stay with her father.

Although she had accepted Lionel, Victoria began 1890 in an agony of indecision, at her 'wits' end', as she wrote in her diary. Should she marry L.C. or L.? 'How the New Year fills me with anxiety; and how well I know which one I would like to marry.' As L.C. continued to bombard her daily with bouquets of flowers from Cannes – anemones, mimosa, roses – Victoria's resolve hardened. In March, they told her father their news, and then the other members of the family. Victoria's marriage to her first cousin solved many problems. It gave her a sense of legitimacy, enabling her to share in her father's inheritance. But it also served a strategic family function, reconciling – for the time being at least – the two branches of the family, the legitimate and the illegitimate, by bringing one of the bastards back into the fold. This was a theme to which she returned soon after her marriage, claiming in a letter to Max that 'marriage has reinstated me altogether from a family point of view', and that now she was married, she felt far less the 'stain' of her birth.

Victoria's father declared himself pleased (as well he might, since part of Victoria's so-called sacrifice had been made specifically in order to care for him). His only worries were that Lionel might not 'stick to' Victoria – how right he proved to be – and that his prospective son-in-law had 'nothing to do or any position in anything'. William Edward was surprised at first, but told his son that he would offer his 'provisional consent' until they had met to discuss his concerns. As he wrote to his brother, 'there are several objections: youth; religion; cousinship &c but I do not think they need stand in the way if they are really attached to one another'.

Victoria was five years older than Lionel, although she downplayed the objection of her fiancé's youth by knocking two years off her age. 'Nobody in the family knows my real age,' she confided in a letter to Béon in March 1890, announcing her engagement to the heir to Knole, 'a very nice, pretty boy . . . a little younger than me'. She told people that she was twenty-five and a half years old, and begged Béon to 'keep well my secret and say I am born in 1864 if anybody asks you'.

Victoria had clearly won her future father-in-law's heart, which was hardly surprising, wrote Lionel's sister Mary, when she was so pretty. But William Edward did insist that any children of the marriage should be raised in the Church of England. This was to be a condition of his consent, along with the demand that Lionel get a profession. To this end, Lionel tried, unsuccessfully, to negotiate an arrangement with Cardinal Manning whereby any boys from the marriage would be brought up Protestant and any girls Catholic.

As to the third objection, marriage between first cousins was becoming increasingly acceptable among the landowning classes during the nineteenth century. At the very least, it kept estates firmly within the family, mitigating any need to make expensive marriage settlements that divided the inheritance. Queen Victoria, that model of propriety, had sanctioned the trend by marrying her cousin Albert. And Charles Darwin, too, who settled at Down House, about ten miles from Knole, had married his first cousin Emma. Although Darwin later came to believe that 'interbreeding during many generations is highly injurious', the evidence of his own family, and research by his son George, suggested that there was little correlation between consanguinity and the incidence of disabilities.

Young Lionel and Victoria at the time of their engagement

There was very little opposition from other senior members of the family. 'My dear Victoria,' wrote Aunt Mary, 'Your letter rather took my breath away – yet it ought not for I heard a rumour last summer which roused my suspicions. If you are happy dear Victoria I am happy too. There is the great objection of the first cousins but I am bound to say I see no others. Lionel's youth frightens me . . . I see a hundred thousand advantages to set against objections which might be raised.' Aunt Mary was particularly happy that there was someone to look after her brother, since she thought it most unlikely that he would ever marry. Even Aunt Bessie seemed contented, and her daughter Ella, Victoria's cousin, hoped that the Duke of Bedford would allow his wife to get to know Victoria before the marriage. In the event, she did not attend Victoria's wedding, but sent a cheque for £500. Aunt Constance was not to come either, as 'nothing', she wrote, 'will induce Uncle

R[eggie] to come to a wedding at Knole', the house that he had lost in a bitter court battle with his brother Mortimer.

On the Sackville side, only Cecilie sounded a note of caution, observing very presciently that Lionel and Victoria would not be happy living with Papa, '*car cela emmène des ennuis inévitables*'. One of these *ennuis*, as Victoria noted, was that 'poor Papa is by no means always in a good mood'. Her father was constitutionally gloomy, a condition exacerbated by the humiliation of the Murchison Affair, and often rude in company, although generally charming in *tête à tête* with his daughter.

To her brothers, Victoria stressed the strategic advantages of her marriage. Announcing her engagement in a letter to Max, she acknowledged that she was 'very much in love', but ascribed her future happiness to the fact that she would now never have to leave her father: 'You know that formerly I could not make up my mind ever to marry, as I felt it my duty to stay with dear papa and take care of him in his old age; now the difficulty is overcome . . . you must remember that later on in life what will be within my means I shall do for you.'

Henry, who had just received £8 from his father to purchase a new heifer (possibly to replace the cow he claimed Max had taken from him) was also pleased with news of the engagement. 'And will still be more pleased,' he wrote to Victoria, in a letter that would later assume great significance:

when I hear of Amalia's engagement. You will then be all safe and there will only remain me for Father to deal with. Victoria, when you come to think of it, a father could not have done more for his children than father has done for us; how kind he has always been towards us. Remember we are his illegitimate children. What pluck he displayed in taking you all over the place so as to enable you to marry well; he could not have done more for us two than to send us far away, we would never have got on in England had we mixed with young men of good families who would only have jeered at us on account of our illegitimacy; thoroughly tried to educate us both in classic and farming matters, and started Max, and is still helping him by sending him a yearly allowance and now he is helping me too. He is a grand old man, this is what I think of him.

The only source of tension with Victoria's brothers was the obvious disparity in their lifestyles. This was to become a continuing theme of dissatisfaction. In Washington, Victoria had been in the habit of sending Max's wife hand-me-down dresses, but even that stopped when Victoria claimed they were 'really too shabby' to send to Mary, posting some fashion plates from the newspapers instead. Mary later complained to Victoria 'in not at all a nice way that I was "horrid not to send her dresses any more, seeing that I was now rich" etc. etc.'. Victoria argued, in turn, that she now lived 'entirely in the country' and had 'only plain woollen and cotton dresses', and that it was therefore distinctly unfriendly of Mary to reproach her in this way.

Victoria's sisters, too, were pleased at first with her engagement to Lionel, for it meant that she could stay with Papa and help look after their interests, as well as those of their brothers. At this stage the sisters were still genuinely fond of each other. Amalia was living at Knole with her father for several months of the year, on equal terms with Victoria. And when she was with Flora in Paris, as she was in the autumn of 1889, they would send Victoria at Knole a copy of *Le Figaro* every day; Victoria would send them vegetables from the kitchen garden in return.

It was not long before chinks developed in Victoria's relationship with her sisters. Their initial enthusiasm at the news of the engagement was tempered by their resentment of Victoria's dominance. Victoria ran the household at Knole, as she had in Washington, and was consulted by her father on most money matters. On the way to Paris in April to buy a wedding trousseau, Bonny, the lady's companion who had been with Victoria

Young Lionel, Victoria and Old Lionel (Lord Sackville)
in the gardens on the South Front of Knole

in Washington, warned her that her sisters were terribly
jealous. Victoria went to see Flora and Flora's month-old son,
another, third-generation, Lionel. The baby was sweet with
deep blue eyes, just like her own, wrote Victoria, claiming as
ever some of the credit; but Flora and Amalia, who was there
too, seemed aggressive and took her to task for marrying a
Protestant. The following day Victoria had another 'stormy
interview' with Flora, who did not want to put Amalia up any
longer. Amalia was far too extravagant, Flora said, and, in any
case, everybody thought her proper place was with Papa.
Victoria, on the other hand, argued that Amalia would be
bored to death at Knole and would feel constantly left out by
the newlywed couple. 'Gab. & Flora are very ungrateful and
don't appreciate all the trouble I go to on their behalf. They
cause me a <u>lot</u> of pain; *l'inquiétude me va droit au coeur.*' Less
than a week later, the Salansons had changed their minds and

said they were prepared to look after Amalia so long as the payment for her maintenance was raised. Nevertheless, wrote Victoria, 'they were still choked with jealousy, and Gab is really very malicious'. Throughout Victoria's visit to Paris – and on trips to buy a bridesmaid's outfit – Amalia was grumpy, and refused to come to Knole until just a week before the wedding; even then she would not conceal how bored she was from the moment she arrived.

Neighbours such as Miss Boscawen thought the engagement 'the neatest thing that could ever happen', and 'such a blessing for Knole' to have Victoria for ever as its mistress. As congratulations arrived from France, from former friends in Washington, from the Prince of Wales himself, Victoria relaxed into her new relationship, enjoying the attentions of her ardent cousin and allowing him ever greater intimacies: not just the *'conversations interminables'* that seemed to pass in no time, the first glimpse of Victoria's naked foot one evening, the kiss that Lionel stole as the train from Sevenoaks to London passed through a tunnel, but also others, more private, that could be referred to only in a code – *'1st n sans n.f & p.m.'*, for example – that has defied all my attempts to crack it.

The marriage took place by special licence in the private chapel at Knole on 17 June 1890. The day before, the Knole estate had been resettled, so that in the event of Lord Sackville dying without legitimate male heirs, it should pass directly to his nephew Lionel. Victoria's position as mistress of Knole was now more than a temporary one.

The bride was led from the sitting room on the arm of her father, along a red carpet that had been specially laid for the occasion, through halls and galleries lined with white lilies, and up the stairs into the chapel. She was wearing a white satin bodice and skirt covered with fine old Brussels lace given her by the groom's sisters, and a wreath of orange blossoms was pinned to her right shoulder.

Victoria was attended by two bridesmaids, Cecilie and Amalia, who, however reluctant, looked 'most handsome' in a dress of pale grey silk, with white silk lace, and a large straw hat trimmed with wild roses and velvet bows. Both bridesmaids carried bouquets composed of stephanotis and lilies of the valley. After the ceremony, the newly married couple retired to the vestry with senior members of the family to sign the register, although, as usual, Victoria's father had no recollection later as to whether Victoria was described as his daughter in the record.

All the finest family silver was laid out in the dining room, and the wedding presents, which numbered some 250, including a lucky horseshoe set in diamonds and pearls from the Prince of Wales, were displayed in the Colonnade. There were presents from Victoria's sisters: a silver peppercorn grinder from Amalia, and a gold quill pen with diamonds from Flora (not to mention '*des bons conseils*' on marriage that Flora gave Victoria in her bedroom a couple of days before the wedding). The Salansons had been staying at Knole the whole of that week, and appeared in particularly good spirits – perhaps because Victoria had recently sent them a cheque for the glassware in their smart new Parisian apartment. But there are no records of presents from Max or Henry.

Other characters, who had played a significant role in Victoria's past, also gave presents: Mr and Mrs Mulhall a fine handkerchief of Irish lace; the nuns of the Sacred Heart a religious picture; Cecil Spring-Rice a silver tea caddy; Bonny a gold cat brooch; Miss Hillier a Spanish lace shawl; and Mr and Mrs Cheston a single diamond pin. The Marquis de Löys Chandieu gave a small watch with rubies and diamonds (he had not wasted any time, and was already married to the equally wealthy Agnès de Pourtalès). The Comte de Béon gave Victoria a single diamond pin. 'You will have to come to my marriage, dear Béon,' Victoria had written to him on her engagement.

'You see that your Victoria has made a good choice. The fortune of Knole keeps on increasing so that our Agent assures me that when my cousin becomes Lord Sackville, he will have between 400,000 and 500,000 francs of rent. It is nice. I will always be able to help my brothers.'

The wedding cake was, according to the *Sevenoaks Chronicle*, 'a rare and unique specimen of taste, elegance and skill', supplied by Mr Henry Ellman, confectioner, of 12 London Road, Sevenoaks, and was 'entirely the work of his manager, Mr F. Fuggle, who deserves the highest praise for this clever and really magnificent specimen of confectionery'. Compressed into a sugar-coated two-foot square was the sprawling four-acre magnificence of Knole. In the centre of this two-tiered marzi-panned model rose the Clock Tower capped with a weathervane dated 1743. The initials of the bride and groom, V.L.S.W., were worked onto three sides of the tower, while above the whole floated a flag, bearing the Sackville motto '*Jour de ma vie*'. At each of the four corners of the base was a stag's head, and on two of the sides were pairs of clasped hands sculpted in icing. The whole was garlanded with tastefully arranged trails of orange blossom, clematis, lilies of the valley, jasmine and stephanotis.

Just before five o'clock, Victoria changed into a smart light-grey travelling dress and donned a straw toque hat trimmed with pale green velvet – part of the trousseau, made at Reuff's in Paris, that Aunt Mary had given her as a wedding present. At five, she and Lionel left Knole for the Earl and Countess of Derby's seat at Keston, near Bromley, where they spent the first night of their honeymoon. '*Jour de Ma Vie*,' Victoria wrote once again in her diary that day.

The wedding was considered a great success by the family, Aunt Mary writing to congratulate Victoria afterwards: 'I cannot say how thoroughly satisfied & pleased I was with the ceremony at Knole. I never saw a Wedding which pleased me so much or gave me such an idea of what a wedding ought to

be. And how perfectly you had arranged everything for I know
you did it all. Every one of the family shared my view. Your
Papa too seemed so happy. Uncle Gummer & Mary stayed at
Derby House afterwards & we did nothing but talk of the way
it all went off . . .'

The couple then left for France, embarking on the sexual
idyll that was to characterise the first year of their marriage. On
2 July they visited Arcachon. It was almost twenty years since
Pepita's death, but Victoria remembered it all perfectly: the
Chateau Deganne, the Casino, the chapel at Moulleau, the
church of Notre Dame where Pepita's funeral had taken place,
and most poignantly of all the Villa Pepa itself. Her heart was
beating terribly on entering the house, she wrote to Max: 'I was
overcome by emotion as I wandered through those rooms;
Maman's portrait is still hanging there, and so is the one of
baby Amalia. *Rien n'est changé . . .*'

5

Sibling Rivalry

On their return from honeymoon, Victoria was forced into daily contact with Amalia, and so began a long chapter of rows and reconciliations. The relationship between these two siblings was always full of conflict. The brothers had been sent away at an early age, first to school and then to the other side of the world, and Flora who, at twenty-one, had been the first of the girls to marry, was now living in France. But Victoria and Amalia were thrown together at home, to endure what for many of us is the longest relationship of our lives: a sibling relationship. They were without a mother and had been, effectively, without a father for the first fifteen years of their lives. From the time their father was posted to Washington in 1881, Victoria had acted as the mistress of his household – a role that she would fulfil at Knole until his death in 1908. Despite giving her occasional cause for complaint, it was a role that Victoria made her own, much to the resentment of Amalia.

Life at Knole was claustrophobic. Lionel and Victoria were quite unrestrained in their newly awakened wedded passion, the details of their sex life minutely recorded by Victoria in her diary. By her own account, they were a 'spoony' couple, kissing and canoodling in front of Amalia and Lionel's younger brother, Bertie, my grandfather. Victoria claimed that they did their best to be kind to Amalia, and not to make her feel too much of a gooseberry, 'but it's very trying for us who just love being alone together'. Victoria could barely contain her irritation: 'We are most unhappy with Amalia who didn't utter a word during or after dinner yesterday and today; Tio [Victoria's pet-name for her husband] told me: "I felt like shaking her." She doesn't try to make herself pleasant when there are guests around, and the only reason we invite young people over anyway is for her. She has terrible bad moods, and I am so patient with her.' Another day, Victoria went to the Library to cry, so disheartened was she that all her efforts on Amalia's behalf and all her attempts to live in harmony with her were rewarded by ingratitude.

After her first married Christmas at Knole in 1890, Victoria wrote in her diary that Amalia was *'la grande ombre dans le ciel de mon bonheur'*, a lowering presence, who would go for days without speaking to Victoria, even when there was company in the house. Amalia would come and go as she pleased, treating Victoria as a complete stranger and rarely informing her of her plans. When Victoria held a party at Knole in honour of the Chancellor of the Exchequer, Sir Michael Hicks-Beach (who was proposing to abolish death duties on heirlooms), Amalia did not even have the good grace to appear – and yet, as Victoria complained, she could so easily have invited someone else in her place.

Lionel, too, did his best to entertain Amalia, playing the odd round of golf with her or taking her to Lord's to watch the cricket. But there was little else to do, except visit neighbours for lunches and dinners: the Wardes at Squerryes, Lord Hillingdon at Wildernesse, the Baillets as Combe Bank, Miss Herries at St Julians. Victoria's father was by now a very gloomy and reserved man in his early sixties, although he appeared much older than his years. When Victoria tried to make conversation at mealtimes – *'Je trouve qu'on a si peu de "small talk" en*

Angleterre' – her husband accused her of talking too much. Victoria was occasionally reduced to tears by her father's grumbling about the expense of housekeeping at Knole. Like other Sackvilles in later life, he had become preoccupied with money, worrying about the cost of keeping up stables for hunting and for carriages, and even considered shutting Knole for the winter and living abroad instead.

One of the causes of resentment between the sisters was Amalia's alleged extravagance. Victoria complained when Amalia was driven in a carriage with four horses to the Baillets, just as she was later to complain about her use of the car to take her hither and thither. Amalia was always asking her father and sister for money, and then irritating them by the ungrateful fashion with which she accepted it. 'It's frightful to have a sister as ill-natured as that,' wrote Victoria. Every now and then Victoria would give Amalia some advice, such as the idea of setting aside £40 a year from her allowance of £140 as a reserve – an idea which Amalia rejected outright. She was not going to save a penny, since having nice clothes was, she claimed, her sole pleasure in life. Victoria found it particularly galling that Amalia owed money to Mrs Knox, the Knole housekeeper, which prompted a testy correspondence between the sisters.

Another cause of resentment was their competition for the affection of shared friends, for Victoria and Amalia moved in similar circles, often attending the same gatherings: a ball of Prince Duleep Singh's, for example, or a garden party at Holland House. On one occasion, Victoria heard from four separate people that Amalia had spoken unkindly of her, and wrote to Amalia to complain. Amalia immediately wanted to know who these people were. On another occasion, the sisters had 'un grand row' when Victoria asked Amalia not to hang around the guests' rooms at Knole so late into the evening; Amalia threatened, in retaliation, to tell all her friends that Victoria had prevented her from even talking to them.

It is hardly surprising that Amalia often felt like a prisoner – a feeling to which she contributed by shutting herself in her room for days on end. She longed to be anywhere else – London, Paris, or the South of France – although even then, Victoria insisted that she be chaperoned. By the end of 1891, Amalia was obviously miserable in England, and equally unhappy staying with Flora and Gabriel in Paris. It was agreed that she should leave for Cannes early in the New Year, with Bonny, a woman 'of forbidding appearance and impeccable integrity', as Vita later described her, acting as chaperone. In her first letter from Cannes, Amalia admitted that she was a little homesick for Knole, and thanked Victoria – to her surprise – for all she had done to try and make her happy there the previous month. '*Enfin!*' exclaimed Victoria in her diary. Amalia was to stay there until the summer when she returned to Knole.

When Lionel and Victoria started staying in London for the season, they also found lodgings for Papa and Amalia. There was still the problem of Amalia's independence: for example, when Victoria and Lionel took a small rented house in Berkeley Square, Amalia came too, but Victoria would not allow her younger sister to stay there on her own while Victoria was at Knole: 'That I cannot permit. She simply does not conduct herself well enough.'

Marriage was one means of escape. The search for a husband was presumably one reason why Victoria was prepared to accompany Amalia to a round of balls that she found excruciatingly boring herself: 'Amalia has simply no idea what an effort it is for me; *j'abomine aller au bal*'. There was a succession of suitors, or Amalia's young 'sparks', as they were described: a Mr Craven with whom Amalia was sent outside to walk in the garden, but whom she found a little shy; then, a Mr Hugh

Walker: '*pauvre garçon, très intimidé, très très bedint, counter-jumper*',* Victoria recorded dismissively in her diary.

Flora and Victoria often discussed whether Amalia stood a better chance of finding a husband in England or France. Squabbling over who was to have Amalia to stay was to be a recurring theme of their relationship. In their attempts to offload Amalia, each of them claimed that her marriage prospects were better in the other country. It is no wonder that Amalia felt 'so unhappy and so unloved by anyone'. Victoria did her best to console her, 'but she simply doesn't understand how unsympathetic she is and doesn't know how to make herself liked'.

A Monsieur Martin, from Paris, could not marry Amalia because he was a Protestant, and this reduced her to tears. Next, there was a Mr Eliot who came for a weekend in October 1893. Lionel, Victoria and Papa did not care for him that much, for whereas some of the other young sparks had seemed too shy, Mr Eliot was too sure of himself, '*un grand blagueur*', or joker. A couple of months later, her attention turned to a Mr Stanley Jackson, who asked her to marry him. But the proposed marriage did not meet with the approval of either father – Mr Jackson senior objecting on religious grounds – and, in any case, Victoria did not think he had enough money to accommodate Amalia's extravagance. Throughout these courtships, Aunt Mary was worried by my grandfather Bertie's frequent visits to Knole, fearful that he would fall in love with Amalia, an idea Victoria found too '*drôle*' for words.

On 17 June 1895, the fifth anniversary of Victoria's wedding,

---

* Bedints were servants in the Sackville family slang – from the German *bedienen*, to 'serve' or 'wait upon'. The term gradually came to embrace anyone the Sackvilles considered common, not just the 'lower classes', but even people of their own acquaintance whom they considered vulgar. It was a term, ironically, that they would soon apply to their own cousins. 'Counter-jumper' was a contemptuous term for a 'shop salesman'.

'*nous avons eu une grande emotion*', Victoria wrote in her diary. For that day, Lionel's younger brother, my great-uncle Charlie, asked Maud Bell to marry him, and a Mr Tobin asked Amalia to marry him. '*Suis si excité ce soir!*' Victoria continued. As before, her sister's romance came to nothing: on the eighteenth, Tobin told Amalia that he could not marry her after all, for he was ruined. A fortnight later, Tobin told Lionel and Victoria at dinner that he was going to give up his mining ventures and settle instead on a job as managing director of a bank in San Francisco on £3,000 a year. Tobin spent several more days at Knole, and Amalia continued to appear very taken with him. In the end, however, matters were decided by the fact that Tobin's mother and uncle (from whom he was due to inherit) were not prepared to give him any money unless he married an American. 'She is so upset,' Victoria wrote about Amalia. 'Poor girl, she really doesn't have any luck.' There was no alternative but for her to return to Paris in December, to care for Flora who had a blood clot in her leg, and who was suffering from some sort of nervous ailment. Amalia, too, was unwell, with anaemia.

―――――

At first the Sackville-Wests and the Salansons got on quite well together, with Lionel arranging for Mr Findlay, the gamekeeper at Knole, to find a dog – named Bruce – for Gabriel. But, despite the reciprocated kindnesses, there were also tensions, and these occasionally flared up over the most unlikely pretexts. Quite soon after Victoria's marriage, Flora wrote to her sister to say that she did not consider her married (since her wedding had been an Anglican one). 'What bigots they all are!' Victoria wrote in her diary; to Flora she replied that it would have been better, perhaps, if she had not come to the wedding since she felt that way. Just before Christmas 1890, Flora wrote back, saying that she wanted to stop all communication with Victoria. '*Comme elle est bête!*'

she noted in her diary. 'She will regret being the one to start this quarrel.' It was not long before Gabriel joined the fray, writing '*une bête de lettre*', in which he laid all the blame for the quarrel on Victoria. Flora, according to Bonny, was too proud throughout to seek a reconciliation, but broadcast her own version of events instead. Some of Victoria's sensitivity on the subject was assuaged when she received a dispensation from Pope Leo XIII, allowing her to have her marriage blessed in a Catholic church without the requirement that any children should be raised as Catholic. On Sunday 10 May 1891, her marriage was blessed by Father Lazzari in the small Catholic church in Sevenoaks. 'At least the Catholics [she was referring to Flora] can no longer reproach me for having got married only in the Chapel at Knole. I am very happy with the way everything has turned out.' The following March, Victoria gave birth to a daughter, who was christened Victoria Mary (but always known as Vita) in the Chapel and brought up in the Church of England.

Mother and baby daughter at Knole

Gabriel fanned the flames of any quarrel at every opportunity. Victoria was particularly '*revoltée*' by the stories he circulated about the sales of three pictures from Knole in August 1890 for £50,000: the Gainsborough portrait of Giovanna Baccelli, and the paintings by Reynolds of *Mrs Abington* and *The Fortune Teller*. According to Amalia, Gabriel claimed that Victoria had pocketed the proceeds herself, a supposition that is hardly surprising given the question of where on earth Victoria's money came from. Victoria was an illegitimate young woman, the daughter of an impoverished lord, and married to a man without either a job or prospects. Yet there always appeared to be money for home improvements, for shopping trips in Paris – the jewellers in the Rue de la Paix, evening dresses from Worth or Redfern, and a '*jacquette d'astrakhan*' from the Ville de Bombay – rented flats in London for the season, or gambling in Monte Carlo. A typical winter's trip to Monte Carlo, such as the one they completed on 30 March 1895, cost £500, '*tout compris*'. Nevertheless, Amalia was persuaded by Victoria that Gabriel's claims were a complete lie, and agreed to explain so to him on her return to Paris, at which point Gabriel denied ever having made such an accusation.

Lionel and Victoria never forgave Gabriel for this calumny. Although Victoria eventually accepted Flora's apologies, and claimed not to bear her a grudge, she wrote that the relationship between the two couples could never be the same again and that they could never all be at Knole at the same time. What tended to happen from then on was that Victoria would visit Flora in Paris every spring on her return from the South of France.

Flora's young son was welcome at Knole, however, and came there for the summer of 1893, where he played sweetly with his baby cousin Vita, giving much pleasure to their otherwise grumpy grandfather. The following summer little Lionel came again, offering his hand '*si solennellement*' in formal greeting to his two-year-old cousin. '*C'etait trop drôle,*' wrote Victoria.

Together, they recited nursery rhymes and went up to London to have their photographs taken. When it was time for bed, Vita would utter a cry of despair on being separated from the infant Lionel.

Money was always at the root of tensions between the Sackville-Wests and the Salansons. Not long after his marriage to Flora, Gabriel had needed money to tide him over the coming accouchement of his pregnant wife. His bank would not accept, as security for a loan, the title deeds from some properties his mother had left him, and advised him to consult his wealthy sister-in-law. In February 1890 – four months before her wedding – Victoria guaranteed a bank loan to Salanson by remitting 2,000 francs to her own account at the same bank as collateral. Gabriel then presumed to draw this money directly from Victoria's account, to her consternation, making her the lender rather than the bank.

Flora's husband, Gabriel Salanson

Given this unsatisfactory experience, it is surprising that Gabriel succeeded, later the same year, in persuading Victoria to invest 5,000 francs in the Société Pégat, a small investment

bank recently founded by a friend of his. Gabriel took the
liberty of enclosing a mandate for Victoria to sign, authorising
him to purchase the shares and to receive the dividends on her
behalf: 'You have absolutely no reason to feel obliged to me on
this account. All I am doing is rendering a service to a friend.'
Within months, she was fretting that she had received no
receipt from Gabriel for the money; over the next three years,
there was a steady stream of letters to Victoria from Jean Pégat
and Gabriel, attempting to reassure her that her money was
safe, despite the evident lack of income from the funds. By
1894, it became obvious that the company had gone bust and
that Victoria had lost her 5,000 francs.

Gabriel was always jealous of Victoria's wealth. Their
dealings were characterised by misunderstandings and
complicated by the maintenance payments made by Victoria
and her father towards the upkeep of Amalia in France. It
particularly irritated Victoria, for example, when Flora
implied to people such as Lady Anglesey that she was looking
after Amalia out of the goodness of her heart (rather than
being paid to do so), and that Amalia did not receive a sou
from Papa. At the same time, Gabriel was trying, *en des
termes pleins de sentimentalité*', to persuade Lord Sackville to
increase Flora's pension. *'Quel homme faux & double,'*
Victoria noted in her diary. Lord Sackville obliged – to the
tune of 5,000 francs a year – but was furious when he heard
that Gabriel had tried to borrow money on the strength of a
life insurance policy that would provide Flora with 30,000
francs on her father's death. Not only was he offended by
the fact that Gabriel was anticipating his death with such
alacrity, but also indignant because this money formed
Flora's inheritance, not Gabriel's.

Relations were just as difficult in 1896. In October, Gabriel
told his wife not to see Victoria at all because he believed that
she had been spreading lies about her: Flora, for her part,

seemed very 'bitter' and envious of the luck Victoria had had in life. 'My sisters are so jealous of me!' wrote Victoria, '*Hélas*! And I do everything I can to be nice to them. I brought masses of things for the children and I'm not even allowed to see them.' The so-called 'lies' which Victoria was alleged to have spread concerned the paternity of Flora's second child, a daughter, Elie, born in 1895 (who died soon after). Victoria is supposed to have suggested that Gabriel was not the father.

In retrospect, Lord Sackville's surprise inheritance in 1888 marked a turning point, not just in Victoria's relations with her sisters, but also with others with whom she had previously enjoyed happy relations. As Victoria took charge of Knole, the others felt excluded. They also scented the existence of money, where previously there had been very little. The tone of everyone's letters begins to change. Béon wrote furiously soon after Victoria's wedding that he had not been pressed more energetically to come to Knole, and, a year later in June 1891, he wrote to Lord Sackville to say that he had not been properly compensated for all his care of the children during the 1870s and that he was owed 110,000 francs. 'What blackmail!' wrote Victoria. 'It's disgraceful and disgusting of him; he who has stolen our furniture and to whom Papa has given so much! *Quelle ingratitude & quel mensonge.*'

The family solicitor, Mr Lawrence, advised Victoria's husband that there was nothing to fear, that there was no proof of such a debt, and that even if there was, it would be too old. Béon, on the other hand, took to writing to members of the family including Aunt Mary, threatening to reveal 'some rather nasty stories if he didn't get paid'. 'Béon's conduct towards Papa is too vile for words,' Victoria wrote to Max in November. He was behaving 'like a pig' and Papa was 'broken-hearted over it'. 'He wants to extort a lot of money out of Papa, and threatens to say all sorts of mean things about our mother. Is it not too mean of him?' When Victoria, Lionel and Papa left for Europe in December 1892, en route to Egypt, letters from Béon demanding money followed them.

By the beginning of 1893, Béon realised that his claims were unlikely to be successful, and that threats of court proceedings were therefore empty. He threw himself on his old friend's mercy: 'I beg of you, my dear Sackville . . . to generously forget that past quarrel . . . You cannot imagine all the terrible troubles and torments I have just gone through . . . If on your side you can oblige me with those 15,000 francs which I have asked you for, you will render me a great service.' Lord Sackville sent 10,000, for which Béon signed a receipt, accepting that this payment was in 'full satisfaction and settlement of all claims and demands'.

———

Victoria wrote in her diary that she often thought fondly of 'poor' Max and Henry, and was relieved that the expense of maintaining her brothers was rather less than that of supporting her sisters: some chickens for breeding one year, money for buying a fine Shorthorn bull the next. To begin with at least, Papa too was pleased with the cups and prizes Max won for his cattle. In 1893, however, Max was £530 in debt and wrote to his father, setting out the financial case: 'I have got into difficulties regarding money matters and my creditors are pressing me.' He had already mortgaged his cattle; the farm itself was in trust and could not be mortgaged; and the creditors had to be kept at bay. It was not extravagance on his part, he insisted: 'I had no labour not a soul for five months and was unable to put in crops for my stock and those crops had to be purchased. My wife and myself had to do everything, from doing up the house, to cleaning the stables, in fact I have never had such a miserable time before, everything going wrong and helping to make matters worse. My luck has been bad and as soon as I tried to improve my stock . . . the bulls have died, bulls which I valued and which cost me all my spare hard earned money.' Papa sent £500 to stave off the creditors – but Victoria could not help complaining to Max's wife that Max had never written to thank him. Privately, she thought that Max had far too many fads, and that they would be the ruin of him.

Henry, too, was running into difficulties and wanted to build himself a house. In November 1893, he wrote to his father asking him to advance in immediate cash the remaining instalments on his farmland purchase, and to let Henry then pay them off as they became due:

> You must not think that I am in any way dissatisfied – I am very much indebted to you for what you have done; I only hope you will live long enough to see that your kindness has not been thrown away. It has been a hard lot for us boys, especially for me, who has felt and can still feel that my presence would not be at all appreciated in England among my own relations. It is a cruel blow to my pride; however, I will endure it for your sake to the bitter end. I will leave aside a subject which is as much painful to you as it is to me. I only hope we will see each other some day after such a long time of separation.

His father would not give him the last five instalments in cash, but obliged with a string of small loans and gifts – including £30 for Henry's share of some imported rams he had bought with a neighbour.

One of the reasons for Henry's repeated requests for money was that he was saving up for a trip to Europe, 'irrespective of support from any one'. As he wrote to his father in November 1895, he was doing this for his own good, 'as I consider the change utterly necessary as I am sinking fast into a state which might lead to my ruin should I continue to lose further interest in my business. You cannot blame me for wishing once more to see my own relations . . . You may rely upon me to be <u>careful</u> when in England as I fairly grasp my position there.' Henry hoped to find lodgings with Amalia in London, and then go to France to stay near Flora. 'I sincerely hope you do not feel against my coming. I am sure I would feel very much disappointed to find that you were, considering the hardships and troubles I have gone through. It has always been my wish to see you all again.'

He also very much wanted to see Knole for the first time. Although he had only the sketchiest conception of the house, he wrote knowledgeably – even proprietorially – about it to his father: 'Knole must be looking itself again now that winter is over', and 'Knole must be commencing to look cheerful now summer has set in'. He had professed himself delighted to hear of the birth of his niece Vita in 1892, but 'at the same time I am sorry that it is not a boy, for it is my greatest wish that Knole may some day belong to one of us [by which he meant one of Papa's direct descendants], and hope that I may live to see it'.

Papa did object to Henry's plans, however, replying from Knole: 'You know very well that I do not wish you to come to England for reasons which you are perfectly well aware of, and if you persist I shall stop your allowance . . . Understand therefore that I forbid your coming.' Victoria added her persuasion:

> Dearest Boy, I am sure he would love to see you, but I am afraid you have offended him very much by taking the law into your hands like this. I should like so <u>very</u> <u>very</u> much to see you, but you know how difficult and painful it would be for Papa. The sad story of his life is hushed up <u>quite</u> so your coming will bring it about again. Take pity on him in his old age dear boy, and submit yourself to his wishes and don't make him unhappy. I am sure you are grateful to him for all that he has done. So many might have given us up altogether and he has done all he could for us all and you in particular.

As a result, Henry delayed his departure until the following year, but wrote to say that he was upset: 'What you have against my coming I am very anxious to know, it seems hard after all these years out here spent in wilderness and solitude [that] I should be stopped from accomplishing an object so long in view.'

At the beginning of 1896, old Lionel relented – possibly because Amalia had told him that Henry would kill himself if he did not see him. He now accepted the fact that Henry was going to travel to Europe at all costs. Towards the end of February 1896, Henry arrived in Paris. It was here that he learned from Flora and Béon more of the circumstances surrounding his birth in Arcachon – and the fact that he had been registered as a *legitimate* son. This revelation was to prove a turning-point in the relationship between the siblings.

Henry did not keep his first appointment with Victoria, but met her at Flora's in March. It was an unsatisfactory meeting at which, according to Victoria, Henry was 'at his most disagreeable and aggressive'. Although Henry 'never mentioned the question of his legitimacy' at his meeting with Victoria, she recorded how 'he complained bitterly of being kept in Africa, whilst I was living in luxury in England, and that my father was nothing but a cad and "a *cochon*". Upon this I said that unless he withdrew these expressions, I should never speak to him again; he not only refused to do so but said he should like to put a match to the old shanty at Knole and burn the lot of us.' In a letter to his father after the meeting, Henry denied having said anything against the old man, and blamed Victoria instead.

In early April, at last, Henry met his father in London before returning to Natal later in the month. It was the first time they had seen each other in ten years. The interview appeared to go well, although when Victoria saw Henry afterwards, she was surprised, after what had passed between them in March, that her brother made no attempt at an apology and simply spoke 'with affected refinement about the weather'. 'I had such a heavy heart on parting from him without a single loving word. I have done all I can and he has not responded to my overtures.' On 12 May, Victoria started to write her diary in English rather than in French, a sign perhaps of the significance of 1896 in the history of the family.

As a result of the meeting between father and son, Lord Sackville attempted to settle the purchase of Henry's other two farms, Hall Cross and Burgundy, as swiftly as possible. On 16 June, he wrote to his son that he had now sent him the full amount (just over £3,000) he had promised him 'for your start', and told him that he must now distinctly 'understand that I can no longer be responsible for any further payments whatsoever in connection with instalments or other arrangements. I shall continue our allowance as usual.' On his return to South Africa, Henry promptly sold his farms – and prepared to launch his claim to be recognised as Lord Sackville's heir.

6

Laying Claim to Knole

By the 1890s, the Sackvilles' year had settled into an established pattern: February and March in Monte Carlo, the summer season in London, July at Knole, grouse-shooting and fishing in Scotland in August, and shooting weekends at great country estates around the country in the autumn. It was an era in which, as Vita later described, 'genealogies and family connections, tables of precedence and a familiarity with country seats formed almost part of a moral code'.

Towards the end of October 1896, Lionel and Victoria were invited to stay by the Iveaghs on their Suffolk estate. Lord Iveagh, the great-grandson of Arthur Guinness, who had founded the brewery, had bought Elveden Hall just two years before, after the death of its previous owner, Prince Duleep Singh. Elveden in 1896 was much as the 'Black Prince', as he was known, had left it: an Indian maharajah's palace, superimposed upon a Georgian country house in the heathlands of East Anglia. Singh's architect John Norton had been instructed to 'decorate the interior with pure Indian ornament', copied from the palaces of Lahore and Delhi. Plaster ornamentation decorated the arches like sculpted icing sugar; a tracery of foliage fashioned from coloured glass and mirrors festooned the ceilings. There was underfloor central heating, and the walls were hung with the tapestries and paintings brought by the new owners (which would later form part of the Iveagh Bequest at Kenwood House in London). The writer Augustus Hare described a similar house party almost exactly a year before the Sackville-Wests stayed: 'the house (with the kindest of hosts) is almost appallingly luxurious, such masses of orchids, electric light everywhere, & c. However, a set-off the other way is an electric piano, which goes on pounding away by itself with a pertinacity, which is perfectly distracting.' In her diary, Victoria remarked on all the fine furniture '*et une armée de bedints*'.

Prince Duleep Singh had developed Elveden as a great shooting estate, where he could entertain his neighbour, the Prince of Wales, who owned the 8,000-acre Sandringham Estate just over the border in Norfolk. The house and its supporting complex of stables, servants' wings, kitchens, and kitchen gardens were all geared towards shooting and the hosting of lavish shooting parties. The birds would be driven out of their hiding places in the trees and hedges towards the guns and blasted from the sky in dense falling flocks by the tweed-suited members of the shooting party. The gentlemen would break for lunch in a heated tent, laid with wooden floorboards, decorated with flowers and gleaming with silver plate. The bag for the three days the Sackville-Wests were at Elveden consisted of 2,445 pheasants, 174 partridges, 104 hares and 491 rabbits – a respectable total, even considering the intense competitiveness of the time.

On their last day at Elveden, the Sackville-Wests received a telegram that threatened to overturn those ancient tables of precedence. Henry, they read, had written to Lord Sackville from Paris, claiming he had documents that proved he was Lord Sackville's legitimate son and therefore heir both to the title and to Knole itself. On Friday 30 October, Victoria and her husband left Elveden in a hurry and, without breaking their journey in London, went straight to Knole to comfort her worried father; the following day, she walked him round the kitchen garden in an attempt to distract him.

In the letter to his father, asking for his legitimacy to be recognised, Henry complained that all his efforts earlier in the year to establish the truth about his birth had been resisted; indeed, that as long as he could remember, he had felt that his 'name and position was being tampered with'. He blamed 'foreign influences' – in particular, his sister Victoria – for encouraging his father to deprive him 'of a place I have every right to have near you as your legitimate son, and all I am asking you in letting bygones be bygones is to restore me my place and social position near you for the future'.

Lord Sackville was later to allege that Henry's letter was the first time he had ever heard it claimed that any of the children were legitimate, 'except as regards the inaccurate statements to that effect in the several Registers of births, marriages, etc.' that he himself had signed. In his written reply to his son on 31 October, he was at a loss to understand why Henry had not alluded to the matter when he had seen him in London earlier in the year; but decided 'to take this opportunity to tell you most emphatically that I never was married to your mother, and that consequently you, as well as your brothers and sisters, are illegitimate children'. He invited his son to meet him at the Lord Warden Hotel, Dover, with 'all the papers and declarations you refer to in your letter . . . when I should have a better opportunity of stating the facts of the case to you'.

Lord Sackville suggested the grandiose Lord Warden Hotel, not just because it took its name from an office held by the Sackvilles in the eighteenth century, but also because it was ideally placed by Admiralty Pier where the cross-Channel steamers berthed. After their interview, he hoped, Henry could be packed straight back to Paris. Henry, however, declined a meeting in Dover on the grounds that the documents – including birth certificates for Flora, Amalia and Henry, stating they were legitimate – were in the hands of his lawyers. In any case, Knole not Dover was, he felt, the proper 'place for a meeting between father and son, considering it is in reality their mutual home . . . and I do not wish bearing your name and being your son to hide myself from the public gaze and knowledge of being the same'. At this point, Lord Sackville felt there was little point in discussing the matter any further, 'as it is perfectly evident that you entirely fail to appreciate or understand that any such statements if made were made solely with the object of shielding your mother, yourself, and your sisters as far as was possible under unfortunate circumstances'.

On Saturday 7 November, Henry telegrammed his father at Knole, threatening to take steps on Monday if no more satisfactory answer was received before then. The same day he also wrote to his cousin Gilbert, the new Earl De La Warr, as head of the family. As the result of a strange sequence of wills, titles and family circumstances – and, in particular, of a provision, known as the 'shifting clause', which precluded the Earl De La Warr from inheriting Knole as well as Buckhurst – Knole had, during the 1870s, mutated from principal family mansion into the preserve of younger sons, while Buckhurst, the home of the De La Warrs, had become the senior inheritance. 'My dear Cousin,' Henry wrote to a man he had never met before, 'As chief of the family I am writing to you for justice, knowing you to be honourable in every way.' He enclosed a circular memorandum and a copy of a letter sent to other members of the family – in which 'you will see, I am sure, the fairness of my demand so cruelly opposed by my father, and notice in his answers the influence under which he is so firmly held of one who is not even his daughter [Victoria], and consequently not one of us, who for the sake of working her own ends has planned, and is executing the ruin of us all'. To his appeal to Gilbert's sense of fair play, he appended a threat: 'nothing whatever will make me renounce a name or interest belonging to me, and the day I am forced by foul play to abandon all I most cherish in this world, then that day I will drag down with me this name I would be ashamed to own then'.

The Sackvilles to whom Henry sent circulars included his uncle, William Edward, and his aunts, the Duchess of Bedford and the Dowager Countess of Derby. He described how he had been for ten years, since 1886, in Africa. Had it not been for his discovery, a couple of months before, of certain facts – and he enclosed copies of the birth and baptism certificates for himself, Flora and Amalia – he might have continued to believe that the three of them were illegitimate and that Colonel [William Edward] Sackville-West was Lord Sackville's heir. 'Now as my father denies all these declarations and facts and above all his own signature, I am fully determined whatever may be the consequence to hold onto my rights to the very end . . . And in ending wish to call your attention to the position of my sister Pepita [Victoria] who alone has benefited, viz., my father's position and existence when she had not even the presumption of having a single act signed by him as shows her act of baptism and the non-existence of her birth.'

There is something rather pathetic about Henry's letter, with all its awkward syntax and malapropisms, and its over-familiarity with barely known relations. Sent from temporary lodgings in the Avenue Malakoff in Paris, it arrived at some of the grandest addresses in England, inviting mockery as well as fear. Even Henry realised this, on one occasion writing self-consciously to Gilbert 'as I hear that my English is much ridiculed by the family'.

People have always been fascinated by tales of pretenders and impostors: from Perkin Warbeck, who laid claim to the Tudor throne in the late fifteenth century, to the Grand Duchess

Anastasia who, it was claimed, escaped the massacre of the Russian royal family at Ekaterinburg, and cropped up at regular intervals throughout the twentieth century. But in no century has the story of the wronged rightful heir, who emerges from nowhere to ask questions about the legal foundations of property and the aristocratic principle, been more popular than in the nineteenth century. Tales of claims to ancient titles, of 'secret' marriages, lost heirs and disputed wills became the stuff of stage melodramas and the staple fare of the so-called 'penny dreadfuls'. Henry's claim had some of the ingredients of the case of the Tichborne Claimant, one of the great *causes célèbres* of the nineteenth century, in which a butcher from the town of Wagga Wagga in New South Wales in Australia claimed that he was Sir Roger Tichborne, the supposedly drowned heir to a Hampshire estate.

The Tichborne Claimant became an unlikely hero of the British working classes. His cause was taken up by the newspapers, and the two court cases – the first to establish his claim in 1871–2 and the second, his subsequent trial for perjury, in 1873–4 – were two of the longest in English history, and fashionable spectacles in themselves, attended by the Prince and Princess of Wales. Even after he had been sent to prison, there were public meetings up and down the country in support of this 'tragic' Englishman supposedly laid low by an aristocratic conspiracy. The Tichborne Claimant died destitute in lodgings in London on April Fool's Day, 1898, but his pauper's burial in Paddington Cemetery was attended by more than five thousand people.

Henry's claim, too, played to the Victorian preoccupation with illegitimacy and identity, and challenged the existing social order in much the same way. Initial reactions from the family were predictably dusty. Lady Derby acknowledged Henry's letter on 13 November and returned the enclosures: 'I am sure you ought to arrange to accept your father's offer to see you quietly as he proposed, and not insist upon meeting at Knole.' From then on, she hoped that all enquiries about the legitimacy of Lord Sackville's children should be filtered through her son, Lord Sackville-Cecil. Aunt Constance, the Dowager Countess De La Warr, returned Henry's papers on the fifteenth, with the excuse that, 'It is a matter in which I cannot interfere'.

Earl De La Warr was more sympathetic, although as he explained in a letter to Henry, the request had put him 'in a somewhat difficult position'. 'But as head of the family,' he claimed, 'I will endeavour so far as I can to see that justice is done to my uncle and his children, and you may rest assured that I am absolutely impartial in the matter.' He handed all the papers to a lawyer friend of his, Mr Marshall Hall, and asked Henry to be 'guided entirely by him before taking any further steps'. The same day, Gilbert wrote to his uncle Lionel explaining what he had done and counselling that, given the apparent strength of Henry's case, 'something ought to be done for him at once, if only to avoid the scandal of a public trial'.

Lord Sackville thought it a pity that Gilbert had answered Henry's letter before discussing it with him, and Victoria, too, feared that Gilbert's actions would serve only to encourage Henry. But Henry was grateful, thanking Gilbert for referring the case to Mr Marshall Hall and expressing the wish that he would 'very much like to know' his cousin. Mr Hall believed that Henry had a fairly strong legal case, as well as a strong bargaining position, since, at the very least, Henry had nothing to lose, whereas Lord Sackville had a lot. He duly met Henry and his brother-in-law Gabriel Salanson at the Hotel Cecil on the Embankment in London. The hotel soon became a headquarters for Henry's camp: the *Morning Post* reported that Mr and Mrs Salanson (née Sackville West) had arrived there from Paris for a few weeks, which alarmed Lord Sackville, and there were reports, too, that persons 'under the names of the Honourable Henry and Mrs West' were staying there. This mystified Victoria, as she had no idea Henry was married (he was not). Was this a mistress, then, or one of his scheming sisters – possibly Amalia, who had temporarily vanished from Knole?

On 24 November, the law firm of Meynell & Pemberton was instructed to take steps on behalf of the Sackville family. Mr Pemberton dispatched a private investigator, Mr John Littlechild, a former CID detective chief inspector and first commander of the Special Branch, to Spain to examine the register in the church of San Millán in Madrid for the marriage of Oliva and Pepita in 1851. He was joined there by Mr John Brain, a junior lawyer at Pemberton's. During the time the Sackville solicitors were collecting their evidence in Spain, and then France, Henry's solicitors were doing the same thing at Bordeaux and Arcachon.

The need to act quickly interrupted the Sackvilles' social life. Lionel and Victoria did not attend the wedding of one of Victoria's closest friends, Violet Spender Clay, on 30 November, and spent the weekend in London instead, mulling over the next legal moves. Crucial to any legal proceedings would be the recollections of Lord Sackville himself, a 'sad, disgusted man', as his great-nephew Eddy Sackville-West later described him, who suffered from 'the temperamental melancholy which dogs all Sackvilles and has driven many of them to end their lives in blackest solitude'. Seeming older than his sixty-nine years, Lord Sackville was now being asked to dredge from the desolate wastelands of his past the details of a passion that had domi-nated his life more than thirty years before – in preparation for a formal statement. The closest he had previously come to betraying his feelings for Pepita had been during an incident recalled by Vita. When old Lord Sackville had once seen Vita holding on to the end of her mother's long hair, he had started and exclaimed: 'Never let me see that child doing that again, Victoria.' It had reminded him suddenly of how Victoria herself had once played with her mother Pepita's luxuriant hair.

It was not long before Henry realised that the friendship between Gilbert and the Sackvilles had not necessarily encouraged Mr Marshall Hall to work in his best interests. Marshall Hall had written to Lord De La Warr, claiming that 'my friendship for you is sufficient guarantee that I should not rashly advise him to do anything to compromise the family honour'. And when Mr Hall heard that Lord Sackville's agents had found the certificate of Pepita's marriage in 1851 to Oliva, he told Lionel – much to Victoria's glee – that this would 'knock Henry's business on the head'.

Henry duly transferred his case from the care of Mr Marshall Hall to the law firm of Day & Russell. On 11 January 1897, the Sackvilles – represented by my great-grandfather Colonel William Edward Sackville-West and his family – his sons, Lionel (with wife Victoria), Charlie and Bertie, and his daughters, Mary and Cecilie – brought 'an action for the perpetuation of testimony' against Henry. This would allow evidence to be collected now to counter any claim that Henry might bring later, on the death of his father: evidence that 'Henry West is not the lawful son of Lord Sackville and is not entitled to any estate title or interest whatsoever, and that Flora Salanson and Amalia West are not lawful children of said Baron Sackville and have no right title or interest whatsoever nor any expectancy of any'.

As the threat of a court case loomed, the battle lines were drawn. Max was initially sympathetic to Henry's cause, at one stage reassuring his younger brother that he was with him 'heart and soul in your work', and Amalia and Flora actively supported it. Max had been much moved by Henry's account of his visit to Arcachon, and the fact that, at the exhumation of their mother, he 'had gazed on her dear face after twenty-five years'. Henry had sent him a lock of her hair. 'I tell you I cried like a child,' wrote Max. Although he was not at all convinced by Henry's case, he was interested in the extent to which Henry's proceedings might work in his own interests, referring in letters to Henry to 'our' case, and arguing that it was necessary to prove the marriage of their mother, Pepita, to Lionel 'before either my birth or yours (before my birth to make my claim any good and before yours to make yours any good)'.

For the first time, Victoria was forced to curry favour with the siblings she had ignored for years. She wrote to Max, wishing him a happy Christmas – a 'very meek and mild sort of letter', as Max described it to Henry – and asking him whether his farm had suffered from the rinderpest and whether his chickens (rather than his children) were thriving, before getting down to business: 'You may have heard what Henry is doing in England. He is making a great mistake. It is so hard on Papa in his old age, as really Papa has always done everything he could for us all.'

'I have your letter of good wishes which I was pleased to receive after your long silence,' Max wrote reprovingly from South Africa early in the New Year;

I am glad to find you still recognise you have a brother in S. Africa & often think of me . . . Yes, the Rinderpest is truly a cloud hanging over me. The Locusts were here last year in swarms & devastated all the crops of the country & ruined me in particular, but there is one thing they proved as provender to my chickens but I am sorry such a fare did not prove congenial to me and my children. Your remark with regard to Henry being in England & making a great mistake I duly note. Henry's move is really what you could have expected, as he finds you are living in the lap of luxury & he was living out here on a pittance . . . I am glad to note that you find it a difficulty to bring up one child & to provide for its future with your thousands a year, while I have three with only £150. I hope you fully realise how much harder it must be for me struggling as it is to make ends meet, & leading at best a hand to mouth existence. Truly my lot is hard, harder than you can imagine.

He then proceeded to ask for a 'present . . . which would further denote, in a tangible form, the great interest you take in me during our troubles in S. Africa, afflicted as we are by every scourge you can think of'.

Max must have been terribly confused. As a result of Henry's researches in Spain, he now had a copy of his birth certificate describing him as the legitimate son of Oliva and Pepita. This was the very document that his father had failed to provide at the time of his engagement to Mary Norton, despite continual requests. It contradicted the information he had been given by his uncle, my great-grandfather William Edward, in Aunt Mary's London house in 1882, that he was the illegitimate son of Lord Sackville.

Max was beginning to believe that he was, in fact, Oliva's son, reassuring Henry that 'if my birth and baptismal certificate is correct, and I quite believe it is, I am not Lord Sackville's son at all, and therefore need not trouble my head at all about inheriting Knole and standing in your way. As far as I am concerned my case seems to be decided, and if I am really Oliva's son I intend to assume the name.' He might even be able to use this information to 'make Lord Sackville disgorge the amount realised by the villa [Pepa], for, of course, under that marriage that property is mine'. Poor Max: of all the siblings, I feel in many ways the most sympathy for him. He had all the eldest child's slightly ponderous sense of responsibility towards his family, and yet the true nature of this family, and with it his own identity, was constantly shifting. Here he was bewildered about his birth, adrift in South Africa, and reduced by circumstances and the rinderpest to milking his own cows.

———

Years of everyday jealousy had begun to take their toll on the relationship between Victoria and Amalia. They squabbled about everything: money, the use of the car for lifts, and most of all for a fair share of their father's affection (a commodity that was in limited supply at the best of times). Amalia kept telling their mutual friends that Victoria would not let her have her own sitting room at Knole. ('What a liar Amalia is,' Victoria retaliated in her diary.) They failed to acknowledge each other's presence as they wandered about the great house, not lifting their eyes from their embroidery as one or the other entered the room.

A list survives, in Victoria's handwriting, of her grievances against Amalia around this time. There were the lies that Amalia had told: that she was staying in Eastbourne with the Stanhopes when, in fact, she was at the Hotel Cecil plotting with Henry; that Victoria wanted her to go on the stage or be sent to a convent. There was Amalia's ingratitude when offered suites other than Cranmer's Room as her private rooms at Knole; her mischief-making over Flora's baby; and her general gossiping to friends such as the Baillets and Mary Galloway. Many people, as a result, including family members, thought that Victoria had treated Amalia badly – Gilbert's wife, Minnie De La Warr, for example, claimed that Amalia was 'the most ill-treated girl in the world'.

Amalia wrote to Victoria from Buckhurst towards the end of 1896:

The last discussion we had on Monday night convinced me more than ever that we cannot possibly get on together. You may say it is my fault, you may say whatever you like, it does not alter the fact that we cannot get on, to try is useless. I have thought about it thoroughly during the last four days & I have come to the conclusion that it is best for you & for me in fact for everybody else that you & I should live apart as much as possible. Knole is my home, as long as Papa is there I must be there too, but I cannot continue leading the life I have led for the last 8 years in constant quarrels it is simply wearing me out, therefore to obtain peace I must see of you as little as possible as we always seem to fight directly we meet. To avoid any more rows in future I wish to <u>have my own sitting room</u>, it is only fair in my father's house that I should have one, you all have one why should I not have one also? . . . I shall always try to fit in my visits so as to be away when you are at Knole & to be there when you are away, but there might be times when we should have to be there together & in the latter case I must have a sitting room <u>of my own</u> . . . Believe me, <u>this is the only way of living in peace under the same roof</u>.

On 2 December, Amalia wrote to her father with a slightly different proposal:

You know how <u>utterly impossible</u> it is for Victoria and I to get on together more so now than ever . . . I am 29 quite old enough to take care of myself & I must have peace my state of health at this present moment requires it. I could not stand any more rows my nerves are simply shattered to pieces. I know of some very nice rooms 3 guineas a week & 7/6 for food per day, if you consent may I engage them? Believe me Papa it is the only thing to do, just as much for your sake as for mine. If ever you wanted me, I should always be ready to come, but to live '*en famille*' again is <u>impossible</u>.

Amalia's position at Knole was made even more untenable by the way in which she had to sneak in and out of the house to scheme with Henry in London. Before she had received an answer to her most recent proposal from her father – who, as usual, was dithering and deferring to Victoria about what was to be done – Amalia had turned up at Knole in a fly (a horse-drawn carriage) at short notice, darted up to her room for a few minutes to collect some things for the Hotel Cecil, and then disappeared just as quickly. Her father wrote that he was 'very much hurt at the surreptitious way you came to K. As you had such an important question to ask me, you should have seen me.'

Amalia in a carriage in front of the Outer Wicket at Knole

Had Amalia asked her father openly about 'the facts connected with her birth', he would have explained all, he claimed, 'but after the letters Henry had written and the telegram he sent me, I strongly objected to her associating herself with him in this matter in secret'.

'It is so miserable to begin the year with this miserable business of Henry, Flora and Amalia,' Victoria wrote in her diary in January 1897, starting the year in English for the first time. At Knole, there was a succession of weekend house parties – with the doings of Amalia and Henry the source of constant gossip and speculation. Mr Kenneth Campbell, a stockbroker friend of the Sackvilles, told Victoria how he had heard from Mrs H. Oppenheim that she and Lionel were going to be turned out of Knole. Mrs Knox the housekeeper was afraid that Henry and his associates would send someone down to Knole to blow the great house up – 'after all', Victoria added in her diary, 'Henry threatened to burn it when I saw him in Paris.'

Neighbours, too, were enlisted in the campaign for hearts and minds. Victoria took particular pleasure in showing her upstairs boudoir to Mrs Arthur Cornwallis and Mrs Battiscombe, and telling them that Amalia had turned it down, as 'it is not fair people should think I refused her a sitting-room'. Mrs Rogers of River Hill House was sympathetic, too, as were old Miss Herries of St Julians and Lady Amherst of Montreal Park; Miss Milligan at Ightham had, it appeared, been told less than half the story by Amalia; the Stanhopes, at Chevening, were amazed by 'how abominably Amalia & Henry & Co had behaved'; and when Victoria heard that Amalia had written to Mabel Alexander, claiming 'there were no differences between her and Papa & that he would be glad to have her back at Knole', she scrawled in her diary 'What lies'.

Early in the New Year, Amalia had left for Paris to stay with Flora, and from there she was encouraged to go to Cannes with Bonny, with Lord Sackville paying her travel first-class and 20 francs a day. This was never enough, complained Amalia, and she kept asking for more, pleading, to Victoria's disbelief and disgust, that she had always been and still was 'neutral' in the matter of Henry's claim. In a letter to her father from the Hôtel Britannique, Amalia explained how she would have to find work, given the uncertainty of her future prospects. She insisted that she was doing this not 'out of spite, far from it; necessity alone forces me to'. Victoria, snowed in at Knole and watching Vita toboggan in the park, was scornful, adding double exclamation marks to the account in her diary of Amalia's threat to earn her own living.

Victoria (*far left*), Lionel (*next left*) and Vita (*seated, centre*) holiday with my great-grandfather William Edward (*centre*) at the family home near Bangor

In February, Lionel and Victoria were told by their solicitor that they could safely leave for a few weeks' holiday in Monte Carlo (while Lord Sackville and Vita were dispatched to Bangor). All the siblings, with the exception of Max, were now on the Riviera, in the country of their birth. Amalia and the Salansons, or so Victoria learned from Amalia's maid, were 'all desperately in debt and fully count upon Papa and I giving in & giving them money to keep their petition out of Court . . . They are determined to do anything.' She also heard that 'Amalia is *tout à fait perdue*': a 'fallen' woman, given that her behaviour with men was so 'perfectly awful'. Henry was being chased by his creditors, including his lawyers, Day & Russell, who were also pressing him to appear in the action for perpetuating testimony; if he refused to do so, they insisted, they would not proceed with the case and would not present his petition for legitimacy. It was not long before Henry had replaced them with another law firm, and was blaming Day & Russell for poor advice.

What particularly bothered Amalia was that she did not have enough to pay for her washing and, despite repeated requests, her father would not advance her the money on her next allowance. On 12 February 1897, she wrote from the Hôtel Britannique:

> Though you have told me not to write to you unless I had something important to say I cannot help answering your letter. It has made me so miserable Papa. I am not going to write much about it, still I do want you not to go on believing whatever has been told you about me. It is all wrong I know . . . I have come to ask you to let me feel once more that you still do care for me & allow me to write to you now and then & show you that I am as ever.

Along with the withdrawal of his love, her father also demanded the return of some family jewels she had taken from Knole. The receipt, which she insisted be made out to the 'Honorable' Amalia Sackville West, listed one gold chain with pearls and rare diamonds, one gold brooch with pearls, two rows of false pearls, one paste necklace, one garnet brooch, one gold bangle with turquoise heart pendant, and one gold ring with three rubies.

News of Amalia's plight filtered back to England, through mutual friends and acquaintances whom she saw in Cannes: the Baillets, for example, and a Kent friend of Mr Pemberton who told him that Amalia is left 'without a sou'. As Lord Sackville finally acknowledged in a letter to Amalia in March:

> something definite should be settled as to your mode of life, the more so as rumours frequently reach me of your utterly unjustifiable complaints to outsiders of being kept without money. You have chosen to leave Knole, and ask me to provide you with the means to live on your own account. Let me

impress upon you the importance of cutting your coat according to your cloth . . . It was your suggestion that you should go as a 'paying guest', and, provided you satisfy me as to the respectability and suitability of the family you propose to enter, I will give you an inclusive allowance of £360 a year . . . You will please understand that this allowance will only continue so long as you conduct yourself properly and live a life of which I approve, and that it must cover <u>everything</u>.

It was quite useless for her to claim that she had been 'neutral' with regard to Henry's conduct. 'Whatever your attitude may be now, I am perfectly well aware of the part you played in that affair.'

Henri de Béon in the 1890s

Béon, too, was in the South of France that winter. It was he who had encouraged Henry in his ambitions the previous year, placing himself, as he boasted to Lord Sackville, at Henry's 'entire disposal', and providing him with the documents that lay at the heart of Henry's case. In February 1897, he wrote once again, refuting what he saw as Sackville's slanderous accusations of betrayal:

> How can it be, Sackville, that you dare to speak of calumny after having taken an unfair advantage of my kindness in every way . . . If you do not act honourably in regard to me whom you called your best friend, be honourable at least towards your poor children who suffer on account of you . . . When your son Henry Sackville West came to me, I gave him a reception altogether natural and from the heart, for I had rescued, received and educated him. It is a noble action that you, their Father, should never have forgotten . . . What have I not done for you? I have sacrificed years of my existence and I have destroyed my future.

He recalled the day when Lord Sackville had thrown himself into his arms, and implored him in 'the most touching terms' to help him out, or he would be forced to abandon his 'poor children and to send them to Spain for your family did not wish to have anything to do with them'. Why was it that Sackville had changed so much since then? For a start, he had not thought back then that one day he would become a lord. And, continued Béon: 'Who is the person who has stirred up this quarrel with me? Who is the person who has made you quarrel with your children?' There was only one person to blame: that 'wicked and ungrateful' Victoria.

> She holds you in the hollow of her hand and makes you do whatever is good for her. You neither write nor say anything without her or by her mediation. Greed of gold devours her. It is inborn in her for when she was a child she would have done anything to obtain a few sous. It is this greed of gold that has

made her change her opinions at the age of 30 years and which has given her this influence over you to incite you to repudiate your friends and your debts and it is this greed of gold which has incited her to separate you from your children.

———

Mardi Gras 1897 was celebrated a little diabolically at a fancy-dress dinner given by Gabriel Salanson in Cannes. All the key conspirators, including Béon, were present, and a strange ditty, scrawled in French on a scrap of paper, records the event. Gabriel came dressed as 'a savage', with a ring on his nose, feathers on his head, and a fig-leaf to cover '*sa modestie*'. Flora wanted to expose all her charms, she said, so her husband suggested she remove her corset and cloak herself in a transparent gown. Henry, '*le Caffre*', came as 'a Negro' and made a speech over coffee, promising that when he became an English milord, he would invite all his guests over to spend the summer on his estate; he would throw 'that' Victoria and her gang out – and good riddance, 'let the Devil take them', echoed Béon.

On hearing that Béon had reappeared in their lives, Max warned Henry that he did not altogether trust him. Béon had threatened 'to say all sorts of things about our mother', he explained; 'It remains now to find out what these things he intended saying could have been, and what it is he knew about her that he hides and does not tell you.' The key to the mystery lay in the Villa Pepa in Arcachon, and one of the very few people who knew (how intimately no one was ever quite sure) the secrets of those shuttered years, who could unearth those buried memories, was Henri de Béon. Joseph Goring Lesnier, a childhood friend of Max from France, also pointed to the importance of Béon's role, informing Lord Sackville that he had seen Henry and Amalia at Béon's apartment in Paris in the spring of 1896 and that it had struck him they were going to blackmail him. Béon, he claimed was a '*maître chanteur* [blackmailer]'.

Another figure from the past who warned of a plot was the enormously wealthy Marquis de Löys Chandieu, with whom Victoria had fallen in love in 1889, to whom she had been 'half-engaged', and whom she had eventually spurned in favour of Lionel. In February, Victoria met her former suitor in Monte Carlo. And the letter she received from an anonymous well-wisher in spring 1897 is probably from him. Löys wanted to help her '*dans cette nouvelle difficulté*' and warned her of a plot to blackmail the family. What puzzled Löys in all of this, though, was the role of the Salansons, who, it appeared, had nothing to gain. 'You are absolutely right to fight this,' he advised, 'despite the scandal with which you're threatened.' Otherwise, what on earth would have been the point of 'so much energy wasted, so many sacrifices made?' It was a poignant reference to all the heart-searching of the early 1890s, when Victoria had agonised between Lionel and Löys, between being 'a marchioness or a peeress', but had eventually chosen Knole – and Lionel – over love for Löys. He explained how Victoria could write to him in Paris, before signing off resignedly. 'Two daughters, *chère Amie*, that's my lot, and I don't want anything more, as I've no energy left.'

Amalia appeared happy at first with the proposed financial settlement of £360 a year but continued to discredit Victoria to Aunt Mary and her daughter, Mary Galloway. In a letter to Aunt Mary on 6 May, Lord Sackville tried to set the record straight: 'There seems to be an altogether wrong impression abroad as to the position of affairs between Amalia and myself. The true facts of the case are as follows – Shortly after Henry's first letter to me Amalia left Knole of her own free will, and wrote to me a few days afterwards informing me she could never return while Lionel and Victoria continued to live here . . . I consider that her behaviour towards me in reference to the part she played in Henry's business has been little short of outrageous.' It was 'utterly false' that Victoria had turned Amalia out of Knole; Amalia had left of her own accord – indeed, 'Amalia's conduct towards me seems to have been somewhat overlooked'.

Amalia was doing more than simply complaining about Victoria to mutual friends and relations; she was also actively stirring up trouble. Amalia told Maie [Mary] Cornwallis-West in Cannes that she had, in her possession, several compromising letters from Maie's husband, William [Cornwallis], to Victoria. 'The liar!!' Victoria wrote in her diary, 'I am not afraid of her threats.' When Cornwallis confronted Amalia with her mischief-making, Amalia wrote to Maie from 10 South Eaton Place, where she was lodging with a lady friend: 'I have just seen Cornwallis and a very painful meeting it was too . . . I write at once to retract every single thing I have told you.' Cornwallis threatened to refer the whole affair to his solicitors, and on 2 July, Amalia drafted a formal statement: 'I, hereby deny ever having stated that I possessed a compromising letter or letters written by William Cornwallis West to my sister Victoria and I have no reason to suppose that any such letter or letters passed between them at any time.' The matter was closed, although relations between the Cornwallis-Wests and the Sackville-Wests remained wary and cool.

———

On 13 April, the day that Victoria started work on a counterpane for Vita's bed, the action for perpetuating testimony opened before Mr E. M. Hutton, Registrar and Master of the Supreme Court at Gibraltar, representing the Attorney General of England. Gibraltar had been chosen for its proximity to Spain, and statements were taken from a motley group of twenty-five Spanish witnesses – of Durans and Olivas, Ramirez' and Rodriguez', Gomez' and Gonzales' – members, friends and former theatrical colleagues of Pepita's family. Pepita's aunt, Micaela, could not sign her own name, and so her son-in-law had to be sent for; others simply left a mark. Alfred Harrison, who had been engaged by Meynell & Pemberton to obtain evidence in Spain, and to arrange for the Sackville witnesses to attend in Gibraltar, reported that lawyers acting for Henry had 'visited all our witnesses at Granada and Albolote and told them not to be led astray by us, that they had a great deal of money for the purpose of remunerating all handsomely, that the matter at issue related to millions'.

The statements prepared in 1897 conjured up the world of Victoria's Spanish ancestors. Some of the evidence, though, was confusing. People were being asked to dredge their memories of almost half a century before, with the result that events might be transposed by up to a decade, muddling the chronology. Other statements were contradictory. One man, Juan de Dios Gonzalez, claimed that he had accompanied Pepita when she left Albolote for Germany in 1856, and then stayed with her in Munich while she danced by day and entertained the 'Prince of Bavaria' by night. Juan de Dios, however, could only have been nine at the time, and the village priest dismissed his claims as the ravings of a 'flighty, romancing' fantasist; other villagers remembered Juan de Dios better as the boy who had been arrested and imprisoned for shooting his stepmother dead. Another feature of the evidence was that much of it was repetitive, with certain phrases cropping up time and time again, as if they had been learned by rote, with a particular agenda in mind and a particular point to prove.

In June, statements were taken from twenty-two French witnesses, at Arcachon and Bordeaux, of many of the people who had been a feature of life at the Villa Pepa: Auguste Desombre and Louisa Dignac, Gustave Hameau and Harry Scott Johnston, Reverend Samuel Radcliff and Madame Vigier. Henry was present at these proceedings, and it was obvious to Mr Pemberton, who was there too, that Henry was determined to go ahead with his lawsuit and to put his father in the witness box.

The Sackvilles spent the second half of June preparing their statements for just such an eventuality. Things were not going that well. As Victoria recorded in her diary, she spent one particular day at the solicitors' 'having our evidence read & questions. Papa makes a great mess of his answers & contradicts himself every minute. It is hopeless and Pemberton thinks he will be a very bad witness.' The following day was not much better. 'We tried to cross-examine Papa last night till one o'cl. It is no good. I am quite worn out by the long sitting from 10.30 till 5 at Pemberton.'

The Sackvilles' visits to the solicitors took place against a backdrop of dinners and dances, of trips to the theatre. Life at Knole continued as before, with weekend house parties and walks to Lionel's farm, where Vita enjoyed feeding the pigs with apples picked in the garden. Victoria redecorated the Ballroom, and celebrated the Queen's Jubilee with a tea party for all of the children on the estate. In London, there were rehearsals for the exclusive quadrille in which Victoria had been asked by Lady Warwick to dance at the fancy-dress ball to be held at Devonshire House. For, despite the murkiness of the story that was emerging in the courts, the Sackvilles placed great public stress on behaving well and keeping up appearances.

Towards the end of June, the examination of witnesses began in the Royal Courts of Justice, as members of the extended Sackville family, former Foreign Office colleagues of Lord Sackville, friends from America, the curate at Withyham, the East Sussex parish where generations of Sackvilles had worshipped, were all questioned about the past. Victoria found Osborn, Henry's new solicitor, 'so common & vulgar . . . [he] did not even know what Papa's name was; he called him Lord West & Lord Sackville-West'. Bonny, Victoria's lady's maid during her seven years in Washington, arrived from France. She contradicted Salanson's claims that he had no idea Flora was illegitimate when he married her in 1888, by recalling the charade of the carefully orchestrated coughing fit at their wedding ceremony.

Victoria and her father made their depositions, and were cross-examined towards the end of July, in Room 278 of the Law Courts. 'They all said I made a splendid witness,' Victoria wrote in her diary after her cross-examination by Henry's counsel, Mr Scarlett, despite the lowering presence of Henry and Gabriel Salanson. Henry, Victoria observed, was the very image of Béon and had 'all his ways', and he and Papa stared threateningly at each other across the court room (Lord Sackville had started to believe that Henry was not his son after all). When her father was examined on 28 and 29 July, he turned out at first to be not quite as bad a witness as had been feared, although he did not listen enough to the questions and was very forgetful. 'Papa has only the truth to tell & he forgets half he ought to say. It is miserable work,' Victoria wrote.

Henry described his father's performance in the witness box to Max even less flatteringly: 'Never, Max, have I been face to face with such awful lies; you cannot realise how he lied. My counsel told me that if the case had been before a jury (instead of being private) they would have stopped the case . . . As for father, he evidently must have been given plenty to drink, for he was wound up like a devil.' Henry went on to reassure his older brother that if he won his case, Max should come to live in England, and he would see him 'comfortably settled down according to your rank in life, for you will be my brother always'. Lord Sackville completed his deposition on 6 August. 'The heat in the Law Courts yesterday was awful,' wrote

Victoria. 'I thought poor Papa wd have an attack of apoplexy; he was so red. He answered very badly & never listened with attention to anything Scarlett was saying.'

After all the statements had been taken and the examinations made, the annual round of life at Knole continued: the Knole flower show, the summer garden parties at the neighbours, and so on. Then it was off, in September, to the shooting parties (with Papa holidaying in Bangor again), and in the winter to Monte Carlo for a few weeks. Here, Victoria met the Prince of Wales once more. They talked about Henry's case, and the Prince 'said what a shame it was on Papa. He said I ought to have a little boy for Knole & that he would be godfather.' He also took the liberty of asking Victoria for a photograph of herself in fancy dress at the Devonshire Ball, and of inviting himself to Knole in the summer.

The visit of the Prince (*seated, third from left*) and Princess of Wales (*holding six-year-old Vita's hand*) to Knole in July 1898. Victoria is seated second from left

With the coming of spring – and as predictable as the social calendar – came renewed hostilities from Amalia. In April,

Victoria learned again of the 'awful' quantity of lies Amalia was telling people. She was astonished, therefore, the following month, when Amalia asked for a rapprochement. Victoria talked the matter over with Lionel, and agreed that he should tell Amalia that she would be forgiven (although never by Papa) if 'she took back all the lies she has told people about us'. When Lionel and Amalia met for a couple of hours on 27 April, it soon became clear that Amalia was seeking to patch things up for the sake of appearances only – and that any reconciliation came with a condition. She would confess to the lies she had been telling, but only if she could show the people to whom she was apologising a copy of Victoria's birth certificate (which described Victoria as the child of an unknown father). Amalia's own humility could only be bought at the expense of Victoria's humiliation. There was to be no reconciliation.

The Salansons' lives were unravelling, too. This glamorous, good-looking young couple had begun to go their separate ways. Within a few years of their marriage, Victoria heard rumours that Gabriel was chasing after other women in St Petersburg, where he had been posted as second secretary, and there were stories about Flora too, spread by Victoria, that Gabriel was not the father of the Salansons' short-lived daughter, Elie. The bustling Gabriel was always restless. He took indefinite leave from St Petersburg soon after his appointment in order to return to France to look after his dying father, but what he really wanted to be was an artist. His financial ambitions were never satisfied by his marriage to the illegitimate daughter of an impoverished peer, and it was only financial embarrassment that forced him to write, in vain, to the Minister for Foreign Affairs in 1897, begging for any consular post, however lowly and however far away.

By 1898, Flora and Gabriel were both filing for divorce on the grounds of adultery – although, in private, Flora also blamed the divorce on the influence of Gabriel's family, 'as there was really no serious quarrel between them, only constant bickering about money matters'. While proceedings dragged on through the summer of 1898 (neither party could prove the other's adultery) Flora was awarded provisional alimony of 500 francs per month. Their son, Lionel, the little boy who had spent a couple of summers at Knole, was to split his time between the parents. If, however, Gabriel were to be successful in his divorce suit – or so the lawyers advised – then he would get custody of the child, with his wife having some access rights.

Knowing that Victoria had her father's ear, Flora wrote regularly to her older sister, asking her to persuade Papa to send her money. Flora owed around 70,000 francs at the time, and the contents of the rented house in which she and her husband had lived had just been seized and sold. Gabriel himself had sold Flora's jewellery, and made off with some pictures belonging to Lord Sackville. Flora's tone is one of desperation, as she shifted from shabby lodging house to hotel – on one occasion having to pay the proprietor 3,000 francs simply to clear her account and have her baggage released.

Flora now thought that she had been punished enough for her wrongs, and that the time had come for her to be forgiven. To the solicitors in Paris, whom the Sackvilles had instructed to talk to Flora, she claimed that she was now on 'very unfriendly terms' with her brother, Henry, and that during the last twelve months no steps had been taken either by her husband or by Mr Henry West in connection with the legitimacy case. Indeed, the two quarrelled the whole time, with Henry on one occasion assaulting the man who had until recently aided and abetted him in his claim.

Victoria sent Flora a little money, which enabled her to give up for the time being her plans to go on the stage. Pemberton, on the other hand, advised Lord Sackville not to give Flora any financial assistance until her divorce was finalised – not even £50 towards her legal fees. Flora could not believe that her own father had refused to help her get custody of her son and defend her honour. If Papa only knew what a terrible situation she was in, he would not have had 'the heart to refuse to help'. 'Abandoned by her own family', Flora did not know what was going to happen, but asked Victoria to remember that, whatever the future held, anything bad 'would be the fault of those who weren't able to forgive'.

Now that legal proceedings were in abeyance, and he had run out of money, Henry hoped that Victoria might help effect a reconciliation with his father that would lead to a financial settlement. Writing from Paris in September, he asked her to forget the regrettable incidents of the past, which he 'deplored', and blamed them entirely on '*cette vilaine créature et infame Salanson*'. He also offered to make peace with his brother-in-law, Lionel: 'My hand is stretched out to you; take it, let bygones be bygones, and let us unite again and in a friendly manner settle everything once for all . . . Knole does not make the slightest impression on me; I do not want it . . . What I want is to go away from a country where everything reminds me of my unfortunate loss and the stain I will have to bear now to my grave.'

A flurry of letters and telegrams to his father and to Victoria, requesting a meeting, followed in early October. Henry stayed at the Charing Cross Hotel in London. From a room perched over the tracks at the railway station, he was poised to make daily, lightning trips to Sevenoaks. He would send messages from the Royal Crown Hotel in town, where he based himself during the day, or leave his visiting card at Knole itself.

On 4 October, Henry wrote to his father, demanding a meeting, and threatening to shoot himself if he did not get a hearing. 'Do you wish now for my death? . . . I am determined at seeing you & at any price.' His life, he claimed, hung 'by a thread', and, in his desperation, he even turned to his aunt Mary, who had rebuffed his approaches a couple of years before:

I am here in an awful stress. I have come over to make it up
with father and Victoria but am afraid they have got very hard
hearted and they mean me harm . . . Will you intervene in my
favour . . . and save me from the awful fate I am bound to
meet, and that of putting an end to my existence at my father's
very feet? How many young fellows are they that have suffered
as I have done – all for the sin of my father. I never brought
myself out in this world, and far better would it have been, as I
wrote him today, had he wrung my neck as a child than make
me undergo today the humiliation, the disgrace, of hearing a
name he denies me now, which has brought me all these evils.

Lord Sackville continued to refuse a meeting, pleading that,
'The state of my health and what took place last year prevents
me from ever seeing you again.' He suggested that Henry go to
see Mr Brain at Pemberton's instead. Victoria, too, excused
herself on the grounds that Lionel would not approve of her
seeing Henry without his permission, but that he was away. On
the fifth, Henry turned up again at Knole at five o'clock in the
afternoon, and insisted upon seeing Papa. Victoria bundled
Vita out of the way to protect her from any unpleasantness,
and the porter Lipscombe told Henry that there was no one
there to see him. Henry started to force his way across the
Green Court, the first courtyard in the ceremonial route that
his ancestor Thomas Sackville had devised for the entertainment of monarchs three hundred years before. Two footmen
hurried to help Lipscombe turn Henry out of the house, stop-
ping him at the Inner Wicket, the entrance to Lord Sackville's
apartments. Here, Henry carried on talking to the servants in a
loud voice for a couple of hours, claiming that Lord Sackville
had been married to Pepita, and that he was therefore the rightful heir to Knole. Eventually he burst into hysterical tears and
left just before the police arrived.

When Henry returned to Knole the next day, he found a

policeman on the door, and he confided to him that he would go to 'extremities' on Saturday if his father did not meet him in London. Lord Sackville, by now, was anxious to settle, and Mr Brain advised that it might be as well to offer Henry an allowance of £100 a year, 'considering Papa's feeling & hatred of being talked about'.

Lionel was away as these dramas unfolded, but Victoria felt that circumstances were serious enough to warrant her wiring her 'darling boy' to return for a meeting with Henry. 'I have been so reluctant to make him give up his stalking,' she wrote, but circumstances demanded the interruption of his sporting season, just as they had at Elveden almost exactly two years before, when Henry first announced his intentions.

Parallel Lives

It is hard not to feel sympathy for Henry, as he moved between England and France towards the end of 1898, trailing his suit-case of papers and 'proofs'. His first visit to Knole, the object of his obsession, had just ended unceremoniously in eviction. His threats, and his awkward English, inspired a sense of amuse-ment and fun, as well as fear, in the members of his legitimate family. He was virtually penniless, and as uncertain as ever of the circumstances surrounding his birth and identity. Only the previous year, his father had claimed, in his deposition, that he was in 'a very different state of mind from the state of mind I had when I was at Arcachon in 1866 . . . my feeling at Arcachon in 1866 was one of great affection both for her [Pepita] and the children, that feeling has now been considerably modified'. Lord Sackville had now begun to doubt whether he was even the father of Max, as well as Henry. What other revelations would be forthcoming?

For the time being, though, all Henry wanted was enough money to live on the Continent 'as a gentleman'. He wrote to Victoria in what she described as 'a very dictatorial way', demanding a meeting. 'What cheek!' she wrote, 'He treats us as if he was doing us a favour to see us but we only condescend to meet him as we pity Papa who is so frightened and weak.' In view of Henry's recent appearance at Knole, Lionel returned early to London, telling Victoria that he preferred her 'peace of mind to the most delightful stalking' (although, as yet, he had not shot any stags), and together they went to meet Henry at Mr Brain's office. Lionel had apparently formed 'the greatest contempt for H', and when Henry repeated that all he wanted was 'an honourable situation', Lionel contemptuously and quietly added, 'like a footman'. Meanwhile, Henry's debts drifted towards the Sackvilles: a letter to Victoria asking for help in paying his hotel bill, a letter to Lord Sackville from his tailor saying that Henry had ordered £20 worth of clothes and given his father's name as a reference. Lord Sackville replied promptly that he would not guarantee payment, a refusal that Henry found 'extremely unkind', even 'more so after what has already taken place'.

Victoria and Vita in one of their first motor cars

Henry outlined his situation to Victoria on 17 October. If it was their intention to compensate him in some way for what he had been 'deprived' of and 'not to do things on the cheap', he was quite sure a settlement would soon be reached:

> If I can get away from here to France . . . with the knowledge I am well provided for and thus be able to live without want I am sure I will leave you Knole and think no more about it. My desire is peace . . . I want to get married and settle down somewhere. I will try and forget what has been done to me so I advise you to earnestly meet me and grant me like honest people what I shall ask you which you can well afford, otherwise you will drive me mad, precipitate matters, and I will get beyond control. Mind you I am not using any threat, I am not blackmailing nor any wish to extort.

Towards the end of October, Henry saw Mr Pemberton, who suggested, on behalf of the Sackvilles, an allowance of £100 a year. At first, Henry described this proposal as 'most absurd', and threatened to come down to Knole again. A watchman was put on the front door to prevent a repeat of events earlier in the month, but Henry never came. Threatened with the prospect of no allowance at all, Henry eventually agreed to the proposal and was persuaded to return to Paris; his father even paid his tailor's bill. Henry soon regretted his decision. 'It was absolutely madness on my part to have ever attempted to start here with only £5 in pocket,' he wrote to his father from the Grand Hotel Terminus on 28 November. He really needed £4 to £5 a week for the first year in order to make a proper start, he argued, and was besieged by creditors who threatened to make his life 'absolutely intolerable until these accounts are settled with'. Three days later he was back in England again, at the Charing Cross Hotel, despite the fact that 'my coming over is looked upon as a breach of the promise made you', in order to 'lay the facts [of his penury] before Mr. Pemberton'. 'Give me the chance of getting out of this mess I am in,' he begged his father, 'and leave the rest to me. You will have no cause to regret it . . . I am short of boots, shirts, and underwear, and require a hat. It will appear ridiculous to you that I should mention all this, but want is necessity.'

From January 1899, Henry was to receive an allowance of £2 a week, to be collected from a bank in Paris, Messrs Demachy & Sellière, to ensure he lived abroad. This was never enough. By the spring, he was working at *Le Petit Bleu*, a newspaper, where, he told his father, he was 'giving entire satisfaction'. He asked him for 300 francs to furnish and pay the first three months' rent on a small room he had found not far from his place of work. It would help a lot because, as he continued, 'I am half fed and half clothed and with a roof over my head that has no comfort, and in consequence feel but unfit for the terrible uphill work before me.'

At the same time, Henry was evidently up to something. In December 1898, he had written defiantly to Max: 'Don't make any mistake, I am far from crushed as people are wont to believe, and you will see me come out on top before many years are over.' Max's predicament was as tragic as Henry's. In February 1899, he was forced to sell his failing farm for £3,000, the proceeds being invested by his trustees to provide him with an income of £180 a year, on top of the £150 he received from his father. As Max acknowledged, his 'painful position' owed a good deal to his own 'carelessness', but it had also been brought on by 'a succession of misfortunes', such as the rinderpest epidemic which killed his cows. This highly infectious virus swept through southern Africa in the 1890s killing, in a couple of years, around ninety per cent of cattle, buffalo and related species from the Horn of Africa to the Cape.

In April, Max's eldest son Lionel died from a brief illness at school, aged fourteen years and eight months. The black-bordered 'In Memoriam' card he sent his father bore the words of his son's last prayer: 'God have mercy upon me, Gentle Jesus take care of me.' 'I am broken-hearted,' Max wrote. 'He was such a handsome, refined, bright boy & would have been 15 years of age in a short while. He was more like my friend & my companion than a son. My God, I wish I had gone instead of him.' Just six months after his son's death, Max applied to the courts in Natal for the surrender of the remainder of his estate on the grounds of insolvency (the proceeds from the sale of the farm were in the hands of his trustees, and therefore could not be claimed by his creditors).

At the creditors' meetings, Max's assets comprised some agricultural implements that were to be put up for auction at his former farm, plus a pitiful collection of items now stored at his house in Loop Street, Pietermaritzburg: namely, one deer head, one aviary, one bicycle, one mealie crusher, three saddles, one churn, eleven head-stalls, one pack saddle. Max himself could not bear to go near his old farm, as he wrote to the receiver, 'because it is so deeply associated with my boy who is dead, who died in such heartbreaking circumstances. The spot where he lived happily with us for 15 years, would remind me of him at every turn; I should expect almost to see him round every corner & it would finally break my heart.' Max's liabilities included outstanding school fees for his children and, pathetically, a debt for £31 19s 3d for the young Lionel's memorial in the cemetery in Pietermaritzburg. Max also owed the undertaker. As he wrote to the receiver, 'My child is lying in the cemetery & the very ground is not paid & I am enduring the tortures of it.'

———————

Flora was in a poor way, too. She had no idea what was to become of her, and at the moment, as she wrote to Victoria, she did not even have enough to pay for her next meal, '*mais c'est un détail, et je n'insiste pas*'. Seeing that her sister was in such 'great distress', Victoria continued to send Flora small sums of money, as she waited for her divorce to be settled: £25 in November 1898, and £10 a couple of months later, towards the rent of her new apartment, at 42 Rue Galilée. Although not far geographically, the lodgings were a world away from the smart apartments in the Avenue Matignon and the Rue Clément Marot, where she had started her married life.

The proceedings of the Salanson divorce are fascinating for the light they throw on the characters, and rackety behaviour, of the two protagonists, and for the predisposition of the court itself. Gabriel's evidence of Flora's adultery was based on two letters written by Mme Salanson, which could leave 'no shadow of doubt on the nature of the relations she enjoyed with the two people cited'. And yet Flora's claim of an affair that Gabriel had had in 1895, while accepted by the court, was seen as purely retaliatory, a direct response to Gabriel's suit. Flora's other grounds for divorce were seen as 'vague and irrelevant'. Yes, the couple may have suffered considerable financial embarrassments, reeling from one piece of bad luck to another, pursued by their creditors; but 'regrettable' though these were, the court judged that Flora could not lay the blame for them on Gabriel. It was, rather, Flora's extravagance and Gabriel's inability to restrain her that were responsible. Gabriel was simply weak and improvident and should never have tolerated his wife's '*attitudes équivoques*' and '*familiarités déplacées*'. He should have snatched her from this '*milieu des moeurs faciles, élégant et malsain, où elle se plaisait*', the 'fashionable and unhealthy world of loose morals, which she so enjoyed'. In granting the divorce, the court found in favour of Gabriel, awarding costs against '*la dame Salanson*', and granting custody of their son, Lionel, to Gabriel.

A Miss Effie Mackenzie Evans, gossipy Paris correspondent for the *New York Herald*, acted as a go-between between Flora

and Victoria. Effie evidently believed that the Sackvilles would
pay the expenses of Flora's lawsuit, and was taken in by Flora's
threats that if they did not, she had two men who would. 'Flora
is always threatening Miss Evans to go to the bad!' Victoria
wrote in her diary. To that end, Effie encouraged Victoria to
meet Flora. A draft of Victoria's letter rejecting the idea survives:
'I have come to the conclusion that, as I can do no more, it is
quite useless having an interview which will be most painful to
both F. & me as I am still dreadfully hurt by all the things she
and her sister & brother have done for many years . . . I have
shown her that I am not revengeful & that I am willing to be
friends at a distance but please don't ask me to meet her.'
Victoria did not want to see Henry either, 'who pesters me all
the time with his letters. I had quite an unpleasantness last
night with Lionel about my charming brothers & sisters. I am
afraid they will be the cause of a good deal of unhappiness in
my married life & my relations with L. That is the worst of it.'
How prescient she was.

Effie hoped that she could keep 'Flora in hand until she
[was] on her feet again', and that a change of climate and
surroundings, away from Paris – and, in particular, away from
Henry – would help Flora get her strength back. 'The sooner
she can get away from him the better for everybody,' she told
Victoria. Effie also hoped that, when she had told Flora all she
had discovered about the past, Flora would 'never again allow
herself to be so deluded'. 'If Flora does not now realise how
much you have done for her I certainly do. I wrote her that
from all I could judge that Henry's place and the best one for
him was to go and live with Béon!'

But Effie's gossip eventually got the better of her. At an interview with Lionel in February 1899, she told him that she was
convinced Henry was not Lord Sackville's son and, even more
scandalously, that he had 'the worst designs on Flora'. When
Flora got to hear of this charge about her relations with Henry,

she threatened Effie with an action for slander, and asked her for 10,000 francs. Furthermore, Flora planned to come to London to confront the Sackville family, and to find out what 'will be done for her'. Effie warned 'that very evil consequences will be the result. That if money is not sent her to come that she will get it "another way". She seems to have lost confidence in my friendship and I am very very sorry to be so misjudged . . . I have been brought into this unfortunate affair and I am too fond of Flora – *malgré tout* – and am too sorry for her miserable and helpless state of affairs not to continue in doing all I can for her and from my sincere convictions of right and wrong.'

In April 1899, Victoria recorded in her diary, with a frisson of horror and sisterly contempt, Effie's report that Flora was looking very 'rich and prosperous', and living 'in a fine appt. & is a common prost[itute]'. Flora had not, in fact, fallen so far, but had become more of a courtesan, like her mother, dependent on a succession of men, as her illegitimacy, her recent divorce, and her lack of independent means pushed her ever closer to the margins of society. Nevertheless, Flora still hoped that Victoria would intercede with their father to give her enough of a pension to enable her to '*vivre honorablement*', accepting any condition that he might wish to impose. She knew that Papa had every right to be severe, but believed that she had been punished enough and would like to be pardoned. She was desperate to be free, and to assume her maiden name again.

———

Amalia moved in similar social circles to Victoria, where she continued to spin her 'tissue of falsehoods' to shared friends and acquaintances – the Sitwells at Renishaw, the Herberts at Llanover. But she did so at a less exalted level, obliged to leave her modest rooms in Ebury Street when the rent went up, or to rely on her father to pay the doctor's bills when she was ill in the summer of 1901 and had to have an operation on her ear. The worlds of the other siblings were more distant.

And yet, their very different trajectories often intersected. In March 1899, while Victoria was in Paris, she spotted Henry driving around the city in a very smart carriage with a man. The following year, she was in Paris once again, to visit the Exposition Universelle, or World's Fair. With around 51 million visitors, the exhibition was the most widely attended event of its kind to date, and it had the effect of pushing up the price of accommodation. Henry was forced, as a result, to complain to his father how the rent for his little room in the Rue d'Edimbourg had doubled, and to ask for his pension to be raised for the duration of the exhibition. Victoria, by contrast, was staying in the Rue Laffitte, and being wonderfully entertained by her new friend, Sir John Murray Scott. In July, she visited the British Pavilion, where 'all the Knole things' were on show.

Each of the exhibition's participating nations had been invited to erect a pavilion, with the British one, according to *The Times*, being designed to 'give a perfect example of a Jacobean house, such as might be the home of an old English family'. Knole was the chief inspiration for the interior. The staircase and landing were a direct copy of the house's Great Staircase, which had been built in the early seventeenth century, with the Sackville family's heraldic leopards perched proudly on the newel posts. The Long Gallery, overlooking the Seine, was modelled on the Cartoon Gallery at Knole, with an almost identical ceiling and chimneypieces, and copies of the X-frame chairs of state arranged along the walls. The British Pavilion attracted 600,000 visitors. One can only wonder whether Henry was among them, strolling through the replica rooms of a house he believed was his, but from which he had recently been physically evicted.

While she was in Paris, Victoria did not see Henry, or Flora, who was now divorced and living in the Rue Galilée. Since her former husband had stopped giving her an allowance, she was threatening 'to settle in London & start a bonnet-shop with her name & Sackville West on the door!' Although Victoria wrote 'very kindly' to her (as she could not help feeling sorry for her), Flora replied that she did 'not want my affection, but my money', and repeated her threat to come over to England as a milliner.

Flora was now threatening again to go on the music hall stage, to perform 'Poses Plastiques', or tableaux vivants. Dressed in skintight, pinky beige body stockings that left little to the imagination, actresses posed as biblical or mythological figures that provided no more than the thinnest veil of respectability to the frankly erotic nature of their art. 'That will never do, as she would have to be in tights,' wrote Victoria. 'It must be stopped at all costs.' Victoria would not see her sister, but when Flora visited England in 1901, 'the poor wretched thing' had an interview with Victoria's husband instead, at her 'miserable lodgings' on the attic floor of 45 Gower Street. 'Lionel says she shows much better feelings now,' wrote Victoria. 'She calls herself Miss Sackville-West! She sees little Lionel Salanson once a week in Paris.' Flora was asking for an allowance of £365 a year, like Amalia's, and for Papa to pay off her debts, which amounted to around £400, in return for which she promised to live peacefully in Paris.

Flora wrote to Victoria after the meeting, thanking her for some money she had sent, '*qui est* of a great help just now', and telling her that she was now going to try to live '*tranquillement*' and to give up her idea of going on the stage. However, knowing that Papa never did anything without asking Victoria first, she hoped that Victoria might be able to get him to help with her debts. The 'most pressing' of these consisted of 1,897 francs for *tapisseries*, 835 francs for the landlady, and 3,000 francs for her lawyers; and she duly received £110 from Papa. 'I am really grateful to you,' she wrote to Lionel, 'for I am sure you managed the whole thing to help me.' In a letter to Victoria, Flora acknowledged that, although she had many faults, she was not 'une ingrate' and would never forget the help she had received from her sister.

It did seem, for a time, that Flora had accepted her lot and decided to stay in Paris, although early in 1902, Victoria received an anonymous letter, warning that Flora was coming to England shortly to induce the Sackvilles to sell some of their paintings and replace them with copies. Rumours continued to reach Victoria that Flora was consorting with a string of unsuitable young men, French counts, and American businessmen, with the relationships often foundering on the twin obstacles of money and religion.

Henry was pleased that Flora was at last divorced, and 'rid of the man that brought about this very sad family quarrel', as he wrote to Victoria. He thought this was now the perfect time, 'while Father is still with us and in good health, that we should be all brought together again and form one link as before', and asked Victoria who is so 'clever and intelligent' to settle the quarrel. What he really wanted was money. In 1900 he wrote to his father, announcing his engagement to a penniless young woman. Could his father raise his pension so that he could live quietly with his wife and bring up a family, possibly in Belgium or Italy where life was cheaper? Or was his father determined to prevent him living honourably and 'd'obtenir dans ma vie brisée les seuls soulagements et la tranquillité [finding the first comfort and calm in his life so far]?' Henry did not receive a reply and wrote again the following year, in April 1901. He still wanted to get married and 'to retire in some quiet spot where I may obtain as a compensation for my present very sad existence, a dear heart that will help me to forget all my past and present sufferings, for you are aware that my life is a most wretched one and that I have terribly suffered both bodily and mentally'. As it would be impossible, claimed Henry, for him to take a wife on his existing means, could he have the same allowance as Amalia? This time, his father acknowledged Henry's letter, adding 'I do not wish to see you', and forwarded the letter to Victoria, who was in Spain at the time. 'I send you a letter from Henry,' he explained; 'He has written to me also wanting me to give him as much as Amalia has to enable him to marry! The old story . . . What a bother he is.'

In the spring of 1904, Victoria was staying with Sir John Murray Scott on one of her annual trips to Paris ('*Toujours* shopping!' she wrote). Her dentist told her that Amalia was in town, and she heard from somebody else that Flora was still leading 'a regular disreputable life!' Papa was there too, but so afraid of bumping into Henry that he rarely ventured out. The whole family then, except Max, was in Paris. But the worlds in which they each moved – the *beau monde*, in which Victoria thrived, and the *demi monde* (at best) in which Flora lived – had diverged completely. After dinner one evening at Prunier, 'the oyster place', Victoria went on to the theatre to watch the Spanish actress 'La Belle Otero' dance. As Victoria complained in her diary: 'she had no chemise or stays on & one could see her figure quite plainly, through the opening of her chemisette; I have never seen anything like that before!' (And she probably had a point, since Otero's breasts were said to have inspired the twin cupolas of the Carlton hotel in Cannes.) Victoria was characteristically blind, however, to the irony of her remarks, given that Flora kept aspiring to a career not dissimilar, and that Otero, like Victoria's mother Pepita, had been born in Spain and presented herself to her adoring public at Folies Bergère as an Andalusian gypsy.

8

Skulduggery in Spain

In the spring of 1901, Victoria visited Spain for the first time. Unlike her daughter, Vita, for whom the country was later to become a place of high romance, Victoria was not favourably impressed. There was 'so little to buy', she complained, and Madrid struck her as being 'wretchedly poor'; the capital's central square, La Puerta del Sol, was very disorderly, 'full of people loafing about all day'. The Alhambra in Granada was similarly disappointing – 'We expected a much grander building' – and the streets of the city were 'smelly & shockingly paved'. She was disgusted by a bullfight in Seville.

Although Spain was the land of her mother's birth, she made no reference to this aspect of her heritage in her diary. Nor did she refer in her Spanish diary to the activities of her brothers and sisters. And yet, in one of those curious near-crossings of paths, Henry was in Madrid at around the same time, researching the circumstances of their mother's marriage at the church of San Millán fifty years before.

On 30 October 1901, Henry's lawyer presented the Spanish courts with a *Denuncia*, a declaration that the marriage records in the church of San Millán had been falsified in such a way as to support his claim of legitimacy. In Spanish law at the time of Pepita's marriage to Oliva in 1851, there had been no civil marriage and no divorce. Marriage was governed exclusively by canon law, with the ceremony performed in church by the parish priest. The only definitive proof of marriage, therefore, was the entry in the register of the parish church where the ceremony had taken place. In 1897, during the action to perpetuate testimony, Spanish lawyers acting for the Sackville family had checked and authenticated the entry in the register of the church of San Millán, which proved 'a marriage valid and canonical to have been celebrated on the day mentioned between the persons named'. If, however, doubt could be cast on the marriage between Pepita and Oliva, then it might be possible to prove that Lionel had, in fact, married Pepita, and that Henry was legitimate and the heir to Knole.

The Spanish newspapers followed the *Denuncia* proceedings very closely, as did the press in England and France. The *Heraldo* was much taken with the way in which 'the fantasies of romance appear mingled with the realities of life', of a heroic young man from a distinguished and aristocratic English family who had come to Spain to defend his name and fortune. The *Correspondencia* also blamed 'the covetousness which stops at nothing' of Victoria and her husband, who had conspired to keep Henry out of inheriting Knole. Another newspaper reported Henry's claim that he had left London for Paris towards the end of 1898 because 'on several occasions his brother-in-law threatened to poison him'. The Sackville family was worried by the tone of the articles in the French press, too, in which, as Victoria complained, she had been 'pretty well libelled'.

The *Imparcial* described how reality had 'taken the aspect of a romantic novel, recalling the boldest inventions of Alexandre Dumas', and its account, like the others, was riddled with errors, particularly about the more distant past. In its extravagant tale, Lionel met Pepita in Madrid:

Lord Sackville fell in love with her beauty, and the impetuous advances of his passion meeting with the resistance of pure honour, he offered to the handsome dancer his hand and his fortune. She accepted the offer, the lord and the dancer were validly married, receiving sacerdotal benediction before the high altar of the parish church of San Millán. Pepita Duran abandoned the stage and fulfilling with the most scrupulous fidelity her marriage vows, demonstrated by an exemplary life her love for the man who had elevated her from the humble social position in which she had been born to the lofty and eminent one suitable to the lineage of her husband.

The newspapers, in general, took Henry's side. But, as the facts emerged, the following sequence of events seemed more likely, and it became clear what Henry, and a distant cousin he had recruited to his cause, had been up to in the spring and summer of 1901. In 1897, a young journeyman printer called Enrique Rophon Ortega, who was then employed at Algeciras railway station, had heard that relatives of Pepita were being sought with the promise that they might be entitled to part of her estate. This, as it happened, was non-existent, and the promise was really no more than an attempt by the lawyers to attract witnesses in the action to perpetuate testimony. As a great-nephew of Pepita's mother, Catalina (and, therefore, a second cousin of Henry), Rophon thought that he might have a claim to some of this estate. It was not long before he realised that there was no property – the Villa Pepa at Arcachon having been sold years before – but by this time he had entered into a correspondence with Henry. Rophon realised that by helping Henry he might earn an, albeit smaller, share of a far larger prize, the Sackville inheritance, and he began to gather evidence in Spain in support of Henry's claim. He started to receive money from Henry 'to make investigations relative to the marriage which was alleged to have taken place' between Lionel and Pepita, and by May 1901 he was working so hard on Henry's behalf that he took leave of absence from his employers to devote himself full-time to the collection of evidence. Rophon interviewed some of the people who had given evidence in Gibraltar in 1897 and were now living in Madrid, including Oliva's brother Agustin and his sister Isabel. His hope was to get them to change the evidence they had given in 1897, and to claim that Oliva had never, after all, been married to Pepita, that all those elaborate accounts of their wedding, and their reception afterwards, had been made up.

By 9 June, when Henry arrived in Madrid with an interpreter called Albert Lens, who ran a translation bureau in Paris, Rophon was confident that Henry had a good case. They had new statements from several witnesses, and they had unearthed a number of technical discrepancies in the paperwork associated with the marriage of Pepita to Oliva. They had a certificate stating that the *expediente*, or file of documents that had to be prepared at the Vicaria, or diocesan offices, before a marriage licence was issued, had been lost. They had evidence that the marriage licence had been signed by a notary other than the one assigned to the job. And, on a third point of procedural irregularity, there appeared to be a blank space beside the marriage entry in the register itself (the 7th Book of Marriages, corresponding to the year 1851, folio 45). Henry and Rophon were all set to take action.

However when, for the first time, they approached a Spanish lawyer, Señor Laguna, with their case, he was not encouraging. Señor Laguna asked Rophon whether he had seen the marriage entry in the church register, whether it was free of erasure or alteration, and whether he had also seen the marriage licence (which would show that the *expediente* must once have existed). Rophon confirmed that he had seen all of these documents. It was at this point that Laguna advised him that the entry was the definitive proof of the marriage between Oliva and Pepita, and that any other evidence was irrelevant. Rophon and Henry despaired at this advice, and on 26 June, Henry left for Paris. Laguna's opinion may, however, unwittingly or otherwise, have encouraged them to destroy the marriage licence, and to scratch out the names in the marriage entry and rewrite them. At the very least, such an action would serve to discredit the entry – the most conclusive piece of evidence in the Sackville case – even if it did not actually prove anything else.

Rophon stayed on in Madrid, and by the time Henry returned to his lodgings at the Café Paris in Madrid in October, with a woman said to be his wife, and an interpreter called Camille Lanquine, who was the nephew of Albert Lens, the entry had been clumsily altered – although not in a way that substantively changed the identity of Oliva, or the fact that he and Pepita had got married on 10 January 1851. Someone must also have visited the Vicaria in the summer of 1901, because another archive had been tampered with by the time Henry returned to Madrid. Minor changes had been made to the Book of Entradas, which recorded all the applications for marriage, and preceded the preparation of the *expediente*. Nothing, however, contradicted the fact that, in December 1850, Oliva and Pepita had visited the Vicaria in order to begin the process that would eventually lead to their marriage.

Henry and Rophon wasted no time in contacting another lawyer, Señor Lastres. They informed him that the marriage entry had been falsified (begging the question of how they knew of the falsification if they had not organised it themselves). And on 29 October, Señor Lastres visited the office at the church of San Millán, where he 'discovered' the altered entry, and then the Vicaria, where he looked at the changes to the Book of Entradas. The next day, a Wednesday, Lastres presented the *Denuncia* to the court on behalf of Henry, formally advising the authorities that records had been falsified and possibly a crime committed.

The Marriage Book Register was impounded, and handwriting experts pored over the entries, examining other parish books of the past few years, to see if they could find writing similar to that which appeared in the falsified entry. In particular, the experts thought that the writing of one Ricardo Dorremocea, who had been a clerk in the San Millán parish office from 1897 to May 1901, resembled the hand which had traced the names above those which had been erased. Dorremocea was duly arrested on 7 November, and placed in solitary confinement.

Suspicion also attached to a former parish clerk, Pedro Cancela, and a warrant was issued for his arrest in Buenos Aires, where it was thought he had fled. It later transpired, however, that although Cancela had left the church in a hurry, he had done so in 1899 – several years before the likely falsification of the register – and his reason for doing so was not that he was fleeing the scene of a crime but because he had eloped with his mistress, leaving his wife behind in Madrid.

The problem with Henry's case, however, was that other pieces of evidence tended to corroborate the authenticity of the original entry. In the municipal archives, for example, there was an extract from the marriage entry in a record kept for the preparation of statistics. Despite the condition of the book itself – some portions of which were 'almost destroyed', the *Heraldo* reported, 'we do not know whether by the damp, or by the numerous mice who have their homes in the walls of our municipal house' – the page containing the extract of the marriage of Pepita and Oliva was found intact and perfectly legible. It was quite clear that these two had been married on 10 January 1851, and, as the *Heraldo* continued, 'that some person obliterated them and came back afterwards to rewrite them, perhaps with the idea that the alteration in the entry would raise doubts as to the legitimacy of the marriage'. There was also the fact that Señor Paredes, a Spanish lawyer who had acted for the Sackvilles in 1896–7, testified on 12 November

1901 that he had seen the entry in the marriage register in 1896, at which time it definitely recorded the marriage of Pepita and Oliva. This evidence was confirmed by another lawyer, Alfred Harrison, who had also seen and authenticated the original entry five years earlier.

Henry's case collapsed. On 8 November, he left Madrid once again for Paris, and on the twelfth, Señor Lastres withdrew over 'a disagreement between lawyer and judge upon a question of law'. In public, Señor Lastres continued to trumpet Henry's good faith, but in private he is said to have told the Chief of the Judicial Police that Henry was a *pillo* (a rascal), and that it was just as well he had disappeared or he would have been put in prison. Although the *Denuncia* proceedings had collapsed, the fact remained that the marriage entry had been falsified, and the perpetrators not found. Ricardo Dorremocea was released from prison on bail, there being no further evidence against him; proceedings were formally suspended the following year, and Dorremocea was acquitted.

Henry's weekly allowance, which he had been collecting once a week from a firm of bankers since December 1898, was stopped in November 1901, on the grounds that he had broken one of its conditions by setting foot in Spain. Little more was heard of him until the following year, when Henry's solicitors, Messrs Osborn & Osborn, informed the Sackville solicitors, Messrs Meynell & Pemberton, that Henry had been making enquiries in Spain and France, 'with the result that an entirely different complexion will now be put on the case'. He had, for a start, statements from various witnesses who had changed their story since 1897. Henry's great-aunt, Micaela, for example, wrote to him in January 1902 to say that she had been misled in 1897 into making 'certain declarations as to the legitimacy of his birth', and that the lawyers had taken 'advantage of their ignorance of the language'; otherwise she would never have claimed that Pepita's children were illegitimate. She now insisted that Pepita and Oliva had never been married, and that their relations had never been other than professional. What she did remember, however, was Pepita's marriage to 'Lord Sackville' in Heidelberg, when she was staying there for her husband's medical treatment, and how the ceremony was cele-brated 'with great show'.

In July 1902, Henry brought his own action 'for the purpose of examining witnesses and taking, preserving and perpetuating testimony', concerning his claim to be the lawful and eldest son of Lord Sackville, and his solicitors signalled their intent to proceed with the matter 'with every possible despatch'. Henry claimed that when the Sackvilles had brought their action for perpetuating testimony in 1897, it had been done at short notice, and at a time when he did not have the 'pecuniary means' to instruct lawyers; that is why he had not had the Sackville witnesses cross-examined in Gibraltar and Arcachon. He now needed to bring a similar action – for the same reason, that many of the witnesses were old and infirm, and their evidence needed to be taken before it was lost for ever. He particularly wanted to refute the provisions of a settlement made in June 1890, the month of Victoria's marriage to Lionel, in which, on the basis that Lord Sackville did not have a male heir, the estate had been disentailed. Under these provisions, his uncle, William Edward, and his sons, would succeed; Victoria would receive an annuity; Victoria's daughter, Vita, would eventually receive £10,000; and Henry would get nothing.

Despite the loss of his allowance, Henry, his lawyers said, now had the financial backing to bring the matter to a conclusion. Henry continued to send Rophon sums of money – and the odd bottle of medicine – in order to continue his lawsuit and to 'make the light shine on all that my adversaries have done'.

Where this money came from is not entirely clear. It is likely, however, that Béon was somewhere in the background. At the time of the *Denuncia* proceedings, the Sackvilles had received a letter from Max's old schoolfriend from Bordeaux, Joseph Lesnier, who was then in New York trying to find a market for his St Loubès wines. Lesnier referred to an article in the New York newspapers about the case in Spain, and laid the blame firmly on Béon: '*c'est Henry de B . . . qui dirige cette affaire. Je le considère comme un triste, bien triste personage.* He should be grateful to you and yet, instead, he's blackmailing you. *C'est ignoble de sa part . . .*' The Comte de Béon, former confidant and keeper of the Sackville family secrets, had recently married the wealthy Inés-Mercédès Sanz at a high-society, high-Catholic ceremony in Paris, presided over by the papal nuncio, the Archbishop of Baghdad, who discoursed on the distinguished histories of both families and the '*nombreux services rendus à la France par la famille de Béon*'.

In June 1901, Victoria received another letter (written anonymously in French, and sent from Paris), warning her 'of a great danger which is threatening both your fortune and your position'. A member of her family, 'who thinks he has a right to all your fortune', the well-wisher continued, had

> found in Paris money and powerful auxiliaries and you are possibly on the eve of great misfortunes. A search has been made in various quarters and compromising papers have been found. I have also heard of more or less mysterious journeys to Spain and Gibraltar . . . If then, dear Madame, you wish to keep your fortune and avoid the insults and scandal of a public lawsuit brought by the 3 remaining members of your family, go as soon as you can to France, try and see and gain to your side Monsieur L'Abbé Estevenet, Vicar of Belmont, near Vic-Fezensac [Gers]. He is the man I have spoken of, who holds all the threads in his hands.

There is a further reference to this mysterious Abbé in a begging letter to Henry, dated March 1902, from his interpreter

Camille Lanquine, asking for money – 'I beg of you to ask for some advance, however small it may be, from the Abbé.' A decade later, the Abbé, a man of independent means, came briefly to prominence when he accused the directors of La Fédération Catholique de France, an organisation he had founded to raise funds for needy members of the clergy, of fraud. Perhaps his involvement in Henry's case was an early experiment in speculation in support of a charitable cause. Whatever the case, the backing Henry received from these sources helped to confirm in Victoria a lifelong suspicion of priests.

Another source of funds may have been the translation bureau, run by Albert Lens. Henry used to visit the office in the Place de la Bourse two or three times a week to have his correspondence with Rophon translated. Lens had travelled with Henry to Madrid in June 1901, and his nephew Lanquine had accompanied him four months later, and got to know Rophon very well. It was later claimed by Matias Paulus, another employee of the bureau, that 'the profits realised by the bureau were utilised in connection with the affair of the inheritance'. Such an arrangement would not have been unusual. Syndicates were often set up to invest in speculative lawsuits, such as disputed succession cases. In a letter to Rophon in 1903, Henry referred to one of these, 'the affair Humbert Crawford', that was doing him a deal of harm: so many people had lost money in it but he hoped, nevertheless, to succeed in his own particular venture. Thérèse Humbert had just been tried and sentenced to five years' hard labour for using a non-existent inheritance, which she claimed had been left her by a phony American millionaire called Robert Crawford, as collateral for large loans. A lot of creditors lost money, and the scandal had given the idea of speculative investment in inheritances a bad name.

In October 1902, after the *Denuncia* proceedings had finally been closed, Mr Pemberton advised the Sackvilles to go on the offensive and to find out who had altered the entry in the marriage register. He proposed to send Mr Brain to Madrid, where he would be helped by two of the other Spanish-based lawyers who had assisted in 1897, Alfred Harrison, who was now living in Barcelona, and Señor Paredes. Key to this investigation were the respective movements of Rophon and Henry between April and November 1901.

In December 1902, John Brain tracked Rophon down to Algeciras, where he was once again in the employ of the railway company. Mr Brain managed to interview a reluctant Rophon, who admitted that he had been in communication with Henry since 1897. The following day, however, Rophon became even more reluctant, 'having slept upon it', and, in view of the justice of his cousin Henry's case, declined to supply any further information. Henry was very pleased with the way Rophon had behaved with Brain, when he heard about the interview: 'You answered him well at his impertinent questions. He is such a scoundrel, and doing his best to work up more of his infamies.' Brain and Pemberton were still no closer to working out who had falsified the register. On 29 December, Mr Brain wrote pathetically from the Hotel de Rusia in Madrid, updating Pemberton on his progress and the substantial costs involved: 'I am writing this in bed before the translation is begun. I can't get up to write because there is no one up to light the fire. Please excuse the pencil . . . I am in the position of a Spanish Prosecutor who has arrived in London to investigate a crime which has baffled the Public Prosecutor and Scotland Yard for more than a year.' He was particularly conscious of the expense of the investigation (£1,250 for him alone over the past five months, and disbursements of £1,200 to Señor Paredes and £400 to Mr Harrison).

Gradually, he began to refine the probable sequence of events between June and October 1901. A man called José Sanchez had, at the time, been the only full-time clerk in the parish office of San Millán, where the marriage registers were kept in an unlocked wooden cupboard. During the after-noons, Sanchez had the office to himself, and it seemed highly likely that Rophon arranged with Sanchez for the names in the register, the 7th Book of Marriages, to be scratched out and rewritten, either in the office itself or in some other place where the book had been temporarily removed under cover of a bulky coat.

In the spring of 1903, Señor Paredes recommended that there was sufficient evidence to apply for a re-opening of the *Denuncia* proceedings, and asked for the prosecution of Henry, Rophon and Sanchez. In July, Sanchez and Rophon were arrested and held until the following month. By this stage, Camille Lanquine had fallen out with his uncle and started offering information to the other side, the Sackvilles: it was Lanquine who had denounced Rophon's activities. Henry at first thought it must have been Lens who had betrayed him and Rophon, and there were violent scenes in the translation bureau between Henry and Lens, whom Henry called a '*canaille*' – a scoundrel.

In October of that year, Henry updated Max on the latest developments, after a 'long silence'. He had never heard whether Max had received the lock of Pepita's hair, which had been cut from her head when she had been exhumed in 1897, washed, shaped into a 'P', and posted in a gilt frame. Henry could only suppose that Victoria or her father had threatened Max. 'It has been her play to separate you and my sisters from me,' he wrote. 'I know and possess the proof that neither Flora nor Amalia can write to me without risking to see their allow-ance stopped immediately by Victoria, and it may be that you are placed in the same position.'

Although Sanchez and Rophon had been let off, further criminal proceedings were launched against the two of them six years later, along with a character called Manuel Anton, who had conveniently gone missing. 'The court was crowded,' *The Times* reported in March 1909, 'as an immense amount of interest is being taken in the case. After the long ceremonies which are customary in a Spanish court, the usher read the indictments presented by the prosecution': the charge of being involved in altering the entry in the marriage register. Although on subsequent days, according to the *Irish Times*, 'most of those present were out-of-work labourers, apparently attracted to the court by a desire to enjoy for a few hours the comfortable temperature of a well-warmed hall', the English press continued to be well represented. They all enjoyed the odd moments of hilarity, particularly when Oliva's brother, Agustin, testified that Pepita had never been married to his brother. So deaf was he that the usher had to bellow the questions in his ear.

Pepita's niece, Catalina, testified too. She declared that Pepita had been married to 'a noble and rich Englishman', who showered the family with gifts of money and was always referred to as 'Uncle Leon' (a Spanish version of Lionel) or 'Uncle Lord' (which he did not become until long after Pepita's death). Catalina described how 'a cértain other Englishman, named Williams, who posed as a brother of Pepita's husband' – possibly, my great-grandfather William Edward – had come on a mission to Spain to destroy the proofs of Pepita's marriage, 'as the union of his brother with the ballet girl dishonoured the family'. Once he had done this, she claimed, he planned to 'simulate' the marriage of Pepita to Oliva.

One of the chief witnesses was Ricardo Dorremocea, the parish clerk who had been arrested and acquitted on charges of falsifying the register back in 1901. His testimony provided a shadowy insight into the underworld of Madrid, as he recalled being approached in the summer of 1901 by a couple of *chulos* (wide boys) sporting dark moustaches, stylish automobile caps (rather than the more traditional wide-brimmed hat), and light jackets with black patches on the elbows. Dorremocea had arranged to meet one of them in a tavern later, and it was here, over a drink, that he was offered a large sum of money to burn

The front page of the *Daily Mirror* features several of the protagonists in the criminal trial of Rophon and Sanchez in Madrid in 1909. Lionel (*top left*) is pitted against Henry (*top right*), while Pepita dominates the centre. The entry in the disputed marriage register runs along the bottom of the page the marriage register, or at least to tear out the page recording the marriage of Pepita Duran. Despite the fact that the *chulo* was carrying a barely concealed revolver, Dorremocea claimed that he had refused to carry out the commission.

The principal prosecution witnesses included Camille Lanquine, who claimed, on the basis of correspondence between Henry and Rophon, which he himself had translated, that it was Henry who had instigated Rophon to commit the forgery. He said that the large sums of money Rophon had received in 1901 had been specifically for what was referred in the letters to 'work' carried out in the parish register at San Millán. Records supplied by the Crédit Lyonnais Bank in Madrid confirmed that Rophon had been sent more than 10,000 pesetas from Paris that summer. Lanquine further alleged that Rophon had told him that it was he who had taken the register and erased some names from the entry, instructing an individual whom he called 'Paco' (almost certainly Manuel Anton) to fill them in again. Matias Paulus, another former employee of the same translation bureau in Paris, also accused Rophon of having falsified the register at Henry's instigation.

A French lawyer named Max Maisonneuve, who had been helping Henry to collect evidence in Spain and who also had an interest in the translation bureau in Paris, cast doubt in court on the profiteering motives of both Paulus and Lanquine. The latter appeared to have changed sides after his falling out with his uncle, and had then been prepared to sell compromising letters to the highest bidder. In contrast to these rather unreliable witnesses, the good-looking Rophon made a favourable impression in the witness box. Although he admitted receiving money from Henry in return for help with his researches, he denied having forged the register. Sanchez, too, protested his innocence, and denied having had anything to do with Rophon. Despite evidence to suggest that Sanchez must at least have known what was going on – evidence that included hand-drawn plans of the parish offices, details of who sat where, and of their typical daily routines – doubts were expressed about the general sloppiness of the security arrangements. It was argued, in effect, that anyone could have tampered with the register. Furthermore, the evidence of the handwriting experts was inconclusive. Sanchez' lawyer played to the populist mood of the court when he asked why it was that 'people of a somewhat vulgar type' (like his client) stood accused, while it was surely those who had paid for the forgery – 'the moral authors of the falsification' – who were really the guilty ones.

The jury was split 6–6, and the defendants were therefore acquitted. The charges were withdrawn by the prosecution and, to Victoria's fury, the suspects released. Lionel, she wrote, had refused to bribe the jury to the tune of £1,000, as their Spanish lawyer Señor Paredes had suggested, and this, she claimed, had worked against them. 'Rophon and all the other Spanish witnesses seem to have been bought & they all contradict what they said in 1897. And also the priests have influenced them greatly [note Victoria's deep-seated suspicion].' And yet Lionel had, quite rightly she felt, refused to offer bribes. 'That is justice!'

———

Throughout Vita's childhood, there was always, she wrote, 'some mystery in the background'. She heard the servants' gossip and her parents' snatched discussions about the looming succession case. She 'realised dimly that a vinegary spinster aunt [Amalia] lived with us for some years at Knole, and annoyed Mother by giving me preserved cherries when Mother asked her not to, also that there was a person called Henry who from time to time came to the entrance and demanded to see Grandpapa, but was not allowed to'. But for most of the time, life at Knole around the turn of the century was very quiet.

Her grandfather certainly was. Many years later, in *Pepita*, Vita attempted to describe this enigma of a man, whom she knew 'as intimately as a child of eight can ever know a very reserved old man of nearly eighty'. 'I knew his little habits and his funny ways. I knew the way in which he would slam his tweed cap down on the settee on the way to the dining-room, stumping along towards luncheon without speaking a word – for he was without exception the most taciturn man I have ever known.' Every night he would leave a plate filled with fruit for Vita in a drawer in his sitting-room for her to collect in the morning. He would spend hours whittling paper-knives from the lids of cigar-boxes, and polishing them with sandpaper till the surface was like velvet. He had a set of little sayings that he invariably came out with whenever the occasion arose. 'Nice fresh taste', he used to say as the first gooseberries of the year were served. And as soon as Midsummer Day had passed, he used to say 'Days drawing in now' – just as my own father did.

Vita's first cousin Eddy often came to stay, and many years later he, too, recalled life in the big house, with its year-round smell of cold wood smoke and the slow, steady tick of myriad grandfather clocks. Every now and then, he remembered, his great-uncle would venture forth from a room, which was bare of all possessions except for a leather armchair and a glass case containing a wasp's nest. 'In this cold and cheerless cell,' wrote Eddy, 'the possessor of some of the finest furniture and silver in England would immerse himself for hours at a time, perusing either Gibbon's *Decline and Fall* or the works of Josephus. These books he read through regularly every year, and as he closed the last volume of either he would remark: "Good book, that." He was never known to vary this comment, nor to enlarge upon it.' Eddy would follow his great-uncle around the house, holding Lord Sackville's hand in one hand and a shawl in the other. 'And so we went very slowly indeed, for he was old and I was not yet at all firm upon my legs – in and out of the dim old rooms and passages, up and down stairs (one step at a time) and along what seemed miles of gallery, with the peak of the shawl trailing far out on the floor behind me.'

Despite the cheerlessness of Lord Sackville's own domestic arrangements, his daughter was transforming the rest of Knole into what she later described as 'the most comfortable large house in England'. On top of these expenses were the shopping trips to Paris, Lionel and Victoria's stock market speculations, and the legal proceedings in Spain and England. By September 1904, the 'case' had cost the Sackvilles £20,000. In contrast to Henry's murky sources of finance, it was quite clear that the Sackvilles were getting their money from Sir John Murray Scott – or 'Seery', as they called him.

Seery was an enormous man, according to Vita, 'six-feet-four in his stockings' and weighing over twenty-five stone, but 'always as fresh and pink as a baby, with his white mutton-chop whiskers, blue eyes, and rosy cheeks'. There was something so monumental about him that he 'made everyone of normal size look mere friskers around him. Perpetually flapping a large silk handkerchief to keep away the flies, he rolled and billowed along on disproportionately tiny feet.' Victoria had befriended Seery in the late 1890s, and he was alternately enchanted and exasperated by her. 'Really, nobody could have failed to love her as she was then,' wrote Vita. 'My mother was adorable at that time in her life. She was tiresome, of course, and wayward and capricious, and thoroughly spoiled; but her charm and real inward gaiety enabled her to carry it all off.'

For the next fifteen years, Seery and Victoria enjoyed a tempestuous, though platonic, relationship. Seery began to lend the Sackvilles money – £18,600, at first, at only three per cent interest, secured on mortgages on the Knole estates. This sum was to grow, to include other aspects of their lifestyle, to around £84,000 in gifts and loans over the course of his lifetime.

Nevertheless, Victoria worried about money. She began to

cut down on improvements to the house at 34 Hill Street in London that Seery had just bought for them. And she tried to make economies at Knole, by shutting the house in the winter months and coming back only for the summer. Her father, after a lifetime of financial fecklessness, had no idea how to make the books balance. When Victoria came down to Knole one evening in November 1906, she found 'Papa very much taken up with the Knole accounts of which he does not understand a word. We must retrench! He has not told us for several years that he was living beyond his income and now the crisis has come . . . The waste in the garden, especially in Vegetables, has been awful.'

Sir John Murray Scott, Victoria's new friend, with a Polish dwarf

The other great trial in the Sackvilles' life was Papa's declining health. In January 1905, 'poor old Stubbs', an elderly retainer, died of delirium tremens and was buried in the neighbouring village of Seal. Lord Sackville was very upset to see all those men in black walking through one of the courtyards at Knole, on the way to the funeral. 'The poor old dear dreads death terribly,' Victoria wrote, and as the last one left of his nine brothers and sisters, he hated more and more to be left alone. He was 'more silent than ever' and increasingly slow at taking things in.

At night his coughing kept Victoria awake, particularly if he had been smoking. 'He almost chokes & frightens us so,' Victoria wrote, 'I do feel so sorry for him, as his cough is terrible at times & he looks at us then, as if he was on the rack – poor dear old mann [sic].'

9

A Death in the Family

Towards the end of 1907, Lord Sackville was diagnosed with prostate cancer. 'Lionel & I are doing all we can & sparing no expense
to save his life' (the operation and nursing home expenses came to
£300), and Victoria felt her own strength breaking down, 'as poor
Papa is so cross and so contrary in every way'. Although the
surgeon did not give him more than a year to live, his immediate
recovery from the operation was marked by the fact that he was
'getting very cross' with Victoria 'over every trifle, as formerly'. He
never spoke at meals, except to say 'something disagreeable'. There
was one advantage of his perpetual cantankerousness: although
Victoria found it 'so sad to see all that want of kindness', she much
preferred that 'he should not be nice to me, otherwise the pain of
seeing him wasting away would be unbearable'.

Victoria was not a natural nurse, finding aspects of his illness,
particularly the incontinence, distasteful. But as distressing as
her father's final decline was Victoria's own sense, growing over
the previous few years, that there 'seems so much ingratitude in
the world'. When her father-in-law had died in the autumn of
1905, she wished that he had left her 'the smallest little souvenir'.
She found her brother-in-law Charlie and his wife Maud mean
(particularly their Christmas present of a book costing 2/6), and
her father himself just as mean. She was fed up with paying for

the house linen when her allowance was too small to cover it. As a result, she began 1906 with a resolution not to wear herself out doing things for other people, especially her family, as she had done till now. 'I shall use a great deal of "judicious neglect". I am sick of the ingratitude I meet on all sides.' In particular, she resented having 'to spend a lot of my own money for Knole and ---- Eddy'. Here were the first signs that she was starting to feel as disinherited, in a way, as her siblings. This sense of injustice would come to dominate the second half of her life.

As Victoria read *The King's Secret*, one of the teenage Vita's many historical romances, she was struck by the fact that the character of Cranfield, whom Vita intended as a portrayal of herself, was in fact much more open than its creator. This had prompted Victoria to think about those closest to her. 'She is very clever and I really think she is perfectly devoted to me,' Victoria wrote of her daughter, 'but she does not let herself give enough. If only she could change and become warmer hearted! It has been rather hard to live all my life with Papa & Lionel who are both so cold on the surface, and now I find the same disposition in my child.' Her husband's '*aridité de coeur*' made her suffer terribly, and her father had 'not an atom of sympathy in his nature'. That is why, she wrote, she had taken to Seery 'as a Father': he was '*sympathetique*', and appealed to the 'Spanish' side of her nature, although he, too, was ageing. When Victoria was in Paris with the two old men in April 1908, she spent 'most of my evenings between Seery snoring and Papa coughing'.

All the while, preparations were being made for the case that would inevitably follow Lord Sackville's death. In October 1907, Henry filed his petition under the Legitimacy Declaration Act, 1858. The following month, Victoria went to hear the Druce case, a notorious succession lawsuit which, she realised, had many echoes of Henry's own case, and indeed of the case of the Tichborne Claimant – including an exhumation, and a limited liability company set up to finance the case of the claimant. (She was particularly pleased to get the claimant's autograph.) High society was taking a similar interest in the Sackville case. Alice Keppel, Edward VII's mistress and a friend of Victoria, quizzed her about Henry. 'I could see the King wanted to know!' The only piece of 'good' news was the death in the spring of 1908 of the Comte de Béon, which 'relieves us of a very tiresome witness in "the Case"'. In June she received a postcard announcing a visit by Henry and his wife (Henry had married Emélie Alexandre in Paris in April 1904), so she gave up a trip to the Opera in order to stay at home with her father, but they never came.

In August, Lord Sackville fell down the stairs to his bedroom, but insisted on keeping that room, despite being barely able to crawl there. Lionel returned to Knole a week later, followed by his younger brothers, Charlie and my grandfather, Bertie. Downstairs, Bertie's vivacious wife, Eva, my grandmother, shocked Victoria by playing polkas and waltzes – behaviour she found most casual, while upstairs, the old man lay in bed, feverish and in pain every time he was moved. He died on 3 September. In her diary, on a page headed 'Papa's Death', Victoria gave a detailed description of her father's last hours, as his mind wandered, his speech thickened, and his breath slowed. She was holding his hand in hers when his breathing stopped. 'In his last look,' she wrote, 'he seemed to beg my pardon for all the harshness and unfairness he had often shown me. I forgave him from my heart . . . I shall never forget the beating of my heart & the awful feeling I had in front of Death, the first time I saw anybody die. But it was such a peaceful Death & I could not have wished it differently.'

———

Victoria spent the day after her father's death in bed, 'feeling quite deadbeat', while her husband made arrangements for the funeral and sent telegrams to close friends and family members.

The list of recipients included Flora and Amalia, but pointedly omitted Henry and Max. Victoria got up on the Saturday and spent the weekend planning a new regime of household economies and answering letters of condolence. One of these was from the King, expressing his 'deep sympathy' and asking whether Lord Sackville had been ill for some time. The letters to Victoria from Violet Keppel, daughter of the King's mistress Alice, were more direct and focused on the court case that would inevitably follow her father's death: 'Of course I know it will be all right but all the unnecessary expenses of lawsuits, it is maddening.' The King, she revealed, was particularly interested in the case, and Violet hoped 'to get all his sympathies on your side where indeed they are already'.

Victoria lost no time in writing to the newspapers, asking them not to cover the impending court case. The editor of the *Daily Mail* replied that although he would be very sorry to publish anything likely to cause her pain, he would be obliged to report the proceedings if the matter came to court. 'In the meantime,' he wrote, 'I have every desire to comply with your request and have given instructions accordingly.'

Vita had been sent to stay with Seery and his sisters in Scotland during her grandfather's final illness. She supposed that 'Mother and Dada knew he would die and wanted [her] out of the way'. He died while she was there, as she later described:

> One of Seery's sisters – the big one, whom her family called the Duchess – came to my room before breakfast with the telegram; she had on a pink flannelette dressing-gown, and no false hair, and I remember noticing how odd she looked. She kissed me in a conscientious sort of way, but I wasn't very much moved over Grandpapa's death just then; it only sank in afterwards . . . Then I went downstairs to Seery's room, and never to my last moment shall I forget the sight he presented, sitting at his dressing-table perfectly oblivious, the twenty-five stone of him,

dressed only in skin-tight Jaeger combinations, and, dear
warm-hearted old Seery, crying quite openly over the telegram.

The sight of Seery weeping unrestrainedly, his sobs shaking
'his loose enormous frame like a jelly', so overwhelmed the
sixteen-year-old Vita that she could not cry herself.

On Sunday night, Old* Lionel's coffin was placed in the private
Chapel at Knole, where my father's coffin rested, too, the night
before his funeral, and Victoria summoned the courage to visit it
there. Just after 11 o'clock the following morning, Monday 7
September, she watched from her bedroom window as 'the sad little
procession', carrying the coffin, left the private apartments and
crossed the Green Court. Her husband walked bareheaded immediately behind the coffin, which was covered with wreaths, with his
brothers Charlie and Bertie on either side of him. Victoria could not
help noticing how very strange it seemed now to be called 'My Lord
and My Lady' – just as, shortly, Vita was to observe how swiftly
'Dada takes his new role very seriously'. At the porter's lodge under
the entrance tower, the coffin was placed on a hand-bier and drawn
by members of the estate staff across the park to the main gate,
where a large crowd was waiting, and into the church of St Nicholas.

On behalf of the Sackvilles, Percy Leigh Pemberton had
asked Henry's lawyer, Mr Fellowes, to discourage Henry from
coming to Knole or attending the funeral. Fellowes assured
Pemberton that Henry would not go to Knole, although he
would attend the funeral itself at St Nicholas's 'as an ordinary
individual' and would leave as soon as it was over, and that he
would make no attempt to seize possession of Knole after the
service (Fellowes took the further precaution of warning his
client that the Sackvilles had 'evidently got a posse of Police' at
Knole to prevent such an event). Nevertheless, Fellowes told

---

* I have used the family epithet 'Old' to distinguish him from his nephew,
'Young Lionel'.

Pemberton that 'they intended to fight for all they were worth', and that the only reason for the delay was that 'the material to be dealt with was so immense that it required time to digest'.

The Funeral of Lord Sackville

Old Lionel's funeral procession makes its way down the drive at Knole towards the church of St Nicholas

In the event, Henry did not attend his father's funeral. Of the five children, only Amalia went to the church (Victoria stayed behind at Knole) and plonked herself in the front pew, where, according to Victoria, Lionel left her alone. After the service, Amalia insisted on walking out of the church immediately behind the coffin and in front of Lionel, which Vita later recorded 'shocked everybody fearfully'. The body was interred in the graveyard beside the church, the only incumbent of Knole – from Thomas Sackville, the 1st Earl of Dorset in 1608, to the 4th Lord Sackville in the 1960s – not to be buried in the family vault at Withyham.

Old Lionel's death was followed by a flurry of letters from Victoria's sisters. Writing in purple ink on black-edged mourning paper, from a rented villa on the coast of Brittany, Flora was very upset that Papa had died without her having seen him again, and anxious about the '*bouleversement sa mort va assurer pour tous*'. She hoped that '*toutes ces vilaines histoires de famille*' would resolve themselves, adding in a veiled threat, '*sans trop de scandale*'. She was particularly interested, however, in what provision had been made for her: although she found it distasteful to raise the matter at '*un aussi triste moment*', she wondered '*quelles sont tes intentions a mon égard?*'

Old Lionel had never had much money, and, on his death, his personal estate consisted only of life insurance policies worth £7,100, which he left to his five children, and a few personal effects. 'Oh, what a mess poor O'Mann [as Victoria described her father] made of everything,' Victoria wrote to Seery, 'but I do forgive him as you know. It is rather dreadful not to provide for his children properly, and to leave it to me to do, alas!' His fecklessness was another reason why Victoria continued to be torn in her affection for her father: 'Just a week since my dear old Papa died. I feel all the time I wish I had been kinder to him in his lifetime, altho' I really did try hard to make him happy, but he had such a reserved and hard nature, so difficult to fathom, poor O'Mann.'

As part of Victoria's economy drive, several of the Knole employees were 'sent away', and plans were made for the family to leave Knole for the duration of the case, leaving only a skeleton staff to ensure that proper care was taken of the house. A couple of weeks after her father's death, Victoria started saying goodbye to her neighbours. The local shopkeepers were particularly cross with Henry for the effect the departure of the Sackvilles would have on trade. Towards the end of October, the family left Knole for their 'long exile'. 'We hated it,' Victoria wrote in her diary. 'I should be very happy there if I did not have the show-rooms to worry me! But I was sorry to go, especially for Lionel & Vita's sake.' Every now and then, the Sackvilles would pop back to Knole. On 3 December 1908, when Victoria returned to pick up some presents, the whole place looked 'very dreary', as I know only Knole can in the depths of winter, and in January, when Lionel and Victoria motored down to Knole with Vita, they found the place 'so cold and bleak . . . We only keep the little sitting-room going.'

Apart from the money from the life insurance policies, which provided his daughters with a lump sum on his death, Old Lionel had made little provision for his children. What Flora and Amalia wanted to know – and they needed a swift response – was what would now happen to their allowances. If these were to be stopped, Flora observed, she would have to give up her plan to get married, as she did not 'have a sou to her name', and she had no idea what would become of her. So would Victoria continue her allowance for the time being?

Lionel outlined the new proposals in a letter to Amalia. In addition to whatever income the girls received from the lump sum left by their father, Lionel and Victoria were each prepared to give them an allowance of £100 a year, totalling £200, so long as 'you will understand that this is entirely voluntary on our part'. Flora was at first much relieved that Lionel and Victoria had agreed to continue her allowance, albeit at a slightly reduced rate, and apologised for *'tous ces détails au milieu de tes préoccupations personelles'*. But it was not long before Flora and Amalia's tone changed.

They addressed their letters pointedly to 'Lionel West Esq.' and 'Mrs West', despite the fact that Lionel had signed the cheques to them in the name of 'Sackville'. As Flora informed Victoria, she was doing so because she believed that Henry's wife, Emélie, was Lady Sackville, '& added many nasty remarks, too long to copy' for good measure. 'I am keeping her letter,' wrote Victoria, 'like many others where she had said she "had nothing to do with Henry." Oh! the ingratitude of them all.' Because Flora insisted on addressing Henry as Lord Sackville, her letters to her brother occasionally got forwarded to Lionel instead, and the extent of her collusion became apparent. She referred to meetings in London of the syndicate backing Henry, and upbraided her brother for becoming demoralised: instead, she begged Henry to '*bien cuisiner le Monsieur*' (literally, to cook Lionel good and proper).

Despite the allowance, Amalia kept on claiming that she received no money from the Sackvilles, and that she was forced to live on charity. Like Flora, she continued to support Henry's case, spreading rumours, based on nothing more than the description of Victoria in her birth certificate as the daughter of a '*père inconnu*', that Papa had picked Victoria up somewhere in Spain and installed her at the legation in Washington. This was the first time, Amalia claimed, that Victoria had ever met Amalia and Flora. No wonder that Victoria found the situation galling and complained at the injustice of supporting siblings 'who have done everything to oust us!'

Victoria considered appealing to Henry's better judgement, and got so far as drafting a letter to him:

> It does seem such a pity that you should not listen to your conscience & to reason, in connection with this sad case you want to bring against Lionel. It is such a hopeless case for you, my poor Henry and I should like you not to be blind [an unfortunate choice of word, given that Henry had just lost the sight of one eye, due to an abscess] to the hopelessness of the whole thing, before you finally settle to throw mud at our Father's memory. There are still so many people living, who were his friends & his colleagues & to whom he never introduced our Mother or spoke about her, you must know, in your heart of hearts, how hopeless it must be to establish the reputation of marriage. Do think well before you act. It is for your own good that I ask you to act rationally. As with the evidence we have got, there is only one possible end to the Trial.

She was, however, dissuaded by the family solicitors from sending the letter. Pemberton argued that the risks of doing so

were too high. 'It is pretty certain, I think, that any such communication would at once be taken as an indication of weakness on
our part, besides the danger that the opportunity would be taken
to circulate statements in the public press that you feared a trial,
and were trying to compromise.' Pemberton was also of the
opinion that, since Henry had obviously made various assign-
ments and commitments to the people backing his case, he was
obliged to pursue the matter to the end, rather than reaching a
compromise, and to that extent he was no longer a free agent. In
addition to rumours that a French priest had financed Henry's
case, there were also reports that the Sackvilles' old butler,
Williams, was trying to raise money on Henry's behalf, at seven
per cent interest. 'Wills' had borne the Sackvilles a grudge for
more than twenty years, ever since he claimed an unpaid commission on some tapestries that Victoria had exhibited, on Béon's
behalf, in the legation ballroom in Washington.

———

Max had been out of touch with the family for some time, but
soon after Old Lionel's death he wrote to Victoria. She was scep-
tical at first about his motives. Although he claimed that he had
nothing to do with Henry, she could not forget a letter he had
written to Henry a decade before, saying he was 'heart & soul
with him & he would do the same, were he in Henry's position'.
'My Brothers & sisters are such liars,' wrote Victoria, 'that one
does not know what to believe' and, as a result, she answered
Max 'very cautiously'. It was not long, however, before she was
attempting once again to engage him on her side.

Max, for his part, was flattered by the attention and desperate for news of the family. 'What is Amalia doing,' he asked on
13 December, 'and how does she live? And Henry? What does
he do for a living? What was the reason of Flora's divorce? Her
fault or her husband's? Is she living quite alone by herself? Is

Henry really married, and is it his wife's money that is carrying him through all this [it was not]? Give me some news.' Max felt that his 'poor little sisters', Flora and Amalia, had been dragged unwittingly into this 'dreadful' business. Even when he heard that Amalia was 'taking active steps in conjunction with Henry', he asked Victoria not to be too 'rough on her, she is a girl, and our sister, and I feel very sorry for her. It's a different matter with Henry, he knows what he is about.'

Max disassociated himself from his brother's stand and, when asked by Henry's solicitors, Nussey & Fellowes, whether he would be willing to help their client in his claim, he 'absolutely' declined. Indeed, he even sent Victoria a letter, addressed to Henry, for her to forward, encouraging him to see the folly of his ways and to give up the case. Once again, Pemberton advised the Sackvilles not to send the letter, 'as it would look as if we had squared Max which we have not done'.

Max's generosity of spirit was reciprocated. 'My dear Max,' wrote Lionel on 12 June, 'I have often thought of writing to you and telling you how much I have always felt for you in your position but until lately have never quite liked to do so as I have always had the feeling, that although it is of course not my fault, I have in a sense reaped the advantage of your misfortune. You have however now shown yourself such a good friend to Victoria & me that I hope you will not think it an impertinence if I write to thank you myself.' Lionel proceeded to blame Béon for inciting Henry in his 'misguided' behaviour, and Amalia for encouraging him.

Lionel's 'generous' letter affected Max deeply. 'It is the letter of an honourable man,' he replied on 13 July,

and it breathes such true feeling and, if I may be permitted to say so, such genuine honesty, that it comes as a most welcome relief after that atmosphere of lies we have all been living in lately . . . Of course I knew all along that the inheritance would come to you, in the ordinary course of things, but I have never owed you a grudge for it . . . I have become reconciled to it long ago. I bow to the inevitable, and I do so without rancour . . . It was only natural that my heart should go out to my sister in her trouble.

He promised to support Lionel and Victoria against his brother. 'What brotherly love I have felt, or might feel, for him, he has alienated from me by the low tricks to which he has stooped.' He had had no idea that proceedings would degenerate into such a sordid, 'and I might say criminal', affair, and blamed the evil influence of Salanson and Béon, the latter having been the only man, besides his father and mother, to know that some of the children had been registered legitimate. 'I have always had deep love and respect for my father,' he continued, 'and I am sorrowful that he should have died without our being reconciled.' As the eldest son, of an albeit dysfunctional family, Max took his responsibilities seriously – not just to his sisters, but also to the memory of his parents. 'When I came to reflect upon his character,' he wrote to Victoria of their father, 'which had made such a deep impression upon me even as a little child, I came to see that in spite of his failings and weaknesses he could not be guilty of the charges Henry was levelling against him.' As for Pepita, he wrote on 8 August: 'Poor mother! I think she was more the victim of circumstances than the author of the cross her children have to bear. She threw away the substance for the shadow, and she exchanged sterling gold for the glitter of brass.'

Over the summer, Max ploughed through all the depositions that Henry's solicitors had taken in June. In September, he addressed the issues raised in these, and gave his own interpretation of events in a series of letters to Pemberton, that amounted to fifty foolscap pages. He was worn out. These letters to Pemberton had 'killed' him. 'My eyes are the colour of red flannel and I am suffering terribly,' he told Victoria. 'My head feels quite

queer and sore, in fact I am quite stupid.' Poor Max often comes
across in his letters as the dutiful and conscientious oldest child,
with more than a touch of the barrack-room lawyer about him.
'I consider that I, as the eldest son, am morally bound to afford
you every assistance in my power,' he wrote to Victoria; 'I think
Henry is doing you a grievous wrong, and I must stand by you.'
He was as keen as Victoria that the proceedings should be
confined to establishing the fact of Pepita's marriage to Oliva,
rather than the broader issues of a marriage by reputation to Old
Lionel, in which their mother's name would inevitably be
tarnished, and attention drawn once again to Max's paternity.
Max gave no credence at all to Henry's depositions – 'the idle
gossip of the riff-raff of Arcachon' – particularly those accounts
of what Pepita had told people about the King of Bavaria. He
reassured Victoria that she was her father's daughter: 'Good
gracious, of course you are! I have not seen you for many, many
years but I often saw the likeness when you were small.' The
sooner the case was finished, he felt, the better.

It was now a year since the death of Old Lionel, and Max
was 'very sad on the anniversary'. But he felt for Victoria, too,
capturing those conflicted emotions she felt for her father:
'How you must miss him, having always lived with him and
been by his side. He left us a legacy of trouble, poor old man!'

Although Henry's claim to the succession crystallised on the
death of his father, it took some time for the case to come to the
courts. In October 1908, Henry petitioned for an official receiver
to be appointed for the income from the Knole estates in Kent,
Warwickshire, Gloucestershire and Sussex, while the action –
initiated in 1907 – to decide the question of legitimacy was
pending. This was, Victoria complained, Henry's 'systematic way
of nagging at us'. As the judge, Mr Justice Eve, acknowledged,
the appointment of a receiver might deprive Lionel of the means
to defend his title, 'doing a grave injustice to the defendant'. Nor
did he think that the estates themselves were in any danger, so

The *Daily Mirror* covers Henry's petition in 1908 to have an official receiver appointed to the Knole estates. The late Lord Sackville (*centre left*) and his nephew Lionel, the new Lord Sackville (*bottom left*), confront Henry (*centre right*) and his wife, Emélie (*bottom right*)

long as they continued to be administered by the current trustees, and no profits were distributed. In November, after at least
one adjournment to allow Henry to go to Paris to visit his sick
wife, he dismissed the motion.

Lionel had attended court and spotted Henry and Amalia
sitting together, despite the fact that she had claimed she had
nothing to do with her brother. Both of them had sworn affidavits declaring that they had always believed that they were
legitimate. It also became clear, during the hearing, that Henry's
case would attempt to prove a marriage between her parents 'by
reputation'; that her father had recognised several of his children as legitimate until 1881, when Victoria went to live with
him in Washington, and that his position had changed entirely
since then. This distressed Victoria on two counts: first, that
her mother's reputation would be tarnished, and second, that
'the whole campaign will be directed against me'. She was
already beginning to hear on the gossip mill, that she had
'turned Henry out of his inheritance by [her] machinations. I
am made out a sort of heartless and clever adventuress.' Vita,
on the other hand, occasionally saw the funny side. In
November 1908, she had gone with Violet Keppel to see a new
play called *The Marriages of Mayfair*, which was obviously
based on the Sackville situation. 'It was amusing because it so
closely resembles the story of my own case; peer who married a
dancer while her husband was still alive, etc.'

As the evidence in support of a 'marriage by reputation'
emerged, it made Victoria, the new Lady Sackville, feel 'quite
wretched & dread the trial more than ever'. She could not 'bear
to think of all the things they will say against my dear Mother'
and to 'dread all those unpleasant revelations' about Pepita's
rackety life just as Vita was coming out as a debutante. Victoria
always thought that her husband was a little insensitive about
these anxieties of hers; that he did not 'seem to understand how
much I mind my poor mother being made out an impropriety

and I want everything to be done to stop throwing mud at her'. Her particular version of her own morals inclined to the prudish (despite her apparent acceptance of her husband's infidelities and a fondness for off-colour jokes, which she recorded in her diary at the end of each year). She prided herself on living up to the family motto of '*toujours* loyal', and on not being a flirt, like many of the fast set who surrounded her. And so it was especially difficult for her to be so dependent on evidence that implied her beloved mother had been rather loose.

Messages of support from friends, such as the American tycoon William Waldorf Astor, provided some consolation. 'I have often thought . . . how anxious & worried you must be,' he wrote to Victoria during the summer of 1909. 'It is a venomous & spiteful attack that is made upon you & were the claimant anyone else I should suspect blackmail . . . I have myself passed from one trouble to another all my life . . . I have always found it best to face the music with courage, & this you will do.' The Sackvilles were also soliciting evidence from former acquaintances of the late Lord Sackville: Lord Weardale, who remembered him at Arcachon; and Sir Hugh Wyndham who was with him in Berlin in 1868, and in Paris in 1871, and swore that Lionel had never introduced Pepita to him or spoken of her as his wife. They also received approaches from people who wanted to sell information, Lionel making a fruitless journey to Arcachon in March 1909 to see a man who had two irrelevant letters from the Comte de Clouet, which he wished to sell for £600.

But the case itself was much delayed. In January 1909, Pemberton told Lionel that 'Henry wants to put off the case again to take more & fresh evidence abroad; he is maddening with his delays'. He suspected that Henry was beginning to realise just how poor his case was. Eventually, in September 1909, Letters of Request were sent by Henry's lawyers to the Courts in Madrid, Granada and Valladolid, asking for permission to examine various witnesses in Spain and to collect relevant documents. These included the 1851 marriage entry, depositions from the *Denuncia* proceedings of 1901, and the record of the withdrawal by the public prosecutor of the criminal case against Rophon and Sanchez in March 1909.

In October, Henry applied for the case to be tried by a jury, in the hope that there would be some sympathy for the underdog. Counsel for the Sackvilles argued that the case should be tried before a judge alone, as it depended upon 'the critical examination of documents' and depositions, amounting to 2,000 folios of evidence, collected over the previous fourteen years and taken in Gibraltar, Bordeaux, Arcachon, Madrid, Copenhagen and London. There would be many complicated questions raised as to the admissibility of particular pieces of evidence. But, perhaps most important of all, it was 'a case which might possibly raise in the minds of certain persons a great amount of prejudice, because it might be said: "Here is a title being taken away from a son and passing to a nephew."' Henry's application was refused.

There seems to have been little action from Henry's solicitors in following up the Letters of Request. Pemberton, who had believed for some time that the other side were dragging their feet, wrote to Nussey & Fellowes to 'place on record the position which I find here at the present time as regards the Letters, and I shall use it at the proper time for the purpose of opposing to the utmost any application which the Petitioner may make to the Court in England to postpone the date appointed for the trial, on any ground connected with the Letters of Request referred to'. As predicted, Fellowes did indeed apply for the trial to be postponed from 22 November on the grounds that Henry had not had time to assemble the witnesses and evidence sought in the Letters of Request, and the case was postponed to February of the following year. 'It is hard on poor Lionel, but I am glad the evil day is put off,' wrote Victoria. Lionel's brother

Charlie, however, was increasingly frustrated: 'Damn. Damn. Damnation . . . What awful bedints the other side are. I saw a fat dirty man who might be a Frenchman there, no doubt fat as a result of being "cuisined".'

As the case approached, there was a last attempt at a face-saving deal by Amalia. In November, she met Lionel at her lodgings in Artillery Mansions, Victoria. She was thinking of getting married and suggested a compromise whereby Henry's legitimacy would be acknowledged, in return for his giving up all rights of succession. Lionel dismissed this as a 'ridiculous proposition', so confident was he now of winning. Flora, on the other hand, was all set on revenge. One of her letters addressed to Henry as Lord Sackville at Hill Street fell into the hands of Lionel and Victoria. In it, she offered Henry 100,000 francs if he needed it, with a further 50,000 available, in order to help him '*à les écraser entièrement . . . N'oublies pas de me trouver un service d'auto très chic à Londres* to take me backwards and forwards from the Courts.' A pathetic postscript begged her brother not to forget to send her some postcards of Knole. Flora was by now set on the path that the rest of her life would take. All her relationships, including a couple of broken engagements, seemed to founder on the twin problems of money (not enough of it) and religion (Flora's divorce made remarriage difficult); her doubtful legitimacy further complicated matters. According to Mrs Cameron, one of the Sackvilles' witnesses, she had, as a result, 'sunk very low indeed & went with pretty near any body – she was now living with a rich young man whom she would probably drop as soon as she had squeezed all the money out of him'.

10

In the High Court

On Tuesday 1 February 1910, the case eventually opened in the High Court in London before the Right Hon. Sir John Bigham. Over the next few days, the 'Romance of the Sackville Peerage', as it had been described in the press, attracted great attention, with its sensational ingredients of ancient wealth and modern manners, English aristocrats and their poor Spanish relations. There was particular interest in the United States, on account of the years the Sackville-Wests had spent at the British legation in Washington.

At the heart of the case was a profound irony: Victoria was put in the extraordinarily ambiguous, and invidious, position of needing her own illegitimacy – a subject from which she had always shrunk – to be proved very publicly in order for her husband to inherit. In *Pepita*, Vita described how her mother usually lived in an unreal world, 'a world of her own creation', but that with 'The Case', she was brought up against facts 'which struck at very deep, real feelings in her early self'. 'For one thing, she cherished a deep devotion to her mother's memory, and could not bear the details of her mother's most private, intimate life being dragged out into publicity. For another, she had an almost morbid shrinking from the fact of her own illegitimacy, and now here she was placed in the position of hearing her illegitimacy and that of her brothers and sisters insisted upon by the very men who were working to gain a superb inheritance for her husband.' As a result, 'she was torn between the most intimate ties that can humanly exist: her mother, her father, her brother, her husband, her home. For, of course, Knole was her home, the only real home she had ever known, and, to all of us [or, more particularly, to Vita], Knole meant as much as any human being.' Victoria herself was not to be called as a witness, but she would have to listen over the coming days as the story of her life was told again, with all its petty snubs and humiliations – beginning in Arcachon where she was not allowed to play at the Villa Pepa with the neighbours' children.

Sir Edward Clarke opened by presenting Henry's petition that 'on a date between the 1st January, 1863, and the 5th day of August, 1867, which date at present the Petitioner cannot give more particularly, at a place unknown to him, Lord Sackville, then Lionel Sackville-West, was lawfully married to Josefa Duran de Ortega; that they lived and cohabited together as man and wife . . . [and] that the Petitioner [born in 1869] is the son of that marriage'. He therefore prayed for a 'declaration of legitimacy'. There were to be two main strands to Sir Edward's case: proving a legally binding marriage between Lionel and Pepita, and proving that there was a 'marriage by reputation'. In the event of his failing actually to prove the former, he hoped that evidence for the latter would be so overwhelming as to prove his case. It was the case for the 'marriage by reputation' that Victoria dreaded.

This argument hinged on a number of declarations by Old Lionel himself: the birth certificates of several of his children, which he had signed as the husband of Pepita, and the marriage certificate of his daughter Flora; the personal correspondence with the Béons, in which he described Pepita as his wife; the fact that he had administered Pepita's estate after her death as if she had been his wife; even the letters he wrote to Pepita herself, in which he referred to her as 'my little wife'. It was as if Lionel's voice was being heard from beyond the grave, as unreliable and as muddled as ever: 'I never described Pepita as my wife . . . I will not swear I never described her as my wife. I did not commonly speak of her as my wife . . . I don't recollect ever saying that I was the legitimate father of Flora. I will not swear I did not.' And so on. At one point, in a reference to a declaration signed at Arcachon, this former representative of Britain to the United States acknowledged that, 'It has not been my habit in life to read documents carefully before I signed them, I have been decidedly careless in that respect.'

There was also the testimony of Fritz Holst, a retired colonel in the Danish army, which had been taken on commission at the British consulate in Copenhagen the previous spring. Holst had met 'Count and Countess West' in Arcachon during the summer of 1868, while he was convalescing from an illness, and had contacted Henry in 1903 when he first read about his claim in the newspapers. Colonel Holst recalled how he would never have introduced his wife to the Wests if he had had any suspicion that they were not married. His evidence also included a letter from Lionel on the death of Pepita, which referred to the very sad death 'of my poor wife', Pepita. Henry's contention that Lionel and Pepita were considered as man and wife at Arcachon in the 1860s was further supported by depositions taken in 1897, in the action to perpetuate testimony, and more recently at Bordeaux in May 1909, from a series of coachmen, painters, butchers, seamstresses, hairdressers, washerwomen and wine merchants.

Sir Edward Clarke was on shakier ground when it came to proving, with documentary evidence, the fact of a marriage, at some place (the petitioner did not know where) and at some time (the petitioner did not know when) between Lionel and Pepita. All he had was an old story that Lionel had once been involved in some sort of marriage ceremony with Pepita; a claim by the former Danish consul in Arcachon, Edward Kirstein, to have read somewhere that they had been married in Madrid; and a piece of paper purporting to show they had been married in Frankfurt. This last was Amalia's Bulletin de Naissance, a document issued for the purpose of information only, to describe the contents of a birth certificate. As in her actual birth certificate, the document described Amalia as the lawful daughter of Lionel Sackville-West and his wife, Josephine Duran de Ortega. But it differed in one significant respect from the original from which it appeared to be abstracted: the state-ment 'Father and mother married at Frankfort-on-Maine' had been added. Despite the fact that Lionel had signed the paper on the back, the judge would not admit the document as evidence. It was not, he argued, an 'authentic' legal document in the same way a birth certificate was; and, in any case, many questions were raised over its dodgy provenance (apparently, it had been given to Henry by the Comte de Béon). Furthermore, nothing had ever come of enquiries made by Nussey & Fellowes into any marriage ceremony performed by diplomatic repre-sentatives in Frankfurt. Indeed, Lionel had denied, when interviewed in 1897, that he had ever been in Frankfurt with Pepita after 1853.

Sir Robert Finlay, the Sackvilles' lead counsel, outlined his case towards the end of the first day. He claimed that Sir Edward Clarke had told only part of the story – and, in partic-ular, that he had ignored the evidence of the late Lord Sackville himself, taken in the action to perpetuate testimony. What Lord Sackville had said over and over again was that any delib-erately misleading statements had been 'made simply and solely for the purpose of saving the reputation of this lady with whom he was living; that there was never a marriage of any sort or kind, and that the children were all illegitimate'. As for Sir Edward Clarke's attempts to prove a 'marriage by reputation', 'I submit that more flimsy evidence was never adduced. It is the evidence very largely of tradesmen – butchers and so on and house painters . . . What you want in order to constitute evidence of reputation is some evidence of persons moving in the same social circle, and more particularly of those who know something of the husband – who are connected with him and to whom he would have introduced the lady as his wife.'

Sir Robert Finlay drew attention to the fact that no English people ever visited Lionel and Pepita in Italy, Paris or Arcachon, and that no members of the Sackville family were present at any of the baptisms – for the simple reason that 'the universal reputation in the family was that this lady was not married to Mr Sackville-West'. In contrast to the 'absolutely worthless' evidence of 'persons in a very inferior position of life', the Sackville evidence was to come from family members and friends, and diplomatic colleagues – witnesses such as Colonel Cornwallis West; Lord Saumarez; the Reverend George Alexander Trevor, curate of Withyham from 1850 to 1857 and a former trustee of the family estates at Knole; Sir Campbell Munro; and the American Mrs Elizabeth Cameron, who claimed that it had always been understood in Washington that the Misses West were illegitimate. When it came to Arcachon, Sir Robert Finlay relied on the evidence of the posher English residents: Harry Johnston, for example, and the chaplain Samuel Radcliff, who said they had known all along that Pepita was Lionel's mistress, not his wife. Many of the people who had known the Sackvilles intimately appeared in court, either in person or as voices, through depositions taken ten years before, such was the eerie effect of the perpetuation of testimony.

The Sackvilles' central argument, however, was that 'for a great many years', Pepita was married to Oliva, and that Oliva did not die until 1888 – of cancer of the tongue, in the arms of his mistress Mercedes, in hospital in Madrid. Therefore, 'during the whole time of this connection between Mr Sackville-West and this lady [Pepita] she was a married woman, and if any marriage had taken place it would have been utterly invalid'. A great chain of evidence supported the fact of a marriage between Pepita and Oliva: the sequence of marriage applications, licences, registers, and so on; and the evidence of those, such as Oliva's sister, Isabel, who had attended the marriage itself in 1851. The alterations to the marriage register in Madrid were simply a forgery designed to discredit this crucial piece of evidence, for it was only if doubt could be cast on the marriage between Pepita and Oliva, that it might be possible to prove that she had married Lionel instead.

Sir Robert Finlay drew attention to the general unreliability of Henry as a character. A particularly damning piece of evidence was the letter he had written to Victoria in 1890, acknowledging his illegitimacy. Sir Robert also referred to the letters Henry had sent to members of the family in 1896, threatening that 'unless pressure is brought to bear to have him declared legitimate, he will make declarations which will drag the honour of an ancient family into the dust'. There were Henry's shabby attempts, after his setbacks of 1898, to apologise and to blame Gabriel Salanson, and then his collaboration with Rophon in 1901 and his efforts to have it put on record that the entry in the marriage register had been tampered with. Although 'it is not for me to bring home to anybody the guilt of doing it', concluded Sir Robert Finlay, 'it is perfectly plain that these alterations were made by someone who was intending to act in the interests of the Petitioner'.

Vita attended the proceedings for the first time on the third day of the case. Victoria had encouraged her to come, against the wishes of her father, and pointed out scornfully to her daughter a group of uneasy-looking people in the courtroom: 'Look at your relations.' They seemed, as Vita later described: 'very drab and black-suited and bowler-hatted, – not romantic at all. My Spanish relations! They looked like plumbers in their Sunday best. Where, oh where, was Pepita, the source and origin of all this wild and inordinately expensive romance? There was nothing left of Pepita but a falsified marriage register and this gloomy troop of Spaniards perching on the uncomfortable benches of the High Court of Justice. And a lot of posters on the railings, and headlines in all the papers. It was all very strange and confusing, and I was too young to understand it rightly.'

This was the day that events took a dramatic turn. Just as the Sackvilles' counsel was about to call their first witness, Sir Edward Clarke asked whether he could read to the court a letter he had just received from the petitioner. In the letter, Henry instructed his counsel to ask the judge for an adjournment of the case until he had received from Spain a number of 'extremely important documents and photographs', which were to be used in the cross-examination of the witnesses. 'Should Sir John Bigham refuse I wish you to retire from the case as I do not care to go any further with such an unfair trial.' Sir Edward Clarke was not prepared to apply for an adjournment, as he could not say the Spanish documents were material to his case, and felt obliged to withdraw from the case. The petitioner's junior counsel followed suit, as did Henry's solicitor, Fellowes, who declared that he could no longer advise Henry as his client had declined his advice not to apply for an adjournment.

When the judge asked Henry what this important evidence from Spain consisted of, Henry was a little unclear and started to suggest documents that the court already had. Was Henry simply playing for time and was, as Sir Robert Finlay implied, his application for an adjournment purely 'vexatious', as even his own lawyers appeared to think? The judge suspended the sitting to allow Henry to consider the situation and, when the court reconvened, Henry said he wished to plead his own case, adding, 'I know that I shall lose, but I will have a good try.' The judge ruled that the case would continue the following day, with Henry cross-examining the defendants' witnesses as best he could. Only if it became absolutely apparent, during the cross-examination, that Henry needed some specific document would he then approve an adjournment while those documents were obtained. Henry was now well and truly on his own, as he told the court: 'I shall have no solicitor or Counsel, my Lord, and in fact I am a stranger in London because I have been for the last few months abroad with my wife who has been very ill – nearly dying.'

Henry was reduced on the fourth day to cross-examining the defendants' witnesses himself, which he did rather ramblingly: quizzing a lawyer called Francisco Ponce de Leon on points of Spanish law; failing to shake the increasingly frail Alfred Harrison, who had seen the unaltered marriage register over ten years before; and being rather bemused by Lord Weardale, who had known Lionel in 1868. 'Do you think he would be capable of making a false registration of his children?' Henry asked Lord Weardale of the late Lord Sackville, to which Lord Weardale replied: 'I can understand a gentleman circumstanced as he was, anxious for the reputation of the lady with whom he was living and the children who were supposed to be his children, and were his children – I can understand his unfortunately making a breach of the ordinary rules which govern gentlemen.'

When the defendants' witnesses had finished giving their evidence, Henry once again asked the judge to adjourn the case, to give him time to bring his witnesses over from Spain and to bring to trial 'the voluminous documentary evidence which has been duly collated by Letters of Request in Spain'. What witnesses might those be, the judge enquired? The whole of the Oliva family, Henry replied. 'But that is very large, you know,' observed the judge. 'These Spanish people are sometimes very prolific.' Even though there were no more than four or five Oliva witnesses, Henry did not know their addresses, nor could he give any idea of what they might say. It is hardly surprising, then, that the judge refused Henry's request for an adjournment. He was 'personally quite satisfied that it would be of no advantage whatever' to Henry. In the light of all this, Henry gave up: 'I can do nothing more, my Lord. I am done. I can do nothing more. I cannot defend myself any further.'

This was confirmed on the morning of the fifth day, when the judge read out a letter written by Henry in Eastbourne over the weekend. Having been refused an adjournment, 'and having no Counsel or Solicitors to advise me and conduct my case, I wish to tell your Lordship that, although it breaks my heart, I retire my petition, as I am unable to fight my case'.

It was left to Sir Robert Finlay to present his case; and for the Attorney General, as co-defendant (because a seat in the House of Lords was at stake), to give his opinion. Although the Attorney General could not 'refrain from an expression of sympathy' for a man who had found that the declaration made by his father on his birth certificate was untrue, he felt that the petitioner had 'wholly failed to make out his case and that Judgment should be given against him'.

In his summary, Sir John Bigham admitted that the strongest parts of the petitioner's evidence were the declarations made by the late Lord Sackville himself. But he believed that these had been made solely to 'please Pepita and to give an appearance of respectability to the life they were leading'. More significantly, he was satisfied that Lionel had never married Pepita – quite simply, because it had been proved beyond all doubt that Pepita had married Oliva.

The evidence which supported this was: first, the entry in the Book of Entradas, which recorded the application on 6 December 1850 for a marriage licence; next, a licence issued by the Vicaria on the 9 January 1851 to the priest of the parish

church of San Millán, authorising him to perform the ceremony; then, an entry in the church register recording the
marriage on 10 January 1851; and finally, an entry of a marriage
on the same date in the civil register, kept by the municipal
authorities in Madrid. Although two of these books had been
tampered with – namely, the Book of Entradas at the Vicaria,
and the register at the church of San Millán – the judge was
convinced that this had been done by someone acting in the
supposed interest of the petitioner, to raise the suspicion that
the entries originally referred to some marriage other than
that of Pepita and Oliva. The problem was that 'the persons
who were guilty of this clumsy fraud had overlooked or had
not been able to get at' the entry of the licence to perform the
religious ceremony or the entry in the civil register, both of
which were in perfect order. Moreover, there was evidence
that entry No. 581 in the Book of Entradas and the entry in
the church register had been seen, authenticated, and copied
in 1896 and 1897, when they were completely free of any eras-
ures or alterations.

As a result, Sir John was satisfied that the two books had
been 'tampered with in recent years, and probably in view of
this litigation'. He had heard of the criminal prosecution in
Madrid, and how the jury had been unable to reach a verdict.
'However this may be,' he concluded, 'the circumstances raise a
suspicion against the Petitioner himself which in my opinion it
was his duty to dispel by going into the witness box and submit-
ting to cross-examination. He did not tender himself as a
witness and the suspicion is not dispelled. I therefore dismiss
the Petition with costs.'

After the collapse of Henry's case, the Sackvilles returned to
Knole in style – their progress lovingly described in a souvenir
edition of the *Sevenoaks Chronicle*. The freshly vindicated Lord
Sackville went to the House of Lords to 'sign his name like the
other peers', before driving down to Sevenoaks in the motor car

with his wife and daughter. At the railway bridge, they transferred from the car into their horse-drawn carriage, and were
driven, as Vita later described, to the top of the town 'by our
incomparable coachman Bond, who wore his top-hat at an
angle a Regency dandy might envy and who had a figure that
any Savile Row tailor might have been proud to dress'. A triumphal arch of foliage, bearing the words 'The Town Welcomes
You', greeted them as they drove up the London Road. The
carriage then stopped for a few words of welcome by the
Chairman of the Sevenoaks Urban District Council and the
Chairman of the Sevenoaks Horticultural and Floral Society.
Lady Sackville and her daughter were presented with bouquets
of flowers – rare orchids for her ladyship, and lilies of the valley
for Vita.

Lionel, Victoria and Vita, riding in a carriage, are pulled through the park

Lord Sackville stood up in the carriage and thanked the
cheering crowds for the warmth of their welcome: 'I can only

say that the enthusiasm and cordiality with which you have received us have touched us far beyond anything that mere words can convey, and the kindly feeling of which this demonstration is the expression will never be forgotten by us . . . I beg you to believe that the memory of this day's reception will be one which time can never obliterate.'

They were all set now for the final leg of the journey. The pair of horses were unharnessed from the carriage and ropes attached instead. With a band leading the way, the carriage was pulled along by members of the local fire brigade in full uniform, across the park and through the front entrance of the house into the Green Court. Here, Lord and Lady Sackville received a hearty welcome from their household: on behalf of the staff, Miss Dorothy Stubbs, the youngest daughter of the head gardener, presented Victoria with another bouquet, and Miss Marjory Bond, daughter of the head coachman, presented Vita with a large box of chocolates. Lionel thanked the firemen for their 'arduous efforts': 'I have had three modes of progress today – motor-car, horses in the carriage, and now you have dragged us up here. I think the last mentioned method of progress has been the most comfortable and safest. It is now 20 years since Lady Sackville and myself were dragged up here in a similar manner to Knole, when we returned to Sevenoaks after our honeymoon. I only hope our weight has not sensibly increased in that interval.' Just as he stopped speaking, the band struck up 'Home, sweet home', a 'most appropriate finish' to the afternoon's celebrations, the newspaper concluded. In the evening, an enormous bonfire was lit just outside the gates to Knole: 'Thus ended one of the most impressive and exciting episodes in the history of Sevenoaks.'

Many of the local inhabitants had taken a day's holiday to celebrate the occasion. As the *Sevenoaks Chronicle* observed: 'After Wednesday, who will accuse the residents of Sevenoaks with being devoid of enterprise; who will say they lack

Vita, Lionel and Victoria, with their bouquets, stand at the entrance to the Green
Court. Members of the local fire brigade can be seen in the background

enthusiasm; who will suggest they are unable to pay due honour
to those they respect and are delighted to welcome home? It
was certainly a red letter day in the history of the old town, but
it was a splendid illustration of what the inhabitants can do
when they are united and in earnest.' Even 'Dame Nature [had]
smiled on the proceedings, for a delightful day was sandwiched
between days of unfavourable weather.'

'Never, before or since, have I felt so much like royalty,'
wrote Vita. Her father, on the other hand, claimed it all 'an
abominable nuisance'.

As a result of the case, the Sackvilles, a family noted for their
reserve, were temporarily the most notorious family in the
country. The case had been blazoned across the newspapers,
appeared in lights in theatreland (*The Marriages of Mayfair*),
and was even to seep twenty years later into *Orlando*, Virginia
Woolf's elegiac novel about Knole. In *Orlando*, the entry in the
marriage register in the church of San Millán became 'nothing

less, indeed, than a deed of marriage, drawn up, signed, and witnessed between his Lordship, Orlando, Knight of the Garter, etc., etc., etc., and Rosina Pepita, a dancer, father unknown, but reputed a gypsy, mother also unknown but reputed a seller of old iron in the market-place over against the Galata Bridge'. When the case was finally settled, 'and the result of the lawsuit was made known (and rumour flew much quicker than the telegraph which has supplanted it), the whole town was filled with rejoicings . . . Hospitals were founded. Rat and Sparrow clubs were inaugurated. Turkish women by the dozen were burnt in effigy in the market-place, together with scores of peasant boys with the label "I am a base Pretender", lolling from their mouths . . .'

There were a couple of postscripts. On 26 February, the judge dismissed Henry's claim to the accumulated income that had been retained by the Knole trustees pending the outcome of the legitimacy case. And in March, Henry presented a motion for a re-hearing of the main case, on the grounds that not all the documents contained in the letters of request to Spain had arrived in time for the case, and that the judge had therefore been wrong to refuse an adjournment; he also objected to the implication that he had in some way been involved in tampering with the marriage register. On 6 April, however, he abandoned the motion for a re-hearing.

An editorial article in *The Times* probed the psychology of claimants such as Henry. It captured the ambivalence at the very centre of their being, and highlighted how they could never accept the marginal status in law to which their illegitimacy condemned them: 'His disappointment is always with him, and he broods over his wrongs. He forgets that for many years he has been treated, and has regarded and spoken of himself, as illegitimate. He looks about for evidence, and he finds people who, quite sincerely and more or less accurately, tell him just what he wants. So a case is built up, it may be with full conviction,

entirely satisfactory to the claimant and his friends, but too
certain to fall, as this case has fallen, like a house of cards the
moment it is exposed to judicial criticism.' This is probably what
happened with Henry, and with Flora and Amalia too. Given
that much of the evidence, in the form of declarations of legitimacy, however false, came from their own father, it is not
surprising they were so confused about their origins. Their
behaviour was not, perhaps, as cynical or opportunistic as it
sometimes seems (such accusations could equally be levelled at
Victoria), but simply lost and bewildered.

Max had been the only sibling to support Victoria throughout the case. Once it was over, relations between him and his
sister cooled, for it was a sad but recurring theme that Victoria
tended to turn off the charm when she had got what she
wanted. Max had been keen to re-establish a rapport with her,
and to assume a role, as responsible eldest child, within the
family. He was due to visit England in the spring of 1910, a few
months after the successful conclusion of the case, as
Pietermaritzburg's representative to the Imperial Pageant, but
promised Victoria that he would not embarrass her. He would
not reveal, for example, that he was in any way connected with
the Sackville family, and would be known as 'plain Mr West,
which means nothing'. The pageant was postponed, due to the
death in May of King Edward VII, but Max came to England
nevertheless, for the sake of his daughter, Vivian, who had
never travelled outside Natal, and to see a specialist for his
throat: 'I have had a wolf or tiger at my throat for the last 5
years and I am only a shadow of my former self.' He was only
just over fifty, but looked, he said, 'sixty or more, and what is
worse I feel it'.

Max and Vivian did meet Victoria for a few minutes in
London. 'I have never had such pleasure in the world,' he wrote
to his sister, 'but it was hard work not breaking down.' Victoria,
on the other hand, was upset that Max would not agree to

disowning his name entirely on a proposed visit to Knole (he was not prepared to travel anywhere under an assumed name). 'You say you want to meet our wishes more than half way,' she wrote to Max, 'and this was our wish par excellence, that you have ignored. I cannot hide from you, dear M., that I have been greatly upset by your resolve and also by our meeting last Monday. My nervous system has been out of order, since this trying winter and now by A. & F. going on the stage. So I am ordered to take a complete rest from all strong emotions, or else I shall buck down . . . So, don't think me unkind if we do not meet very soon.' She was relieved that the specialist had told Max that he did not have cancer, and sent him a cheque.

Max pleaded with his sister not to think harshly of him: 'But do not do me the wrong of thinking that I wished to hurt your feelings in any way. When will you recognise that I am fond of you, and that I have from my heart always felt for you? Do you think that I would willingly add to our trouble? . . . But I am very heartsore and bitterly disappointed. It was indeed a load of sorrow and of shame that father left us. How it has eaten into the heart of us all.' Max was never to visit Knole – the only one of the siblings not to.

11

'Sackville Tragedy in Paris Flat'

In the small hours of the morning of 3 June 1914, a woman and her husband were found dead in their sparsely furnished lodgings at 75 Boulevard Suchet in Paris's 16th arrondissement. Their names meant nothing to the concierge of the apartment building, or to the police. All the concierge could supply, by way of meagre details, was that the deceased had been a quiet, rather melancholy man, but seemed very kind and good-hearted nonetheless.

It was only when the husband's former brother-in-law, Gabriel Salanson, learned of the tragedy a few days later, and sent news of it to England, that the sorry story emerged, despite attempts to cloak it in secrecy. Reports surfaced in the English press a fortnight after the deaths, and the identity of the couple was made public.

'Sackville Tragedy in Paris Flat: Grief-Stricken Claimant's Suicide after Wife's Death' is how the *Daily Mirror* described the story on 16 June. The wife, Emélie, had died after a long illness at 3.15 a.m. on 3 June, and her husband, Ernest Henri Jean Baptiste Sackville West (Henry, for short) had stood for a moment by the bedside looking at her body. He asked one of the nurses whether all was over, and when she confirmed that his wife was dead, he is reported to have remarked: 'It is fate. It is finished now for both of us.' Reverently, he covered his wife's face with a sheet, and 'distracted with grief', walked into the next room and shot himself in the head at 3.30 a.m. Max Maisonneuve, a Parisian lawyer and close friend, who had advised Henry throughout the legal proceedings in Spain, was with him when his wife died. 'As I followed him from the room,' reported Maisonneuve, 'I was horrified to see him raise a pistol to his head. I sprang towards him to seize the weapon, but was too late. He fired, and fell back into my arms.'

On 15 June, the *New York Times* reported an interview with Henry's sister Amalia, who summarised her brother's troubles since 1910, in particular his distress at the illness of a wife whom he adored. 'I have a letter from a very close friend of my brother,' Amalia claimed, 'in which it is stated that immediately he was sure his wife was dead he went into another room and shot himself before any one could interfere – that is just what Sackville [a pointed reference to what she believed was his proper title] would do.' Under the heading, 'A Love Tragedy: Peerage Claimant's Despair at Wife's Death', *The Star*, too, stressed the depth of a husband's love for his 'young' wife (Emélie was, in fact, forty-five years old), and published photographs – dating from the time of the court case – of a proud-looking man with a bristling moustache, and the wife to whom he had been passionately devoted.

Other newspapers emphasised different reasons for Henry's despair. The 'Tragedy of Great Peerage Romance' (the *Weekly Dispatch*) recalled the loss of a major lawsuit four years before. In the *New York Times*, Maisonneuve was quoted as saying that Henry 'never accepted the finding of the English court as to the legitimacy of his birth. A few weeks before his death he had decided, as soon as he could find sufficient funds, to make an attempt to bring the matter before the courts again. He was much embittered at the loss of his suit, and could hardly think of anything else. His wife's illness came as a final blow.'

Whereas the Sackvilles had returned to Knole in style after their victory, to take possession once again of the house that had been their family home for more than 300 years, Henry was greatly diminished. Stripped of the swagger that had distinguished earlier portraits, he had returned to France with his documents and his proofs, and a photograph album of his father's castle in his suitcase.

It seems that, for a few years, he and his wife ran a lodging-house in Monte Carlo. And it was here, in February 1911, that Victoria had a terrible fright on her annual trip to the Casino, when she spotted Henry and his wife in town. Her sister-in-law, Maud, ran after them to make quite sure that Victoria had not been mistaken. 'What a bore!' Victoria wrote in her diary. She had netted some £500 the previous month, and continued to be delighted by the day's winnings, 'But H has spoilt everything now.' This was Victoria's last reference to her brother in her diaries until his death over three years later.

Emélie, however, had been diagnosed with cancer, and after a major operation her condition worsened to such an extent that she and Henry decided to move to Paris in search of better medical care. In April 1914, they rented a flat in the Boulevard Suchet, overlooking the Bois de Boulogne. No. 75 is now a modern apartment block; if its surviving neighbours at this end of the Boulevard Suchet are anything to go by, it was probably then a relatively modest three-storey villa.

By now it was clear that Emélie's end was fast approaching. Henry's funds were severely depleted by the expenses of his wife's illness – in particular, the two nurses he had engaged, and his desire, according to the reports, to gratify his wife's 'every whim in the matter of delicacies'. By the time of their deaths, they had just 10 francs in their possession, a simple bed, a few chairs and a table for furniture.

Over the past decades, the progress around Paris of the illegitimate Sackvilles had traced, topographically, the gradual decline in their fortunes: from the Rue de Monceau, where the convent was located in a street of '*hôtels particuliers*' backing onto that most elegant of Parisian parks, and the smart apartments near the Champs Elysées, where Flora and Gabriel lived soon after their marriage, to less fashionable areas, where in the late 1890s Flora and Henry dodged their creditors and lodged either together or within a few minutes' walk of each other, encouraging each other in hopes of inherited wealth and hatred of Victoria. Henry's final address in a shabby apartment completed that downward trajectory.

A few days after their deaths, Henry and Emélie were buried side by side – as Henry had requested in a note he left behind – in the vast suburban cemetery of Bagneux, a couple of miles from Vanves, where Henry had attended the lycée and from where he had written Victoria those charming schoolboy letters in the 1870s. Their simple funeral was attended only by a sister and a nephew of the dead woman. Not a single relative of the dead man was there to mourn Henry. I have visited their modest grave – in the 26th Division of the cemetery, Ligne 9, Tombe 34 – the plain stone slab, paid for by a member of the Alexandre family, a contrast to the more ornate baroque memorials all around. Scraping the lichen off the stone to expose the names engraved in the granite, I was struck by the irony of the misspelt 'Sakville': Henry had spent half his life trying to establish a claim to the name and title 'Sackville', and yet even in death he was denied it.

There were no reports of the deaths in the Parisian press. Here, the newspapers were dominated by international events – just over a month before the outbreak of the First World War – by outrage at the latest excesses of the suffragettes, or '*femmes sauvages*' as they were known, and by reports of the terrible storms in the city. Buildings had been struck by lightning, the Place de la Concorde flooded, and the streets themselves destroyed by landslides and subsidence, with holes up to twenty feet deep opening in the pavements of Paris.

There was, however, one reference in the French newspapers to Henry's sister, Victoria. Lady Sackville happened to be in Paris, staying at the Hôtel Edward VII, on 16 June, the day the story about her brother's suicide in penury broke in the English press. '*Une personne des plus estimables et de beaucoup de goût*', she had just sold the art collection she had inherited from Sir John Murray Scott to the French dealer Jacques Seligmann for £270,000. The reporter from *Le Gaulois* catalogued the Gobelins tapestries, the paintings by Boucher and Le Prince, and the magnificent furniture, '*ébloui de tant de merveilles*'.

Sir John had himself inherited this collection from Sir Richard Wallace and his wife, who had employed him for many years as their private secretary. On her death in 1897, Lady Wallace left the English half of the collection to the nation, forming what is now the Wallace Collection. But the French half she left to Sir John. This collection was housed at No. 2 Rue Laffitte, on the corner of the Boulevard des Italiens, not far from the hotel where Vita's grandfather Lionel had first made Pepita's acquaintance. It was here that the Sackvilles often stayed on their trips to Paris. Vita described this treasure house, which drew visitors 'from every part of Europe', in *Pepita*:

> Room after room opened one into the other, so that, standing in the middle, one could look down a vista of shining brown parquet floors and ivory-coloured *boiseries* on either side. Here, indeed, one had the eighteenth-century illusion at its height. The traffic might rumble down the boulevard outside and the cries of Paris echo muffled beyond the slatted shutters, but inside the rooms there was no hint, even in the smallest detail, of the modern world. No telephone, no electric light; nothing but wax candles in the heavy ormolu candelabra on the tables and in the sconces on the walls; no bells, save those that one could jangle by pulling a thick silken rope ending in an

BEAUTY AND THE BEAR

The Hon. Victoria Sackville West, daughter of Lord Sackville, with "Ivan the Terrible," the three-months'-old Russian bear, which she has tamed at Knole Park, Sevenoaks

Vita plays with the bear cub given to her by Ivan Hay, beside
the pond in the garden at Knole

immense tassel. Even on the writing-tables the little sifters were always kept full of sand, and the pens were long quills, with a knife laid ready to sharpen them. All around, silent and sumptuous, stood the priceless furniture of the Wallace Collection. Chairs and sofas of brocade and petit point; tables and consoles with the voluptuous curves of Louis Quinze or the straight lines of Louis Seize; the bronze sphinxes of the early Regency; the tortoiseshell and buhl of Louis Quatorze; the marqueterie of rose-wood and lemon-wood; the ormolu mouldings of Caffieri, sporting into shells and cupids, into the horned heads of rams and cloven hoofs of satyrs; endless clocks, all ticking, and all exactly right, chiming the quarters together; the library full of rich bindings, all stamped with the Hertford crest; the faded gilt of the panellings; the tapestries where hirsute gods and rosy goddesses reclined on clouds; the heavy curtains, – all was untouched perfection of its kind, even to the exquisitely chased fastenings to the windows and differently modelled keys to every door.

On his death in 1912, Seery left Victoria £150,000 and the contents of Rue Laffitte with the intention that these precious objects should be housed at Knole. The bulk of his fortune of £1,180,000 was to be divided between his two brothers and two sisters but, despite this, the Scott family contested Seery's will, claiming that Lady Sackville had exercised 'undue influence' over Seery in his dotage. Before the case – dubbed 'The Million-Pound Lawsuit' in the press – was settled, the house on Rue Laffitte was placed under legal seal, and none of the objects within could be viewed. Nevertheless, Jacques Seligmann agreed a price for its contents sight unseen, on the basis of the sketchiest of inventories and his knowledge of the Wallace Collection, and committed to purchasing them in the event that Victoria won the case, which she did. Seligmann's gamble had paid off. His son Germain described with relief the moment

they were allowed at last to inspect the collection at 2 Rue
Laffitte. It was 'like entering Ali Baba's cave . . . All over the
floors, piled up in corners, some carefully covered with slips,
others wrapped in papers or, more often, with only a heavy
coating of dust to protect them from sight, were some of the
greatest sculptures of the eighteenth century and luxurious
pieces of furniture made for the royal family. There, rolled in a
corner, was the famous set of tapestries after cartoons by
Boucher, now in the Philadelphia Museum . . . Yonder was the
superb Houdon bust of Sophie Arnould, now in the Louvre.'

Lord Sackville on his way to court for the Scott case

As Victoria, then, was finalising her deal with Seligmann for
what was one of the finest collections of eighteenth-century French
sculpture and furniture in private hands, and planning how to
spend the proceeds, her brother lay dead on the other side of Paris
in possession of a simple bed, a few chairs and a table.

Victoria herself barely commented on her brother's suicide in her diary. 'Henry wrote for money which we sent him to help with his wife's illness and he committed suicide on the 3rd after her death, poor fellow. The papers are full of it today . . .' was the extent of her summary of recent events. She was equally taken up with the storms in Paris, the sale of her Scott inheritance and the arrival from Constantinople en route for London of the pregnant Vita and her husband Harold Nicolson. They had married the previous year and appeared so wrapped up in each other that Victoria felt barely wanted. 'Great storm in Paris yesterday,' she wrote in her diary on 16 June, 'great chasms on account of rush of water; I was very near the very place yesterday, trying to sell Napoleon's *service de campagne* . . . for £10,000.'

The next day, Victoria went to the studio of Auguste Rodin, with whom she was conducting a mildly flirtatious relationship. Here she found the great sculptor 'miserably unhappy' with his companion of fifty years, Rose Beuret. Victoria had become friends with Rodin when he visited London in May 1913, and Rodin came to Knole the following month. By November she was sitting for him in his studios in Paris and the South of France. Rodin adored the flattery – and money – of the Society beauties who sat for him, and Victoria, who always craved adulation, was equally flattered by the attentions of the seventy-four-year-old sculptor, although she had no real appreciation of his art (she frequently criticised his work, much preferring the style of the French eighteenth century – the style of the works of art in the Rue Laffitte – to the rougher, more realistic style of Rodin). Rodin compared his relationship with Victoria to that of Michelangelo and Vittoria Colonna, the Roman noblewoman to whom the great Renaissance artist had addressed some of his finest sonnets. He kept telling her how beautiful she was – '*Quelles belles épaules*', he muttered repeatedly – 'and yet the bust is perfectly hideous up to now', thought Victoria, 'I look like a fat negress with pouting lips.'

Victoria's letters to Rodin over the next few days, signed '*votre modèle*', referred to the suicide of '*un très proche parent*' and the debts he had left, but as an inconvenience among many other '*ennuis considérables*' that prevented her from spending the day with the sculptor; and she berated him for not sending a single word of sympathy on her bereavement.

The following week, Victoria was back in London, consulting the family solicitors about paying Henry's debts and the expenses of his funeral, such as they were (in July she sent £100). She instructed Pemberton not to write to the papers to contradict suggestions that she had failed to help Henry. But by July she was more preoccupied with the Scott family, who continued to create difficulties over Victoria's share of the Wallace Collection. '*Ces Scotts!*' she wrote to Rodin, '*Je les voudrais au fond de la Seine!!*'

Henry's suicide had an effect on Victoria more profound than she was prepared to admit at the time. The last entry in her diary for the year 1914 was on 5 September, and she did not take it up again until the following July. In the intervening months, she obviously suffered a nervous breakdown. In January 1915, when she first sought treatment from Dr Woods, she was, she claimed, 'depressed enough to take [her] own life'. She hated 'that horrid war' and Lionel's departure for the Dardanelles; Vita's preoccupation with her own husband and newborn baby; Harold's rudeness; the installation of Lionel's mistress, Olive Rubens, with her complaisant husband Walter, in a flat at Knole; and the 'dreadful hurricane' at Knole after Christmas, in which a tree fell on the car carrying one of their guests back to the house. But top of her list of worries had been the 'shock' and 'worry' of Henry's suicide, including the money she had paid for his expenses.

Victoria credited Dr Woods with having given her a 'new

lease of life'. By July 1915, she claimed that she now accepted 'life more or less as it comes' and was 'very much more philosophical in every way'. 'I want to be happy,' she wrote, '& radiate happiness and have "Peace within".' Any 'Peace within', however, must have involved the suppression of all memories of her brother; of the childish letters he had written her, describing how much he had cried when she left for her convent in Paris; of the shopping trips on which she took him to outfit him for a new life in South Africa; of the shared gratitude he admitted to her once that he felt towards their father; and, finally, of the furious figure glaring at her across the courtroom. And any 'Peace within' must also have come at the expense of her other siblings, of whom, after Henry's death, there is barely a mention in her voluminous correspondence or diaries.

Victims of Circumstance

After the court case, relations between Victoria and her sisters were strained to breaking-point. In less than a month, Amalia was writing to Lionel to ask whether he and Victoria intended to continue the allowance of £200 a year they had given her since 1908. Lionel replied that, at the time of her father's death, he had not been aware of the 'active part' she had played 'in helping Henry to bring his action against me and involve me in all the unnecessary expense which this lawsuit has entailed'. Under the circumstances, he continued, he must decline to make her an allowance, 'however much I regret the circumstances in which you find yourself'. Nor, as he told his friends, had he been aware at the time of the large sums of money Amalia had received from her friends for 'the express object of helping H. to pay his legal expenses'. It was, he felt, up to 'these friends to help her now that she finds herself, through her own ill-advised conduct, in such unfortunate circumstances'.

Amalia turned for assistance to her very grand first cousins: Gilbert, 8th Earl De La Warr, and Herbrand, 11th Duke of Bedford. For whatever reason – genuine concern at Amalia's near destitution, some sympathy with Henry's claim, or a desire to avoid more scandal engulfing the extended Sackville family

– the Duke of Bedford offered Amalia £200 a year, on condition she lived abroad. Amalia – unfoundedly – blamed Lionel for persuading Herbrand to make this condition, which she described as 'absolutely downright wicked'. 'It is no doubt your wife's wish to get me out of her way,' she wrote to Lionel; 'She knows it is absolutely impossible for a girl to live abroad alone without running the risk of having the worst said of her. I am fully aware knowing the hatred she bears me that such a move would be a great feather in her cap but for my father's sake I decline to afford her that pleasure.' Her letter ended with a warning: 'There will come a day when you will have to part with all your worldly possessions that you cannot prevent happening & all I pray for is when that day comes God may spare you both the punishment such cruelty deserves.' In the end, Amalia turned down the Duke's offer.

Every now and then, there would be reports, secondhand, of the sisters' slanders: a note from Flora to the newspaper proprietor Lord Northcliffe, or a heap of letters written by Amalia to the Countess de Baillet, vilifying Victoria, which somehow found their way to Victoria after the Countess's death. Victoria, on the other hand, felt that she had always treated 'that vile Amalia pretty well', having topped up her allowance and given her an extra share of Papa's insurance money after his death in 1908. Lionel was outraged, on his wife's behalf, by the fact that 'Amalia has neglected no opportunity of abusing Victoria and uttering the most abominable calumnies about her ever since, by her own wish, she left her father's house.'

Relations were further complicated by the fact that Amalia and Victoria continued to move in some of the same social circles. In May 1911, Vita and her father attended a fancy-dress ball at the Savoy Hotel in aid of Middlesex Hospital. Lionel was dressed as Thomas Sackville and Vita as an 'Orientale', while Amalia, as Victoria observed sarcastically, 'had the good taste to be there in a Spanish dancer's dress' – Victoria clearly thought that Amalia lacked judgement in drawing attention to her origins in this way. That evening, Vita 'had a curious experience with Amalia': as Vita sat down at a table reserved for the 'Hon Miss S. W.', thinking it was hers, 'a lady came up & claimed it, declaring "You are not the only one bearing that name, Vita!"' The lady turned out to be Amalia, and so Vita slunk discreetly away.

There was also some overlap between their professional circles. By a strange coincidence, several family members were among the crowd of over a thousand packed into the Galerie des Glaces in the Palace of Versailles on 28 June 1919 for the signing of the treaty which brought the First World War to an end. Amalia's first cousin, my great-uncle Charlie, was the British Military Representative to the peace conference. Amalia's niece's husband, the young diplomat Harold Nicolson was there, dressed in tails and a black slouch hat, as a member of the British delegation, and it is to him that we owe some of the most poignant descriptions of the day: the splendour of the French Republican guards, their sabres flashing as they saluted the guests, in contrast to the defeated German signatories being led from the hall 'like prisoners'. Amalia's husband-to-be, a French diplomat called William Martin, was there, too. As Keeper of the Seals, Martin was responsible for collecting, in advance, all the state seals of the signatories to the treaty and then transporting the treaty itself from the Quai d'Orsay to the Palace of Versailles.

William Martin had entered the French diplomatic service in 1888, and his personnel file is full of consistently good reports from his superiors: '*parfaite éducation*', '*excellente conduite personelle*', '*excellente caractère*' and so on. He spoke good English and Spanish, and had had postings in Lima, Belgrade, St Petersburg and Madrid, before his appointment in 1913 as Ministre Plénipotentiare Chef du Service du Protocole, Introducteur des Ambassadeurs. It was in this role, predominantly social and ceremonial, that Martin had his moment of glory, a couple of months before his marriage, in the Galerie des Glaces.

On 23 August, Harold wrote to Vita from the British delegation to the Paris Peace Conference, 'your aunt Amalia is engaged to the Chef du Protocole here – one William Martin (a French man – sort of Lord Chamberlain to the Republic). He is a dip. by profession – so one day she will be an ambassadress – & in any case she will have a big official position here. Isn't it a joke?' On hearing reports of Amalia's engagement, Victoria told Vita how lucky Amalia had been to get anyone to marry her at her 'tender age'. '*Il sera bien volé* ['he will be well and truly fleeced'], *l'âne Martin, mais c'est son affaire; & j'espère qu'il a un peu de* filthy lucre *a lui offrir.*'

Amalia and William were married in Paris at the end of August. Although the wedding was celebrated '*dans l'intimité*', according to *Le Gaulois*, the witnesses included Monsieur Stephen Pichon, the French Minister of Foreign Affairs, and Sir George Grahame, the British chargé d'affaires – a high-level diplomatic turnout reminiscent of Flora's marriage in Paris thirty years before. Victoria noted dismissively that Amalia was now fifty-one, and her husband fifty-four, and therefore, as she described it, 'no blooming virgins' – just as she had scoffed a quarter of a century before at Amalia's young 'sparks', many of whom, she claimed, were 'counter-jumpers'. It was ironic, though, that Amalia was getting married just as Victoria's own marriage was coming finally to an end. For twenty years, Victoria had turned a blind eye to her husband's affairs, but she could no longer ignore the presence in their lives of the latest, and most long-lasting, mistress, Olive Rubens. The other irony, as Harold had hinted and Victoria noted, was that there was talk of William Martin getting posted to England, in which case Amalia might 'come as Ambassadress to England! *Ce serait drôle!*'

In 1920, Martin was appointed Ambassador to Lisbon, but the humid summer climate did not suit either him or his new wife, and within months he was asking for a couple of months' leave in France. He left Lisbon for good in 1921, barely a year after taking up the post. From that point, his career rather petered out – in postings as the French delegate to various international commissions in Eastern Europe. But his ambitions – and certainly those of Amalia – were undiminished, particularly as, he told his superiors, she was the daughter of a former British ambassador and closely related to the great aristocratic, political and diplomatic dynasties of Salisbury and Derby. There were even links, through the De La Warr family, with the government of Ramsay Macdonald.

By 1924, Martin was begging for an appointment to crown his career – Spain, perhaps, which he knew very well; England, where his wife was well connected, he claimed, and tirelessly promoted France's interests in conversation with prominent '*hommes politiques*'; or the United States, where Amalia had spent several years as the daughter of the British Minister. Poor William Martin certainly did not want to retire at sixty, but in the end he had to settle with being made a Grand Officier de la Légion d'Honneur in 1925, and a pension of 12,000 francs a year. For the rest of their life together, he and his wife lived in genteel poverty.

Many of these years were spent in East Kent: at first, tucked away among the woods near the church in Doddington, in a one-storey lodge with Gothic windows; then in the village of Lyminge. The writer Sir Sacheverell Sitwell recalled meeting Amalia in the Lord Warden Hotel in Dover, where she was staying between houses, in the late 1920s. He had not seen her since he was a boy in the early 1900s, when Amalia, whom he remembered as 'very Spanish and very charming', used to stay at Renishaw Hall in Derbyshire with his mother Ida. Amalia was at the hotel with

her husband, 'a very distinguished old Frenchman with beautiful manners', and told Sitwell that she had come to live
there 'because it was near Knole, which had been her home'.
Sitwell had found this 'very pathetic', and Amalia 'the victim
of circumstances over which she had no control'.

Amalia nursed her resentments into old age. In December
1934, she wrote to her brother Max, after a long silence, thanking him for his letter and for sending a photograph of himself
(which resembled their father so closely that at first she thought
it was him). 'We were waiting for each other to write,' she
began, before embarking on her version of the past. 'O! dearest
brother what tragedy lies behind all this . . .' She recalled the
day in 1896 when her father received Henry's letter, asking for
his legitimacy to be recognised. She had been alone with her
father at Knole – and 'that awful woman Victoria was away
with her husband on a shooting visit'. 'Father turned deathly
pale & handed me the letter saying: "I am in a fine hole".'
Although she had persuaded her father to write 'a nice, kind
letter' to Henry, he changed his mind as soon as he had done
so, claiming that he could not send it 'without Victoria seeing
it'. At that moment, Amalia had immediately known that 'all
was up & that the most terrible case was in front of us'.

In Amalia's skewed version, Victoria was not their father's
child at all, but simply the '*fille de père inconnu*' her baptism
certificate described her as – '& in that lies all the vengeance,
cruelty & revenge of that woman'. Victoria, Amalia continued,
'knew she was <u>nothing</u> & she was determined to be something'
– specifically, Lady Sackville. But 'what <u>she is no one knows</u>':
she had not been brought up with the others, and had been
sent off to the convent when their mother died; and yet, she
'had a terrific influence over father. He could do nothing or say
nothing without consulting her. He was terrified of her.' 'I now
understand why,' she added darkly. The judgement in Henry's
case had been a 'blot on English justice'. And if ever the papers,

proving Pepita's marriage to their father, fell into her hands, Amalia promised, she would reopen the case, 'shattering to pieces that <u>infernal plot</u>'. Their father, 'cowed by that woman', may have behaved 'shamefully' and 'wickedly', but had he lived, she argued, and been put in the witness box, he would have told the truth.

At the very least, their mother's honour would have been spared. Amalia reassured Max how loved and respected Pepita had been in Arcachon, and told him that she had paid for their mother's coffin not to be disinterred, and for a woman to tend the burial plot. As for Victoria, 'where is she now, some say shut up, mad others say. She is queer & sees no one. I don't know & I don't care.' Amalia herself, on the other hand, was 'happily married not rich but holding my position all the same & Willie is beloved by all his "*collègues*", he is retired, pensioned off & alas! the pension is small but better than nothing'. Most important of all, 'I have proved by my marriage to the world we are legitimate because had I not been so I could not have married Willie his position was too great. I have done that woman [Victoria] in the eye & when she read in the papers I had been at a banquet at Buckingham Palace & received by the King & Queen she must have had a fit . . . O! the tragedy of it all dearest brother but O! the victory I have had over that woman.'

There is the most tantalising reference in this letter of 1934 to another of the 'victims of a woman's ambition': the middle sister. 'Poor Flora,' wrote Amalia, 'died 9 years ago in abject poverty she had gone to the bad, I tried to save her but it was no good, she left a son who is not much I am afraid, her husband is still alive but no one sees him, he behaved so badly to her etc.'

After the collapse of Henry's court case, Flora at the age of forty-four had gone on the stage. 'She has already made her debut in Paris,' reported the *Daily Mirror*, 'where, dancing in bare feet, she had a wonderful reception.' Amalia was quoted on Flora's lessons in Paris with Professor Teresa Cerutti, 'who is undoubtedly the leading exponent in France of what is known as the "mimed" dance', in which the dancer 'expresses different emotions and incidents'. Amalia went on to tell the papers how she, too, proposed to go on the stage very shortly, making a pointed reference to Pepita's legacy: 'You see, the stage is in our blood – that part, at least, of our inheritance is undeniable. It is now absolutely essential that we should earn our living, for the expenses of recent litigation have left us practically destitute.'

Towards the end of 1910, Flora moved from Paris to London to try her luck there. She had a little postcard printed of a pencil drawing of herself, her eyes half-closed, a smile on her lips, and a wreath of roses haloing her head and blooming on her breast. 'The Honourable Miss Sackville West', it is captioned, beneath a Sackville coat of arms floating in the top left-hand corner. The serenity of the image belies her state of mind that Christmas. What we know about her movements and her mood comes from a correspondence with a Monsieur Vidal, with whom she had recently embarked on a relationship that was partly professional – he was, purportedly, her manager, her '*tyran au théâtre*' – and partly something more, a man whom she wanted to become her '*grand ami*'. As so often in Flora's letters, the tone is rather desperate, full of '*le spleen*', as she traipses for auditions from theatre to theatre, several of them fairly small and some distance from the centre of town. She even considered, in an attempt to win sympathy, offering her services for free at a charity concert in aid of the families of miners killed in the terrible Pretoria Pit explosion in Lancashire in December 1910. She began to despair of ever finding in London someone who could sing in French to accompany her dancing – to recruit a singer from France would cost too much money. She was worried, as a result, that she would have to cancel her audition with the great theatre manager, Alfred Butt.

A postcard of Flora, 'The Honorable Miss Sackville West'

At this time, Flora felt that the world was against her. Her brother Henry was no help: he had disappeared for the time being and, according to Flora, needed to pull himself together after the failure of his lawsuit. She was also concerned about what the Sackvilles and their lawyers might be up to, convinced that she was under surveillance by a private investigator. Suffering from a terrible cold, and constantly racked by bouts of crying which left her feeling drained of energy, she was all alone in a deserted capital. '*Tout est mort*,' she wrote to Vidal: it must be the English way of celebrating Christmas. She was also very discouraged by Vidal's distance and apparent indifference. He had not sent her any money in order to help her stage her act – money for the set, props and accompanist, and for her accommodation at the Hôtel Metropole – but she also felt let down by him as a friend. It 'only goes to show,' she wrote, 'that you can't rely on anyone in this world . . . What a dreadful thing life is for those with no luck.'

In January, Flora was shown an article in a small English paper about a woman who had announced her imminent debut on the English stage under the assumed name of an old English family, claiming she was the daughter of a peer. The source of the story had not dared to name the woman or the family, but Flora naturally suspected that the story had been placed by the Sackvilles (possibly through an intermediary, the journalist Basil Tozer, whom Flora later threatened to sue) in an attempt to distance themselves from the shame of Flora's debut.

In March 1911, Flora made her English debut at the London Palladium. The Palladium had opened on Boxing Day 1910, just a few months before, to provide a new style of entertainment for the middle classes: entertainment that was popular – there was seating for up to 3,000 people – and yet also contained elements more 'cultured' than the staple music-hall fare. A typical 'variety' bill of a dozen acts might include Cockney comedians and circus performers – jugglers, tightrope walkers, tumblers and so on – as well as scenes from Shakespeare, potted versions of opera, and 'ballets divertissements'.

In a cultural sense, then, Flora's divertissement in *La Danse des Fleurs* followed in her mother's dainty footsteps. *The Playgoer and Society Illustrated* noted 'Flora Sackville West's sensational Oriental dancing fantasy . . . The whole of the fantasy has been arranged by the artist herself, while the exquisite music is specially composed by Mlle Jeanne Vieu, the celebrated French composer.' According to the *Observer*, her performance 'proved to be quite pleasing, although it was not marked by any high development of terpsichorean skill. What Miss West had to do was to pose as the Houri of an Arab Prince's dreams, and this she did very prettily if with hardly sufficient technical accomplishment to provide the title with a raison d'être.' The papers also noted her aristocratic connections. The *New York Times*, in April that year, published a photograph of the beautiful Flora, dressed exotically, under the headline 'Peer's Daughter as a Dancer'.

Peer's Daughter as a Dancer.

Flora as an 'houri'

Victoria was staying in the South of France when she read of Flora's debut. 'What a worry!' she wrote in her diary, although she did concede that 'the Harem skirt' which Flora was wearing was considerably 'better than the thin gauze she first intended to wear!' Two weeks later, pictures of Flora dancing at the Palladium appeared in the *Sketch* and made Victoria 'boil with indignation. She has no shame!'

The following year, according to a notice in *The Times* in February 1912, Flora and a Mlle Phine de Nocker were performing a series of six '*causeries littéraires musicales et dansées*' at Marble Arch House, in London, illustrating 'song and dance in many countries and ages'; the first subject was to be 'Athens and the Athenians', followed in subsequent weeks by the song and dance of 'The Directoire, Ancient Egypt', and 'Japan and the geishas'. They took a version of their show to Spain a couple of months later, as Flora hoped to launch her career in the homeland of her mother. A sympathetic interviewer from the

Heraldo de Madrid was very taken with Flora on the day before her debut at the Trianon Palace in April, and even more taken with Phine de Nocker who sang, out of sight, while Flora mimed her Persian, Bohemian and Greek dances on stage; the interviewer thought this was a great shame, as he would have liked to see more of Mlle Phine's beautiful, mysterious eyes. The interview appeared in a regular column, appropriately entitled 'Las Luchas por La Vida' ('Fighting for Life'), and Flora described her struggle to be recognised as legitimate, how she, a peer's daughter, had been forced to earn her living on the stage. She referred to the case she had recently brought against her sister Victoria and her brother-in-law Lionel for defamation – presumably, for circulating those stories that she was a mere fortune-hunter, capitalising on the family name.

After that, references to Flora are patchy: a note in the records of the High Court that Flora had changed solicitors in her case against the Sackvilles, but no reference to its outcome; a letter from Lionel to Victoria celebrating some clever 'move' by Pemberton that had dealt with Flora for good; a photograph, dated 1912, of a semi-clothed, bosomy Flora, her dress parted provocatively at the top of the thigh, that suggests she had succeeded in her threat to the family to 'go to the bad'.

Other than that, Flora's trail goes frustratingly cold. There is nothing in Victoria's diaries, no letters, no further newspaper reports, no court records to cast their cynical slant on a person's life. But sometimes, perhaps, the gaps, the silences, and the disappearances are as revealing and resounding as the written record. The next reference to Flora is the sentence in Amalia's letter to Max, implying that she died around 1925. I had hoped to find her through the surviving members of her family. Her daughter Elie had died tragically young, but what became of Lionel Salanson, the solemn little boy who had come to stay at Knole two summers running in the 1890s, who had played so sweetly with his cousin Vita that she cried when it was time to go

Flora poses in 1912

to bed? Even old Lord Sackville, so bleak and reserved in his dealings with grown-ups, had looked on indulgently as his two grandchildren struggled to play croquet or to converse in French.

After his parents' divorce, Lionel Salanson had been consigned to the custody of his father, Gabriel. He was called up soon after the outbreak of the First World War and served as a cavalry officer before being seconded to an air squadron in the Somme as a spotter. Reports in his military dossier praised him regularly as an energetic and conscientious '*observateur*', '*plein d'allant*' and '*plein de sang froid*', flying on many photographic missions over enemy lines in bad weather and under attack from German planes. He was Mentioned in Dispatches on two occasions in 1916, and was awarded the Croix de Guerre. Photographs of him around this time show a swarthy, stocky young man, standing beside a boxy biplane in a muddy airfield in the Somme. Something in his direct gaze and the slightly sardonic downward twist to his mouth recalls the blustering swagger of his father and the dark smoulder of his mother.

Flora's son, Lionel Salanson (*middle row, third from left*), on the Somme in 1916

In 1917, Lionel formally transferred to the fledgling airforce (the Aéronautique Militaire) and began training as a pilot in Chartres. But a plane crash during training in April, in which he badly injured his arm, rendered him '*inapte à tout service de Guerre*'. It was suggested, instead, that he might put his excellent knowledge of Russian to good use and act as an interpreter. And so, in September 1918, he was sent on a mission to Siberia to help train Czech pilots who had joined the fight against the Bolsheviks in the Russian Civil War. After catching typhus and dysentery in Vladivostok, he was demobilised in 1919, after which his movements, like those of his mother, become hard to follow.

In 1920 he was drafted into the 34 Régiment d'Aviation as a reservist, and in 1925 he married Odette Derminot and went to live in Avoine in the Loire, joining his father there as a wine-grower. Gabriel died in Avoine in 1935, but Lionel stayed on as a '*propriétaire viticulteur*'. What little we know about him now comes from his military dossier. In 1937, as France seemed yet again in peril, Lionel wrote to the military authorities asking to be accepted back as an officer in the reserves of L'Armée de l'Air. His application was rejected on the grounds that, in 1927, he had been dismissed, and stripped of his rank as a reserve officer, for having failed to notify the authorities of a change of address and thereby made himself unavailable for service for well over a year. Police searches to trace him at various addresses in Paris and Sèvres in 1925 had been unsuccessful.

Having served throughout the First World War with some distinction, Lionel found all this very painful, and wrote that he would be only too happy to place on record the testimonials of his comrades from the French front and Siberia. Nevertheless, the authorities ruled on appeal that because he had been in L'Aéronautique for only two years, and because he had shown no interest '*aérien ou militaire*' since then, and because of his age (he was now forty-seven), he could not rejoin the reserves. He should consider applying, instead, to rejoin the cavalry, '*son arme d'origine*'.

There is no record that Lionel Salanson had children, and so, with his death in 1954, the last of Flora's lineage was laid to rest. Like Flora, Victoria had only one child – Vita – and neither Amalia nor Henry had any. It was Max and his descendants who multiplied.

Over the two decades before the court case, Max had suffered a series of calamities in South Africa. His fine, thoroughbred herd of cattle had been carried off by the rinderpest in the 1890s, and by 1899 he was bankrupt. His eldest son Lionel had died suddenly the same year. It was a tribute to his general equanimity, and to the love of his family, that he had been as supportive of the Sackvilles as he was in the run-up to the case.

He had known all along, he wrote, that the inheritance would go to his brother-in-law in the ordinary course of events, but he had never borne them a grudge for it.

Although Max's life was never quite deranged by bitterness in the way that the lives of his siblings had been, there were, of course, complaints. In 1924, when he was discharged from his bankruptcy, he sued Cracroft Nourse and Edward Greene for mismanaging the trust established for his benefit in the 1880s, and in particular for a disastrous investment in a hotel in Pietermaritzburg. After the forced sale of Max's farm in 1899, his trustees had invested £2,000 – two-thirds of the proceeds – in the Camden Hotel. Although this appeared a reasonable investment when run by its original proprietor for a principally military clientele, the business suffered after the end of the Boer War in 1902 and the death of the owner in 1905 (his widow had no experience of the business). In 1908 the trustees decided to take on the mortgage and manage the business themselves. They made advance payments to Max on account, in lieu of interest, but by 1912 were unable to continue doing even that. Max was too poor at this stage to take legal advice.

Max and Mary in South Africa with their granddaughter Daphne's son, Vere

When he heard from his friend Mr Kufal, in October 1912, that the Camden had gone 'cronk', Max wrote to Colonel Greene to register his concerns: the interest payments had stopped, and the underlying value of the investment had slumped with the Pietermaritzburg property market. Max and his wife continued to feel that they were being kept in the dark, as the trustees vainly 'nursed' their investment back to health. 'When they found that they could not put things right, and no wonder for a worse investment you could not think of, then they had to let the cat out of the bag.' In 1923, the trustees sold the hotel for less than their original investment. The trustees did, however, use the balance of the original proceeds from the farm, around £1,000, to purchase a house in Pietermaritzburg called Fairview for the couple in 1917.

'Trust funds have no business to be invested in an hotel,' Max had written to Colonel Greene's solicitors in 1923.

> Hotels are always going smash, changing hands, and are places where everything depends upon the management. You could not have a worse security. And the proof of the pudding is in the eating! . . . What a difference it would have made to my life, during the last 11 years, if I had received what was due to me. We have had to live on £100 a year, the miserable pittance that Lord Sackville allows me. Out of this we have had to feed, clothe ourselves (three persons!) and educate our daughter.

'I have consulted my son, and my wife and children,' he concluded, 'are all agreed that if this request is treated in the same manner as the previous ones we shall have to move the Court, and place the whole thing before it, as the attitude displayed towards me is tantamount to persecution.' The solicitors wrote back, stating that they were 'sick and tired of receiving letters from you couched in the terms of the one under reply', and denying his charges.

Max was very bitter towards Colonel Greene, but blamed the other trustees far less. As he wrote to his friend 'Cra' Nourse:

> all I can say is that Greene has led me the life of Hell. I have no words to describe to you the depth of misery and destitution to which Greene has condemned me. I have been deprived of all means of livelihood for the last 11 years, and had it not been for the little remittance from England, we should have absolutely starved. I am afraid my poor father little knew what stone he was tying round my neck when he created that Trust. I am sure I could have arranged my affairs a long way better than Mr Greene. I tell you I have had a life that a kaffir would curl his lip at: and Greene, out of sheer spite, seems to have taken a fiendish delight in 'rubbing it in'.

When the case came to trial, the court eventually awarded Max damages of £640 for unpaid interest, with costs. In 1931, Max, by now in his seventies, was back in court, this time suing his wife Mary and son Guy, who had replaced Greene and Nourse as trustees, for using Max's trust funds of around £1,800 to build a house in Pietermaritzburg – with Max's knowledge and consent – but failing to provide adequate accounts. Some of the money, Max claimed, had been used without his permission to pay Guy's personal debts.

The fact that Max shared the Sackville tendency to litigiousness has probably skewed the emphasis of his family story. The survival of court records and legal depositions from Max's lawsuits in 1924 and 1931 tended to bring out the drama of personal conflict, and to ignore the humdrum contentments of everyday life, the satisfaction Max got from his knowledge of Jersey cows or from his beloved daughters, Vivian – with her large and flourishing family – and Ruth.

Seen through the prism of the court records, the story of Max's son Guy's life is similarly one-sided. In 1925, after his first wife Therese had left him, Guy installed his two daughters, aged four and seven, in the care of a housekeeper, Mrs Grier, in a house on the coast, while he commuted to his job as a clerk in the Office of the Registrar of Deeds in Pietermaritzburg. Over the summer, complaints that Guy and Mrs Grier (who often called herself 'Mrs West') mistreated the girls came to the notice of the Child Welfare Society. Mrs Grier, already known to the society as an undesirable character ('not suitable either morally or physically to have the care of young children') would thrash the girls on the hands and legs with sticks and brushes. The society asked the authorities to investigate, but there was insufficient evidence for the police to proceed.

© Nicolson family

Guy Sackville West

Life for the two girls became even more miserable after Guy married a woman called Daisy in 1928. That year, the elder daughter, Zelda, who had long been described as 'of doubtful intellect' was committed to an 'institution for the feebleminded' in Cape Town. And two years later, Guy applied for his nine-year-old daughter Carmen to be committed to an institution, too, 'where she will be under proper supervision'. 'The child is out of control,' he wrote; 'She cannot be trusted to go anywhere alone.' Carmen had been sent to several schools in Pietermaritzburg 'to see if she would improve, but she appears to have made up her mind not to submit to any discipline'. She had been sent, soon after Guy's second marriage, to stay with his octogenarian grandmother, 'Granny Norton', at Greytown, but returned a few months later as she was found to be unmanageable. Part of the problem lay in the tension between Carmen and Daisy. Despite a series of whippings, Guy wrote, 'the child is disobedient and defiant to her step-mother'. There were also reports 'that the child had misconducted herself with a boy at school'.

The Child Welfare Society supported Guy's application, confirming that Carmen had had a very unsettled childhood, that she was thrashed at home by her stepmother, and that her father and stepmother did not live in harmony. 'I am of the opinion,' their officer concluded, 'that a committal to an Institution where there is proper discipline will benefit the child. I consider that the step-mother will never do anything with this child; she illtreats the child, and I have personally seen marks on the child which were the result of a severe thrashing.' As a result, Carmen, like her sister, was sent to an institution on the other side of the country, the House of Bethany, in Cape Town. It was not until 1932 that Therese learned the fate of her two daughters. By now she was settled and financially secure with a new husband, Mr Butler-Deane, and applied for custody of Carmen. Now that she was displaying 'a keen and satisfactory interest in her child, visiting her regularly and furnishing her daughter with a musical education', that her 'domestic life and social surroundings' were eminently respectable, and 'that little interest has been displayed towards the child by her father Mr Sackville West', it was decided that Carmen should be released from the House of Bethany in 1937 into her mother's care.

Guy was a poor husband and father, and by 1932 he was having trouble with Daisy, with whom he had two young sons, Cecil and Reginald. Once again, he applied to the Child Welfare Society for an order placing the boys in care. 'I have had serious differences with my wife,' he wrote, which 'culminated this morning in . . . my wife in a rage throwing plates at my head & I left the house . . . I know that she will not properly care for the children but leave them for long periods in the care of Natives & I ask that they be placed at the Peter Davis House in the care of the Child Welfare Society.' Had this application been successful, it would have resulted in all four of Guy's children being in care. (When I mentioned this to Adam Nicolson, the grandson of Guy's first cousin Vita – expecting him to be taken aback by the contrasts in the lifestyles of the different branches of the family – Adam only half-jokingly compared the standard of parenting to Vita's own care of her sons, Nigel and Ben.)

The Child Welfare Society did not feel there was enough evidence to warrant the removal of the boys; and the magistrate pointed out, furthermore, that since Guy already had 'two other children in Institutions in the Union' and that he was heavily in arrears with the payment for their maintenance, it would be very unusual for more of his children to be admitted to homes.

On several occasions in the 1930s, Guy brought actions for divorce – later withdrawn – against Daisy on the grounds of her adultery and violent behaviour towards him. At stake was the custody of his sons. In a letter to the magistrate in November 1932, he claimed that his now-estranged wife was a 'woman of immoral habits and that four nights last week she did not

return to her room until midnight'. Surely, he wrote, this justi-
fied him in 'pressing for the custody of these children from a
woman who does not care a straw what happens to them!' He
had also heard that the children, who were living with Daisy,
had had only one bath that month. 'All this can only have had
a bad effect on their health and, in after years, they will probably suffer. Besides, Mrs West's language is dreadful and the
children, who are both talking, are picking up bad words. The
influence which Mrs West has over them is of a poisonous
nature and the children ought to be removed and placed into
respectable quarters. The whole affair,' he concluded, 'is too
squalid for words.'

Cecil and Reginald had a miserable childhood, fought over
– but neglected at the same time – by their parents. As a result,
the boys spent much of their time at boarding school. Cecil
eventually worked on the South African railways as a fitter, and
lost contact with Reginald, who emigrated, it is thought, to
Canada. Until his death in 2009, Cecil was the last known
surviving grandchild of Max to bear the name Sackville West.
After her death, photographs of Guy and Reginald were found
tucked away in a drawer in Vita's study at Sissinghurst, where
they must have lingered for decades without explanation or
acknowledgement.

Guy's story is a shabby postscript to his father's story: an
illustration of the very different trajectories that applied either
side of the succession struggle. Vita's first cousins included, on
the one side, the 'illegitimate' side, the hapless Guy and the
elusive Lionel Salanson; and on the other, 'legitimate' side,
completely oblivious of the other branch, two future Lord
Sackvilles and inheritors of Knole.

Slaving Away at Knole for Nothing

The month after Henry's suicide, as Victoria sunk into a depression that would last well into the following year, she wrote in her diary: 'I have slaved away at Knole to keep everything together & I get no help or kindness from Lionel. These eternal pin-pricks & difficulties & his eternal flirtations and love affairs making life extremely unpleasant, especially now that my Vita is married & naturally away so much. What am I to do eventually? I feel so ill. How long can I stand it?'

She had already started to think of buying herself a bolt-hole. But even this was not without its humiliations. When Lionel asked her what she planned to call the house she was proposing to buy in Hampstead, she replied, 'Sackville House, of course!' 'And why?' he asked. 'Because it is my name.' 'No! it is not; it is mine,' he insisted.

Victoria's husband was beginning to deny her the name that was hers by birth and by marriage in much the same way as she in the past had attempted to deny it to her siblings. To Victoria, who had been particularly sensitive on this subject ever since childhood, it was as if her husband was taunting her with her illegitimacy.

In contrast to Lionel's plea to his wife a quarter of a century before to remember 'this is your house, Vicky', Victoria was being progressively eased out of Knole. She was being forced to confront the spectre, in the longer term, of her own disinheritance. Her brother-in-law Charlie was already making his expectations clear, writing 'a very pompous letter' in 1918, to advise Lionel and Victoria not to sell any more heirlooms. 'Poor Charlie!' Victoria noted. 'He used to be so nice!' And on a visit to Knole, Victoria's nephew, Eddy, at this stage a precocious teenager, stated his intention of altering the Orangery at Knole when he became the owner. 'He speaks quite freely about being here!' Victoria noted.

Her frustration reached such a point that, on 23 November 1917, she devoted a separate entry in her diary to her many resentments: 'I feel so much like leaving my home tonight and yet restraining my offended feelings, that I must put it to paper, as some relaxation for my misery.' That very evening Lionel had been rude to her in front of Olive Rubens. Cheerful, warm-hearted and gentle – the temperamental antithesis of Victoria – Olive had at first been treated as a family friend by Victoria, who encouraged her confidences in much the same way she had those of her husband's other lovers. But by the end of 1917, Victoria's tolerance was strained. Olive had been staying at Knole for the past month while Lionel was home on leave (occupying a room, at his insistence, right below his and connected to it by a private staircase). During dinner, Lionel was 'full of *petites attentions* for Olive, even offering to share a pear with her, and it is a fruit he <u>never</u> eats'. He then proceeded to speak slightingly of Victoria's friends, particularly those with an artistic bent, such as Edward Knoblock and Osbert Sitwell.

What's more, he had stopped consulting Victoria about the rearrangement of certain rooms: 'Formerly, he never moved a table without consulting me. Now, his mistress does what she likes.' Particularly hurtful was the removal from his bedroom, in deference to Olive, of the two photographs of Victoria aged four and twenty-three, which had been hanging there since

1889, and which were now left lying around on the floor in the passage outside. Victoria was feeling so unwanted, like 'an unpaid housekeeper', that were it not for her social position and her 'duty to Knole', she 'should gladly go'. 'Married life under these circumstances even in a magnificent house, is miserable work. I feel absolutely miserably unhappy and I want to go away miles & miles from Knole and put some great barrier between him and me. *A quoi bon* to struggle on,' she asked herself, when all that she could see was 'a long vista of years with that misery ahead'.

In a letter to Vita, written years later, Victoria wondered how she could have put up with Olive being such a regular visitor to Knole, often in the company of her husband, Walter, and all 'that scale-singing that went on for hours in the Court, when I was still in bed' (Olive was a singer by profession). By 1918, Walter was ill with tuberculosis (he died two years later),

Lionel in the Stone Court at Knole, with his two grandsons, Ben (*left*) and baby Nigel

and Victoria had his room disinfected every time he left Knole, for fear that her grandsons, Nigel and Ben, would catch it. There were fresh suggestions that the Rubenses should be installed in a flat in the Green Court, with Walter becoming manager of a tapestry-weaving firm based in the Stables. One of the other Knole properties suggested was the former School House, in the nearby village of Godden Green. When Victoria went over to view it in the spring of 1919, she suffered '*un serrement de coeur*' to see 'la Maîtresse' about to be installed so close. '*Enfin! il me faut prendre mon parti et tâche de tout comprendre et de tout pardonner . . .*'

As she entered her fifties, Victoria was being relieved of her roles as wife, mother and chatelaine of Knole by her husband's heirs and by his mistress. She also felt that she was being edged out of family events, including my own father's christening in March 1919. She had asked Olive 'point blank' not to attend, 'as she was not a relation', but Olive went all the same. 'It is too bad of L. and O. as they know how much I mind the Aunts gossiping and all the neighbours seeing her at the party. Still, I won't make a row. *A quoi bon*,' she concluded resignedly.

The following month, Victoria arrived at Knole unexpectedly one Saturday afternoon, and discovered Lionel and Olive in each other's arms, kissing under one of the tulip trees in the garden, 'just like any soldier and his girl in the Park . . . an occupation [that] was not much in accord with their both saying to me that their friendship was purely platonic'. On 17 May, when Lionel had ignored her request not to have the Rubenses to stay the following week (on the grounds that Walter was so infectious), Victoria finally decided to leave Knole. Lionel, she thought, ought to have considered 'his wife's wishes in her own home, where she has done <u>so</u> much & where I was absolute mistress for 20 years, till Papa died . . . I am really too unhappy here since the evil day that he fell in love with Olive, who has unconsciously changed him.'

The final insult had been finding them under the tulip tree. 'Oh! The misery and the humiliation of these 6 years! I love Knole & the possession of the finest place in England. It was so uncomfortable & different when I went there in 1889 & I have made it so comfy and brought it back to healthy life like if it had been a sick child. But I am so unhappy with L. & his systematic treatment of me, that I had better go. And I shall go on Monday.' On Monday, escorted by her friend, the architect Sir Edwin Lutyens, she duly left her 'beautiful and beloved Knole'. Victoria believed that after her departure, 'poor old Knole [was] doomed henceforth'.

Victoria found a fleeting visit to the house on 13 August, in order to pack her possessions, 'most painful': 'I simply could not go near the garden or in any of the rooms except my bedroom.' Some of the servants told her that 'Knole is lifeless and quite dead without me, that I have made, by my absence, all the difference in the world . . . I left my beautiful Knole without looking back once. I had to harden my heart & I feel more than ever that this chapter of my life is closed.'

It wasn't. For Victoria had already established, through the family solicitors, that she could go to Knole whenever she liked. On another occasion, as she described to Vita, she

spent a dreadfully sad afternoon at Knole of which I took final farewell. I don't think I shall ever go there again. I was stupid enough to feel a *serrement de coeur* when I passed through the dining room, to see one solitary place. But then I remembered, as a palliative, all the *méchancetés* and deep wounds I had received and I [went] on in to the old French Library and that part of the house where I had lived since 1889. Going through my clothes was also very painful; finding the dress he proposed to me in, and my wedding dress and orange blossoms. Well, let us draw a veil over all this, child.

She did not like the way changes were being made to the decoration of particular rooms, finding the reception rooms, and especially the Colonnade, 'very stiff'. She heard that Lionel had told Harold he was 'glad that Knole was his at last & he could do what he liked there! (as if I had ever prevented him to do so!)'

Although returning to look at her old belongings made her feel 'like a ghost', Victoria kept going back to make lists of things to take with her to the house she had bought in Brighton. Each time, she insisted that she would never spoil the rooms of 'my dear old Knole' by taking away too much, and hinted that this visit would be her last. She even suggested, a couple of years later, taking Knole for a couple of months every summer, while Lionel was away shooting and fishing. 'If Lionel refuses,' she argued, 'he puts himself in the wrong as I have done nothing to deserve that my dear old house should be shut from me altogether.' But Lionel, as she had probably anticipated, obligingly put himself in the wrong by not taking her up on the offer, since two months a year was not long enough; he wanted a full-time tenant.

Knole has always inspired a sense of ownership in its inhabitants, however transient their stay. This has often taken the form of a competition for the person who loves and understands it the best, or whose legacy is most enduring. Now that Victoria had left the house, the struggle to establish – or erase – her legacy was on. She had been helping the American Charles Phillips with his two-volume history of Knole and the Sackvilles. In 1920, Mr Phillips told Victoria that when he had shown her husband a draft of the last chapters of his book, describing Victoria's installation of electric lighting and bathrooms at Knole, Lionel had simply crossed through those passages with his pencil. 'How petty!' Victoria complained. 'I am part of the history of Knole, having lived there 31 years and having done a lot for Knole in every way.'

She returned to this theme in the 'Book of Happy Reminiscences for My Old Age' that she added to her journals on 23 September 1922, her sixtieth birthday. She recalled, for example, the first delightful years of her marriage, when she drank 'at the Cup of real Love till I felt absolutely intoxicated . . . I have had the most perfect happiness with Lionel that any woman may wish for or expect from a man, being her husband or her Lover. He was both to me during those ten years.' But the other source of great happiness in her life had been Knole. She had inherited from her mother, she wrote, her 'love of beautiful things and of great comfort' and then 'had a fine field to work upon at Knole'. Her husband may have wished her contribution to be forgotten, but she described how she had 'made Knole the most comfortable large house in England, uniting the beauties of Windsor Castle with the comforts of the Ritz and I never spoilt the old character of Knole'.

Reflecting many years later on the different ways in which she and her parents related to Knole, Vita perfectly captured her mother's legacy. For Vita, love of her birthplace 'transcended' her love 'for any human being'. Her mother, however, never 'felt like that about Knole; not quite; not as my father did. She never got its values right; one could not have expected that of her. She was too Latin, somehow; too unreal; too fantastic altogether; too un-English. She exploited it for the wrong reasons; invented stories which were really not necessary to enhance the authentic legend. But still, it was her home, and in her own way she added her own legend to its grey historic walls.' Although Victoria made Vita and her father clench their fists in silence whenever she talked about Knole, Vita could now see that 'she contributed beauty to it in her own way, and influenced people, and showed them beauty in a way which mightn't be truthful, and mightn't be ours, but which was certainly her own, and was not the less gracious for that'.

At the time of leaving Knole, Victoria was still an attractive woman, with the smoothest of complexions. Like her mother, Pepita, she had grown rather fat – she was particularly fond of pâté de foie gras, steak with sauce béarnaise, soufflés, fine clarets, and always a glass or two of Château d'Yquem to round things off – but she disguised her *embonpoint* with her stylish choice of clothing. As her daughter's lover Violet Keppel recalled, 'her voluminous, ambiguous body was upholstered, rather than dressed, in what appeared to be an assortment of pattens, lace, brocades, velvets, taffetas'. There was always something exotic – foreign – about her, for she never lost her French accent or was fully assimilated into English society. The other thing people always remembered about her was the perfume she wore, leaving a trail around the house of essence of violet or heliotrope ordered from Paris. But what they remembered most, of course, was her charm – albeit manipulative. 'I must get my friends moulded in my way or else I can't get on with them,' she wrote in her diary. Vita recalled a friend of hers who had compared her to a 'powerful dynamo generating nothing'. The problem was 'there was no driving-belt attached to her whirling wheels'.

Victoria's idiosyncratic taste extended to her houses, too. Like Pepita, she had a passion for acquiring and renovating properties. She had bought her first bolt-hole in Brighton in 1918, 'an impossible barrack' in Sussex Square, according to Vita, consisting of three houses knocked into one. The result, after spending £50,000, was 'a great echoing mausoleum of a house', with twenty-four bedrooms. She also owned two houses in London, the Hill Street property she and Lionel had bought with Seery's help, and a house in Ebury Street she had bought for Vita and Harold. By 1923, she was tiring of her Brighton house, and bought a smaller villa, White Lodge, on the cliffs overlooking the English Channel at nearby Roedean, and commissioned Edwin Lutyens to remodel it.

There was even what Vita described as a 'short but unfortunate period', in 1929, when she owned a house in Streatham, 'a singularly hideous villa of yellow brick, which for some reason she said was like an Italian palazzo'. For all her taste in interior decoration, Victoria never shared her daughter's horticultural expertise. When Vita was coming to lunch with her one day in the Streatham palazzo, Victoria realised that the garden looked a little bare – so she simply planted £30 of artificial flowers in order to 'buck' things up.

Victoria remotely monitored the comings and goings at Knole from her clifftop villa, furious, for example, to hear that Olive had sat in the front row of the Great Hall at a concert put on for the estate staff: 'It is too bad of Olive to appear brazenly before all the servants and workpeople of our Estate, & bad of Lionel to ask her or sanction her.' Nevertheless, she continued to refuse Lionel a divorce (he had even threatened to cite Lutyens as co-respondent). She did not want the 'fine' family name being dragged yet again through the scandal of a court case. But more than that, she simply could not contemplate having 'that woman at Knole in my place . . . indeed <u>NO</u> to that terrible and quite unnecessary humiliation of that <u>snake in the grass</u> in my place at Knole'. 'Olive,' she wrote to Vita, 'is not the proper person to be at Knole'; it made Victoria 'sick' to think that it could have been a gardener, rather than her, who had come upon Lionel and Olive in that dreadful compromising position in the garden. It was only because they had begged her to avoid a scandal that she had not left that very night. 'I left soon after, though!' And although it was she who had left, Victoria always felt that she had been driven away from the home in which she had lived first with her father and then with her husband for the past three decades: 'yes, it was <u>my</u> home and I had done all I could for it . . .'

On a visit to Penshurst in 1922, Lizzie de Lisle told Victoria how much everybody wanted her to return to Knole, and asked her if she could not forgive Lionel. 'I said it was not a case of forgiving him,' Victoria replied, 'but that he did not want me, and I had just read some of Vita's book on Knole (which she will publish in the autumn) and every Sackville had always dismissed peremptorily his wife or his mistress, and alas Lionel was no exception.'

———

When Lionel and 'the bountiful womanly Mrs Rubens' came to play tennis at Long Barn, where Virginia Woolf was staying with Vita in 1927, Woolf described my great-uncle: 'He is a smooth worn man, inheriting noble nose & chin which he has not put much into himself; a straight young-looking man, save that his face has the lack lustre of a weak man whose life has proved too much for him . . . I found him smooth and ambling as a blood horse, but obliterated, obfusc, with his great Sackville eyes drooping, & his face all clouded with red and brown.' Six months later, this 'decayed, dignified, smoothed, effete' man was suffering from health complications caused by influenza. Victoria still resented the presence at Knole of the 'snake in the grass' and felt that she should be there instead to nurse her dying husband. It also brought back painful memories of her own father's death twenty years before. 'I am not wanted,' she wrote; 'I feel sad that they must torture him, as they tried to torture my poor O'Mann, and in the same room!'* Her sorrow did not stop her, however, from having her maid ring Knole, where her husband was on his deathbed, to say that she too had had a dreadful day: she had been thoroughly disturbed by the housemaid sweeping the carpets.

———

* Archbishop Bourchier's Chamber, now the Pheasant Court Room.

'The day I became a widow' is how she began her diary for Saturday 28 January, 1928, the day of Lionel's death. 'So the end has come after 15 years of misery.' The repercussions were to be wide-ranging.

Victoria hated the idea of her brother-in-law Charlie's second wife, Anne, taking over Knole. Anne was an American divorcée and former actress, described by Victoria's friend, the illustrator George Plank, as a 'bed-to-worse young lady'. 'What a mistress for Knole! and no money,' wrote Victoria. In any case, Charlie was thinking of living abroad. 'The whole thing to me is too dreadful on account of my beloved Knole and what it means to the ruin of that lovely place which Vita can't inherit unless Eddy makes a rich marriage.'

This was most unlikely since, as Victoria knew, Eddy preferred young men to women. Equally unlikely was Victoria's hope that the entail might be broken, to enable Vita to inherit Knole, which Vita 'adores and which she would adorn much better than Anne or Eva!'* Victoria claimed to have heard a rumour of an even more improbable plan – or was this purely wishful thinking on her part? – that Vita should divorce Harold and marry Eddy, her first cousin (just as Victoria herself had done), in order eventually to become Lady Sackville.

Instead, Victoria offered to rent Knole from Charlie for a couple of years – and was rather put out when he refused. She squabbled with him, too, over the return of some items of Knole furniture (seven van-loads had travelled to Brighton), and claimed that Lionel's estate owed her money for 'loans' she had made her husband during their life together. As Eddy wrote to Virginia Woolf, 'there seems no end to her [Victoria's] stylised behaviour. I hear from Raymond [Mortimer] that she is busy spreading the most unkind stories about us all & our treatment of her; meanwhile she writes to us all in turn, to get

---

* My grandmother, the wife of Lionel's youngest brother, Bertie.

round us. She has now claimed part of the family regalia &, if she doesn't get it, will no doubt try to hew every bathroom tile out of Knole, since she put them there. What a woman!'

Charlie was evidently under the impression that Vita was siding with her mother, and so, in an attempt to calm family tempers, Harold wrote to Charlie a few months after Lionel's death: 'Any such impression would be completely false . . . We are dealing with a lunatic [Victoria] who will stop at nothing to gain her revenge. We must therefore all stick together if Knole is to be protected. And we shall <u>stick</u> together. Best love to Anne. She must think she has married into a rather eccentric family.'

Vita, too, felt disinherited. It was with a certain insincerity that she wrote to her cousin Eddy, the heir apparent, after her father's death: 'Knole is now to you what it used to be to me; but I know you love it as much as I do.' Years later, in a letter to Eddy, she acknowledged that the house had always been 'an awful and deep block. I suppose my love for Knole has gone deeper than anything else in my life. If only you had been my brother this block wouldn't have occurred, because I shouldn't have minded in the least if you had succeeded to Dada, in fact, I should have liked it.'

Virginia Woolf was more straightforward in her description of Vita's feelings, writing in her diary a fortnight after Lionel's death: 'Lord Sackville is dead & lies at Withyham, & I passed Knole with Vita yesterday & had to look away from the vast masterless house, without a flag. This is what she minds most.'

In a letter to Harold in July 1929, Vita compared her 'voluntary exile from Knole' to the end of a liaison with a beautiful woman, who never, from force of circumstances, belonged to me wholly; but who had for me a sort of half-maternal tenderness and understanding, in which I could be entirely happy. Now I feel as though we had been parted because (again through force of circumstances and owing to no choice of her own) she had been compelled to marry someone else and had momentarily fallen completely beneath his jurisdiction, not happy in it, but acquiescent. I look at her from far off; and if I were wilder and more ruthless towards myself, I should burst in one evening and surprise her in the midst of her new domesticity. But life has taught me not to do these things.

Harold understood his wife's feelings and her resentment of the new regime at Knole. The changes there, he wrote, 'are superimposed upon Lionel's memory. They are the little dead leaves which, falling, falling, will gradually efface the imprint of his footsteps. They are the dust of change settling on your childhood . . . Knole knows that it belongs to *you* more than to Charlie.'

One of the first people on whom Victoria turned in her fury after Lionel's death was her daughter. Vita and Harold discouraged Victoria from attending his funeral in the local parish church of St Nicholas, and were very relieved when Victoria resigned from the executorship of her estranged husband's will. Lady Sackville found their attitude unsympathetic, and claimed in her diary that Vita had treated her 'abominably' for the last few years: 'I had loved her so. I have finished with that monster of ingratitude.' The break between mother and daughter – during which Victoria often refers to 'the Vita' as 'the Vipa' – lasted nearly two years. There was one particularly dreadful scene in the offices of the family solicitors, Pemberton's, when Victoria accused Vita of stealing the pearls she had in fact given her daughter on her marriage fifteen years before, and forced her to hand them over. 'She was like a mad woman,' wrote Vita, 'screaming Thief and Liar, and shaking her fist at me till I thought she was going to hit me.'

© Nicolson family

Vita Sackville-West in the 1920s

It was only after Vita had spent 'a bloody afternoon' at Knole in December 1929, at the wedding of her cousin Diana, Eddy's sister, to Lord Romilly that relations improved. Victoria sympathised with how Vita must have felt returning, out of duty rather than pleasure, to Knole and the chapel in which she herself had been married. Vita wrote sweetly and sadly to her mother, describing her emotions and the comfort she had taken from the older Knole servants who had understood, too, how she had been feeling. Early the following year, what Victoria called 'the Awful Nightmare' of her estrangement from Vita was over, and she returned the pearls.

'Such vicissitudes fell to the lot of all those who came into any intimate contact with her,' Vita wrote of her mother. 'Her friends bore it with patience and pain; but other people, such as servants, secretaries, tradesmen, and professional men with their reputation to safeguard, did not at all relish the wild allegations she broadcast about them.' At any one time, there were so many lawsuits pending – for slander, summary dismissal, or unpaid bills – that Lady Sackville jokingly rechristened her house the 'Writs [Ritz] Hotel'. There are echoes in these Sussex County Court cases of Pepita's regular trips to the magistrates' court in La Teste in the 1860s, to settle her differences with the servants and tradespeople of Arcachon, another provincial seaside town. Vita often drew attention to her mother's 'rapscallion Spanish background', to Catalina's money-making schemes, and to Pepita's volatility – 'the vindictive grievances, the storms', all of which were 'far better suited to Albolote than to Knole' or Brighton.

After her departure from Knole in 1919, Victoria's health deteriorated steadily. She was diagnosed with diabetes in 1925, and in 1926 suffered another nervous breakdown. Her diary became more and more self-pitying, and was often written in French – always a sign with Victoria that she was under severe emotional strain.

What had originally been mere eccentricities became mad obsessions. Her passion for fresh air had first manifested itself at Knole, where she bought a door-stopper for almost every door (many of them still there) to keep a constant cold draught whistling through the house. When she moved, her clifftop house on the south coast, White Lodge, 'caught the full force of the Brighton gales', Vita recorded, which suited her mother 'perfectly as the mania for fresh air had never deserted her and every door was still propped open and every window tied back with string'. She took to taking her meals outdoors, even in winter when it was snowing, well wrapped in furs and girdled with hot-water bottles.

Her parsimony became more pronounced, like her

grandmother, Catalina's. Vita chronicled her mother's later years with a mixture of adoration and exasperation, ridiculing Victoria's money-making schemes. In order to repair the roof of White Lodge, she sent a circular letter to all her friends and acquaintances asking them to contribute enough cash to buy a tile for her Roof of Friendship Fund; she was extremely irritated when the painter William Nicholson took her at her word, and sent a tile wrapped up in a paper parcel. The chaotic ambition of Victoria's building projects, and the scale of her acts of personal generosity, were increasingly matched by great meanness. Her letters were scrawled all over the backs of old circulars and stationery – in themselves, a record of her enthusiasms, obsessions and favourite haunts: Lady Sackville's Fund for Kent Prisoners of War, notepaper snaffled from hotels or from Fortnum and Mason, catalogues for her defunct interior decorating store Speall's, with its advertisements for candles and lampshades, silk cushions and screens. She once wrote to Vita on lavatory paper filched from the ladies' room at Harrods, 'Regarde, comme ce papier prend beaucoup mieux l'encre que Bromo'. 'A stranger recommendation for a toilet-roll was surely never devised,' commented Vita. Postage stamps she found 'ruinously expensive', and was for ever getting people to go out of their way to drop letters or notes off for her.

As she grew older, her sense of time – which had always been sketchy – became more erratic. Meals were served at odd hours of the day, and Victoria would stay up half the night talking to whoever would listen, and rising late the following day. 'The incredible disorder of her bedroom balanced the general disorder of her life,' wrote Vita. 'No picture of her would be complete without a picture of the untidiness and indeed squalor in which she elected to live.' Vita ascribed this to her mother's suspicious mind – inherited, she suggested, from 'her riff-raff Spanish ancestry'. She now suspected everybody, to an extent that was neither 'normal nor hygienic'.

It meant, in effect, that she would never have her bedroom touched or dusted . . . that she kept odds and ends of food standing on tables because she declared that if it were taken away it would be stolen. The most expensive bottles of pickled peaches from Fortnum and Mason stood there, half empty, for weeks. Tins of truffles from Strasbourg, jars of French mustard, pots of jam from Tiptree, samples of bath-salts, scent from Coty and Molyneux, boxes stacked with old 1/2d. envelopes intended for re-use, a stray bottle of Kümmel or cherry brandy; and then, on her bed, letters, stationery, diaries, note-books, handbags, fly-whisks, eye-shades, unopened parcels, so that the general accumulation left her only about a quarter of the bed to lie in. Yet she never seemed to notice the discomfort. She was far more concerned with the idea that the servants would read her letters and diaries, or would move her possessions out of her reach.

Victoria's final years were a descent into darkness. As her sight failed, the letters that she scribbled late into the night, the litany of resentments, the collection of 'Thoughts', became increasingly illegible. Her world closed in. There were no references to the siblings who had once dominated her diaries and her correspondence, but which now consisted simply of updates on her health, gossip about her few remaining friends, and accounts of the squabbles with her servants. It was a terrible irony how the sibling who so cynically secured the inheritance through a judicious marriage half a century before had become, in the end, as disinherited as the others: bitter, bedridden, and almost blind as she dreamed of her lost domain and unlikely schemes of reclaiming it.

Although mother and daughter had been reconciled in 1930, after their two-year rift, their relationship had the occasional flare-up, Victoria's letters to Vita veering wildly from affection to vituperation. During one of these, Victoria told her

Victoria, Lady Sackville, at Brighton in about 1920

eighteen-year-old grandson, Ben, all about his mother's affairs with women, including Violet and Virginia, and his father's affairs with men. Many years later, Ben tried to explain to himself Victoria's gratuitous mischief-making: 'She may just have wished to give vent to her misery and loneliness – this blind old woman with a gardener on a cliff, with nothing to keep her alive but dreams of Washington, Knole and her lost beauty – by poisoning an innocent grandson's mind.' Virginia Woolf's reaction was blunter: 'The old woman ought to be shot.'

In January 1936, Vita heard that her mother was critically ill, and rushed to her bedside at White Lodge. Lady Sackville died soon afterwards, on the thirtieth, leaving, according to Harold, who arrived a few minutes after her death, 'a pathetic typewritten note' saying that she was to be cremated and her ashes flung into the sea. 'Vita is much harassed and shattered, but inwardly, I think, relieved,' he wrote. A sense of perspective, if not relief, is evident in a letter Vita wrote to her son, Nigel: 'I do feel that

Grannyma's life was a fitful fever but that now she sleeps well. I feel also that all her faults are forgiven her, and only her virtues are remembered. That is what I prayed for, whenever I knelt at her bedside. You were both so good to her and understanding . . . and my only regret is that you didn't know her in the days when she was really gay and charming. You would have really loved her then, as I did.'

The day on which Victoria's ashes were due to be scattered at sea, 8 February, was bitterly cold, with a strong east wind. Harold lunched at the Metropole with Victoria's secretary, Cecil Rhind, before picking up the urn containing the ashes from Mr English's oyster shop in Brighton. They had been kept there overnight for fear that the press, who had got hold of the story, might picket the undertakers and take snapshots of Harold and Mr Rhind as they carried out the urn. But it was felt that Lady Sackville would have approved of her penultimate resting place, as Mr English was a particular favourite of hers, and she had often taken guests to eat oysters at his shop. The urn was then transported by car to a large open fishing boat waiting on the shingle, with two sailors. Clutching the little container in its brown-paper parcel, they clambered into the boat and, heads bent against the spray, they chugged along the coast until they were opposite White Lodge, some two miles out. At that point, as Harold described in his diary, 'The two men stand up and take off their hats. So does Cecil. I kneel by the gunwale and spill the ashes over into the sea, saying, "B.M. [short for Bonne Maman], all who love you are happy that you should now be at peace. We shall remember always your beauty, your courage and your charm." It is merely a handful of dust which slides out of the container into the waves.'

There is also a stone in her memory, as the 'beloved daughter' of the 2nd Lord Sackville and the wife of the 3rd Lord Sackville of Knole, in the churchyard of St Nicholas's in Sevenoaks. It bears an inscription in the sort of doggerel

Victoria always appreciated: 'A kindly thought is all I ask, But if remembrance be a task, Forget me.' Victoria's stone stands just a few feet from the grave of her father, which she used to visit regularly in the years before she left Knole. She would have been surprised to find that another name had joined her father's, long after his death, on one side of the base of the Celtic-cross memorial: that of Charlie's unpopular second wife Anne, who died in 1961. Charlie himself, who died the following year, chose to be buried in the family vault at Withyham, leaving his wife to share a grave with his uncle.

Days after the death of her mother, Vita received a strange letter from her aunt. Amalia was writing to 'rectify' a notice she had seen in *The Times*, which stated that the late Lady Sackville had been the eldest daughter of Lord Sackville: she enclosed a copy of her letter to the editor, 'which may reveal to you (if you do not already know it) that your Mother by birth had no right to the name of Sackville West'. Her letter to the editor claimed that Victoria 'was not his daughter, but the child of "father unknown",' and in it she reserved the right to reopen the case 'at any time . . . if I deem it necessary so in the interest of the family', particularly if the paper continued to publish 'misleading statements'. Vita wrote to Mr Pemberton, whose firm had represented the Sackvilles during the succession case and who still represented her uncle Charlie. She was worried that Charlie's dignity and rights as Lord Sackville might in some way be affected by the publication of Amalia's letter either in *The Times* or in some more scurrilous newspaper, and took it upon herself to act on his behalf as he was, at the time, on a boat to Havana. Pemberton duly wrote to Amalia, warning her that Uncle Charlie would 'take a serious view of the publication of any matter which makes any suggestion of this sort'. On other occasions, Amalia — for whom fact and fiction were always curiously intermingled — claimed that Victoria's father was a Jew who had been murdered in Spain, and a Basque goatherd. Vita's lawyer simply dismissed Amalia's rants as 'the vapourings of an ill-balanced mind'.

The older brother, Max, died aged seventy-eight in Pietermaritzburg, just a few months after Victoria, perhaps the only one of the protagonists in this story not to have been completely destroyed by the past, as the romantic tale of the 'English milord and the Spanish dancer' had turned to tragedy. Henry had been driven to suicide by his failed succession case; Victoria had ended her days feeling cheated and dispossessed, after all she had gone through to secure her legitimacy and inheritance; Flora had gone to the bad; and Amalia, hoping via marriage to achieve some of the diplomatic and social cachet to which she believed her ancestry entitled her, had continued to denounce Victoria after her death.

So it was Amalia, the sibling with whom Victoria had had perhaps the most explosive relationship, who was now the lone survivor. Amalia had lived in East Kent since the 1920s, and her final home was a cottage in Hythe, its paintwork blistered by the wind and spray, and its peace disturbed by the cries of the seagulls. (Hythe, incidentally, is twinned with Berck-sur-Mer, the seaside resort in northern France where Victoria had spent her summer holidays with the nuns in the 1870s.) No. 4 Hillside Street, like White Lodge, had views over the Channel towards the country of the sisters' birth. And there is a sense that Amalia (with her French husband) was always, like Victoria whose ashes swirled in the sea, caught between the two countries, switching between the two languages, and never quite at home in either.

Amalia died in September 1945, in a nursing home in Folkestone, about as close to France as you can get. The notice of her death, which appeared in the *Daily Telegraph* on 17 September, observed all the niceties of title that were so important to 'Amalia Marguerite Albertine, beloved wife of Richard William Martin, G.C.V.O., G.B.E., C.M.G. [Willie, or his widow, had evidently awarded him some bogus British honours] and younger daughter of the late Lionel, 2nd Baron Sackville'. An identical notice appeared in the *Folkestone, Hythe and District Gazette* the following week, buried among the marriages of homecoming servicemen, the tables of tide times, and a report that 'sixty members and friends of the Folkestone branch of the Newsagents' Federation held their first outing for six years on Wednesday'. As Folkestone resumed its peaceable activities, the last of those warring Sackville siblings was laid to rest, within sight of the country where their story had begun and where so much of it had taken place.

Notes

In most cases the sources of quotations are made clear in the text. With the help of the Select Bibliography, interested readers will be able to trace them without undue trouble. The following notes are intended, where sources are not self-evident, to help indicate where I have found additional information, and to provide ideas for further reading.

Introduction

The starting point for this book is *Pepita* by Vita Sackville-West, although detailed quotes are taken from the witness statements to be found in the National Archives (TS18/247). For the writing and publication of *Pepita*, see Glendinning. For the background to Knole and the Sackville family, see Robert Sackville-West (*Inheritance*). For mid-nineteenth-century Spain, see Ford; and for 'Spanish' dancers, in particular, see Seymour. For a playful essay on Pepita, see Girouard (*Enthusiasms*).

Chapter 1: The Villa Pepa

Again, one of the principal sources for this, and subsequent chapters, are the statements taken in 1897 'for the perpetuation of testimony', in the National Archives (TS18/247). For Arcachon during the Second Empire, see Daney, Dejean, Fauduilhe, Garner, Hameau, Lalesque, Lee, Massicault and

Roth; and for its villas, in particular, see Cottin (whose family owned the Villa Pepa from the 1870s to the 1970s). If you are ever in Arcachon, I highly recommend a guided walk of the Ville d'Hiver and its villas. For the reactions of the Sackville family to Lionel's secret family, see Sackville Mss U269, in the Kent History and Library Centre, and the diaries of the Earl of Derby.

Chapter 2: Lost in Translation

For Argentina in the 1870s, see Mulhall. For the Rue de Monceau, see De Waal; and for information on the convent itself, I am grateful to the Sisters of St Joseph for opening their archive. For South Africa during the Zulu War, see O'Connor and Williams. For Knole and the extended Sackville family at this time, see Robert Sackville-West (*Inheritance*) and Vita Sackville-West (*Pepita* and *Knole and the Sackvilles*); also, Bentley, Blakiston and Cecil. For Stonyhurst, see Gerard, Henderson, Hetherington and Hewitson. For the correspondence between the Sackville West siblings, see TS18/247.

Chapter 3: Continental Drift

For a rich evocation of diplomatic Washington in the 1880s, see Alsop (Susan Mary Alsop was a political hostess as well as a writer, and as a result gives a particularly sympathetic account of Victoria's years in the capital in *Lady Sackville*); see also Adams, James, Sackville-West (*Pepita*) and reports in the *New York Times*. For an assessment of Lionel Sackville-West's skills as British Minister, see Spring-Rice, and for his own account, see Sackville. Victoria's 'Book of Reminiscences' is in the Lilly Library, Bloomington, Indiana. I am grateful to the Mooi River Farmers' Association for information on farming in South

Africa in the 1880s. For all family correspondence, see Heard and TS18/247.

Chapter 4: The Surprise Inheritance

Victoria began her diaries in 1888. These can be found in the Lilly Library and are a major source of reference for this, and all subsequent chapters. For relative wealth of landed estates, see Bateman. For general information on Knole and the Sackvilles in the 1880s and 1890s, see Robert Sackville-West (*Inheritance*) and Vita Sackville-West (*Pepita* and *Knole and the Sackvilles*); for the fire, see Sackville Mss U269. For cousin marriage, see Anderson and Kuper. For Victorian views on illegitimacy, see Collins, and *Legitimacy and Illegitimacy*. For family corres-pondence, see TS18/247. For Victoria's wedding, see *Sevenoaks Chronicle*.

Chapter 5: Sibling Rivalry

Principal sources for this chapter are Victoria's diaries, and family letters to be found at TS18/247 and among private papers.

Chapter 6: Laying Claim to Knole

For Elveden, see Aslet and Hare, and for Edwardian country houses, Gardiner and Girouard. For the twists and turns of the Sackville inheritance, see Robert Sackville-West (*Inheritance*); and for the broader tradition of pretenders and succession claims, including the Tichborne Claimant, see McWilliam. For the Duchess of Devonshire's ball, see Murphy. For Gabriel Salanson's career, see the Archives des Affaires étrangères et européennes at the Centre de la Courneuve, Paris. For family correspondence and for all proceedings relating to the 'action for the perpetuation of testimony', see TS18/247; also Victoria's diaries.

Chapter 7: Parallel Lives

For details of Max's bankruptcy, see papers in the Pietermaritzburg Archives Repository, and also TS18/247. For Flora's divorce, see 'Le jugement de divorce Salanson/Sackville en date du 8 mars 1900' at the Archives de Paris, Boulevard Sérurier. For the representation of Knole at the Paris Exhibition of 1899, see Leathes. For Victoria's friendship with Sir John Murray Scott, see Alsop. For all other quotations, see Victoria's diaries.

Chapter 8: Skulduggery in Spain

For the proceedings in Spain, see TS18/247, Vita Sackville-West (*Pepita*) and the Spanish and British newspapers. For events at Knole, see De-la-Noy, Edward Sackville-West, Robert Sackville-West, Vita Sackville-West (*Pepita*). For Sir John Murray Scott, see Alsop and Vita Sackville-West (*Pepita*). For other quotations, see Victoria's diaries.

Chapter 9: A Death in the Family

For Vita's early writings, see Glendinning. For the flurry of letters after Lord Sackville's death, see TS18/247. For other quotations, see Victoria's diaries.

Chapter 10: In the High Court

For 'the case', see the transcripts at TS18/247 and Victoria's diary for 1910 (the only year not at the Lilly Library, but in the care of the National Trust at Sissinghurst). For the mythical implications of the case, see Woolf (*Orlando*); and for Vita's reaction to the case and its aftermath, see *Pepita*. For the Sackvilles' triumphal return to Sevenoaks, see *Sevenoaks Chronicle*. The letters between Max and Victoria are to be found in private Nicolson and Sackville papers.

Chapter 11: 'Sackville Tragedy in Paris Flat'

For reports of Henry's death, see British and US newspapers. For Sir John Murray Scott and the Scott case, see Alsop, Vita Sackville-West (*Pepita*) and Seligman. For Victoria's friendship with Rodin, see Ben Nicolson, and Victoria's letters to Rodin at the Musée Rodin, Paris. For all other quotations, see Victoria's diaries.

Chapter 12: Victims of Circumstance

For Harold Nicolson at Versailles, see Rose. For William Martin's diplomatic career, see the Archives des Affaires étrangères et européennes at the Centre de la Courneuve, Paris. For Vita's memories of Amalia, see *Pepita*. For Flora's theatrical career, see British and US newspapers; and for the London Palladium, see Woodward. For Lionel Salanson's military career, see the Archives de l'Armée de l'Air, Service Historique de la Défense, Chateau de Vincennes, Paris. For court records relating to the lives of Max and his children, see Pietermaritzburg Archives Repository. Other quotations were taken from Victoria's diaries and private family papers.

Chapter 13: Slaving Away at Knole for Nothing

For Victoria's old age, see Alsop, Sackville-West (*Pepita*) and – particularly for her relationship with her daughter, Vita – Glendinning. For Victoria's friendship with Sir Edwin Lutyens, see Lutyens and Ridley. For Violet Keppel's memories, see Trefusis. For Virginia Woolf's memories, see Virginia Woolf's diary. For Eddy Sackville-West, see De-la-Noy and for Vita's letters to him, the Berg Collection. For Lady Sackville's death, see Harold Nicolson (*Diaries and Letters*). Other quotations were taken from Victoria's diaries (and the 'Book of Happy Reminiscences for My Old Age') and from letters in private family papers.

Select Bibliography

Archives

Archives de l'Armée de l'Air, Service Historique de la Défense, Chateau de
    Vincennes, Paris
Archives des Affaires étrangères et européennes, Centre de la Courneuve, Paris
Berg Collection, New York
Kent History and Library Centre, Maidstone, Sackville Mss, U269
Lilly Library, Indiana University, Bloomington, Indiana, Diaries of Victoria,
    Lady Sackville
National Archives, Kew, TS18/247
Nicolson papers, Sissinghurst
Pietermaritzburg Archives Repository, South Africa
Sackville papers, Knole

Published Sources

Adams, Marian, *The Letters of Mrs. Henry Adams, 1865–1883*, ed. Ward
    Thoron (Longmans, Green, 1937)
Alsop, Susan Mary, *Lady Sackville* (Doubleday, 1978)
Anderson, Nancy Fix, 'Cousin Marriage in Victorian England', *Journal of
    Family History*, xi (1986), p. 290
Armstrong, Lucile, *Dances of Spain I: South, Centre and North-West* (Max
    Parrish & Co., 1950)
Aslet, Clive, *Elveden Hall: the Property of the Earl of Iveagh* (Christie's, 1984)
Bateman, John, *The Great Landowners of Great Britain and Ireland* (Leicester
    University Press, 1971)

Bentley, Michael, *Lord Salisbury's World* (Cambridge University Press, 2001)

Blakiston, Georgiana, *Woburn and the Russells* (Constable, 1980)

Bourne Taylor, Jenny, 'Representing Illegitimacy in Victorian Culture', in *Victorian Identities*, ed. Ruth Robbins and Julian Wolfreys (Macmillan, 1996)

Cecil, David, *The Cecils of Hatfield House* (Constable, 1973)

Cicirelli, Victor, *Sibling Relationships across the Life Span* (Plenum Press, 1995)

Clifford, Lady Anne, *The Diaries of Lady Anne Clifford*, ed. D. J. H. Clifford (Alan Sutton, 1990)

Collins, Wilkie, *No Name* (Penguin, 1995)

Cottin, François et Françoise, *Le Bassin d'Arcachon: à l'Age d'Or des Villas et des Voiliers* (L'Horizon chimérique, 2003)

Daney, Charles, *Sur Le Bassin D'Arcachon à L'Epoque de Napoléon III* (Cairn, 2008)

Dejean, Oscar, *Arcachon et ses Environs* (Bordeax, 1858)

De-la-Noy, Michael, *Eddy: The Life of Edward Sackville-West* (Arcadia, 1999)

Derby, Edward Henry Stanley, Earl of, *A Selection from the Diaries of Edward Henry Stanley, 15th Earl of Derby (1826–93) between September 1869 and March 1878*, ed. John Vincent (Royal Historical Society, 1994)

———*The Later Derby Diaries*, ed. John Vincent (University of Bristol, 1981)

De Waal, Edmund, *The Hare with Amber Eyes* (Chatto & Windus, 2010)

Faduilhe, Charles-N., *Du climat d'Arcachon au point de vue de quelques maladies de poitrine* (1866)

Ford, Richard, *Handbook for Travellers in Spain* (John Murray, 1845)

Gardiner, Juliet, *The Edwardian Country House* (Channel 4, 2002)

Garner, Alice, *A Shifting Shore: Locals, Outsiders and the Transformation of a French Fishing Town, 1823–2000* (Cornell University Press, 2005)

Gerard, John, *Souvenir of the Centenary Celebration, Stonyhurst College, July 1894* (Marcus Ward & Co., 1894)

Girouard, Mark, *Enthusiasms* (Frances Lincoln, 2011)

———*The Victorian Country House* (Yale University Press, 1979)

Glendinning, Victoria, *Vita: The Life of Vita Sackville-West* (Weidenfeld & Nicolson, 1983)

Hameau, Gustave, *The Climate of Arcachon, A Treatise on its Influence on Certain Diseases of the Chest*, trans. Samuel Radcliff (London, 1874)

Hare, Augustus J.C., *The Story of My Life* (George Allen, 1896–1900)

Heard, Amy, *Amy Heard: Letters from the Gilded Age*, ed. Robert Gray (2005) at ee.stanford.edu/gray/amy

Henderson, Andrew, *The Stone Phoenix: Stonyhurst College 1794–1894* (Churchman, 1986)

Hetherington, Percy Fitzgerald, *Stonyhurst Memories; or, Six Years at School* (R. Bentley & Son, 1895)

Hewitson, A., *Stonyhurst College, Present and Past* (Preston, 1878)

James, Henry, *Letters*, ed. Leon Edel (Harvard University Press, 1974–84)

Kuper, Adam, 'Incest, Cousin Marriage, and the Origin of the Human Sciences in Nineteenth-Century England', *Past and Present: A Journal of Historical Studies*, 174 (February 2002)

Lalesque, Fernand, *Ville d'Été, Ville d'Hiver* (Paris, 1886)

Lee, Edwin, *The Health Resorts of the South of France* (London, 1865)

Lees-Milne, James, *Harold Nicolson* (Chatto & Windus, 1980–1)

Legitimacy and Illegitimacy in 19th-century Law, Literature and History, ed. Margot Finn, Michael Lobban and Jenny Bourne Taylor (Palgrave Macmillan, 2010)

Lutyens, Mary, *Edwin Lutyens* (John Murray, 1980)

Massicault, H., *Guide illustré d'Arcachon et du littoral avec notice anglaise by S. Radcliff* (Bordeaux, 1872)

McWilliam, Rohan, *The Tichborne Claimant* (Hambledon Continuum, 2007)

Mulhall, Marion, *Between the Amazon and the Andes, or Ten Years of a Lady's Travels* (E. Stanford, 1881)

Murphy, Sophia, *The Duchess of Devonshire's Ball* (Sidgwick & Jackson, 1984)

Nicolson, Ben, 'Rodin and Lady Sackville', *Burlington Magazine*, January 1970

Nicolson, Harold, *Diaries and Letters*, 3 vols, 1930–62, ed. Nigel Nicolson (Collins, 1966–8)

Nicolson, Nigel, *Portrait of a Marriage* (Weidenfeld & Nicolson, 1973)

O'Connor, Damian P., *The Zulu and the Raj: the Life of Sir Bartle Frere* (Able Publishing, 2002)

Ridley, Jane, *The Architect and His Wife: A Life of Edwin Lutyens* (Chatto & Windus, 2002)

Rochegude, Felix de, Marquis, *Guide pratique à travers le vieux Paris* (Paris, 1903)

Rose, Norman, *Harold Nicolson* (Cape, 2005)

Roth, Mathias, *Medical and Other Notes, Collected on a Holiday Tour to Arcachon, Biarritz, Pau and the Principal Watering Places in the Pyrenees* (London, 1879)

Rowe, Dorothy, *My Dearest Enemy, My Dangerous Friend: Making and Breaking Sibling Bonds* (Routledge, 2007)

Sackville, Lionel, Lord, *My Mission to the United States 1881–1889* (for private circulation, 1895)

Sackville-West, Edward, 'Sketches for an Autobiography', in *Orion: A Miscellany*, vol. 3 (Nicholson & Watson, 1945–7)

Sackville-West, Robert, *Inheritance: The Story of Knole and the Sackvilles* (Bloomsbury, 2010)

Sackville-West, Vita, *The Letters of Vita Sackville-West to Virginia Woolf*, ed. Louise deSalvo and Mitchell A. Leaska (Virago, 1992)

——*Vita and Harold: The Letters of Vita Sackville-West and Harold Nicolson*, ed. Nigel Nicolson (Weidenfeld & Nicolson, 1982)

——*Pepita* (Hogarth Press, 1937)

——*Knole and the Sackvilles* (William Heinemann, 1934)

Seligman, Germain, *Merchants of Art, 1880–1960* (Appleton-Century-Crofts, 1961)

Seymour, Bruce, *Lola Montez* (Yale University Press, 1996)

Spring-Rice, Cecil, *The Letters and Friendships of Sir Cecil Spring-Rice*, ed. Stephen Gwynn (Constable, 1929)

Stonyhurst College, *Stonyhurst Magazine* (Stonyhurst, 1881, etc.)

Trefusis, Violet, *Don't Look Round: Reminiscences* (Hutchinson, 1952)

Williams, Stephanie, *Running the Show: Governors of the British Empire 1857–1912* (Viking, 2011)

Woodward, Chris, *The London Palladium: the Story of the Theatre and its Stars* (Northern Heritage, 2009)

Woolf, Virginia, *Orlando* (Penguin Books, 1993)

———*The Diary of Virginia Woolf*, 5 vols, ed. Anne Olivier Bell (Hogarth Press, 1975–80)

Newspapers and Journals

American: *New York Times*

English: *Daily Chronicle*; *Daily Express*; *Daily Herald*; *Daily Mail*; *Daily Mirror*; *Daily News and Leader*; *Daily Sketch*; *Daily Telegraph*; *Evening News*; *Evening Standard*; *Folkestone, Hythe and District Herald*; *The Globe*; *The Graphic*; *Illustrated News*; *Lloyd's Weekly News*; *Manchester Guardian*; *Morning Post*; *News of the World*; *Observer*; *Pall Mall Gazette*; *People*; *Playgoer and Society Illustrated*; *Reynolds's Weekly Newspaper*; *Sevenoaks Chronicle*; *The Scotsman*; *Sphere*; *Standard*; *Star*; *The Sunday Times*; *Tatler*; *The Times*; *Weekly Dispatch*; *Westminster Gazette*

French: *L'Aurore*; *L'Action Française*; *La Croix*; *La Presse*; *L'Echo de Paris*; *Le Figaro*; *Le Gaulois*; *Le Matin*; *Le Petit Journal*; *Le Petit Parisien*; *Le Temps*; *L'Humanité*; *L'Univers*

Spanish: *El Liberal*; *Heraldo de Madrid*; *La Correspondencia*

Unpublished Sources

Leathes, Richard, 'Knole at the Paris Exhibition', unpublished paper, 2012

Acknowledgements

Just as I was beginning to research this book, in March 2011, I received a letter from Vayle Wolstenholme, a South African now living in Australia. She was hoping to carry out a promise made to her late mother: to hand back to Knole, and a member of the Sackville family, a couple of letters written to her mother's grandfather, Max, in South Africa a century before. As a young woman, her mother had noticed an important-looking envelope, with a red wax seal, amongst the pile of papers being consigned to a bonfire during a clear-out of the family home. She had no idea how much was incinerated that day – furniture, as well as old papers – but she suspected that these two letters would mean a lot to an historian of Knole and the Sackvilles in the future.

Her suspicions were correct. The letters she had plucked from the fire (and goodness knows how much else went up in flames) referred to a series of events that took place at the turn of the nineteenth and twentieth centuries, and were the subject of the book I was writing. They were both addressed to Max Sackville West: one was from his brother-in-law, my great-uncle Lionel, and the other was from his sister, Amalia.

I entered into a correspondence with Vayle, which resulted in her coming to Knole with the letters, to fulfil the promise she had made to her mother. Throughout her life, Vayle had heard stories about her great-grandfather, Max, and the disputed succession to a stately home in Kent. In the 1930s, Vayle's mother, Daphne, and grandmother, Vivian, had visited

England and had had lunch at Sissinghurst with Vivian's first cousin, Vita Sackville-West, and her husband Harold Nicolson. Vita had been shocked when she was shown a photograph of her uncle Max in South Africa – not simply because he was by now an old man, but because he was the spitting image, or so she claimed, of her grandfather, Lionel, the 2nd Lord Sackville.

As an illegitimate child, and a potential source of embarrassment to the family, Max had been packed off to South Africa by his father, Lionel, in the 1870s. Vayle was as intrigued as I was by his story. She quizzed members of her family, and spent hours in the afternoon heat of Pietermaritzburg, scrabbling about on her hands and knees, searching for the grave of Max (who died in 1936). She located the last remaining person in South Africa to bear the surname Sackville West: an elderly woman, Lea, living in a nursing home in Johannesburg.

Vayle was occasionally dismayed by the behaviour of her antecedents, and fearful of re-opening old family wounds – or causing new ones. For the fault-lines ran not just between the 'legitimate' and the 'illegitimate' branches of the family, but also within those branches themselves. Why had no family member, Lea wondered, attempted to track down her late husband, Cecil, one of Max's grandsons, during his lifetime? Why had he been disowned and abandoned by his uncles, aunts and cousins? Why was it that, among Max's descendants, Vayle's side of the family had had so little to do with Cecil's? These were just some of the questions Vayle wished she had asked her parents.

I am, as a result, indebted to Vayle, Lionel and Pepita's great-great-granddaughter on the 'illegitimate' side, for all her researches; just as I am to Adam Nicolson and his sister, Juliet, Lionel and Pepita's great-great-grandchildren on the 'legitimate' side, for all their help and friendship. They gave me complete access to the family papers at Sissinghurst, and to the trunks of letters, which their grandmother Vita had used to write *Pepita*, the starting point for this book. I thank them, too, for giving me permission to quote from the published works of Vita Sackville-West and Harold Nicolson. I am also grateful to the National Trust staff at Knole and Sissinghurst for their expertise and willingness always to answer a question or supply a photograph.

———

My curiosity as to what became of Pepita's children began several years ago when I was writing *Inheritance*, the story of Knole and the Sackvilles, who have lived there for the past 400 years. But whereas *Inheritance* chronicled a fairly well-documented family – there is, for example, a family tree at Knole that traces the Sackville lineage back to the early Middle Ages – *The Disinherited* tracks down figures far more fugitive, people who left just wisps of themselves behind. The evidence consists not of heirlooms – those portraits and objects, freighted with emotional and historical associations that are a feature of *Inheritance* – but of certificates of birth, marriage, divorce and death, of censuses and court reports, newspaper accounts, diaries, and letters.

Some of these documents are to be found in the town halls of France, the staff of which have been unfailingly helpful in providing copies; others in magnificent repositories on the fringes of Paris and London: the Archives des Affaires étrangères et européennes at the Centre de la Courneuve; the Service Historique de la Défense at the Chateau de Vincennes; and the National Archives at Kew. The papers at Kew, on which much of this book is based, have survived as the result of a technicality. Because the family saga culminated in a court case in which a title – that of Lord Sackville – was at stake, the court reports were preserved with the records of the Treasury Solicitor at the National Archives. I have my friend

Guy Philipps QC to thank for pointing me in that direction and for providing me, unwittingly, with the key that unlocked this story. He could not have prepared me, however, for the excitement of finding that it was not just the transcripts of the court proceedings that were preserved at Kew, but all the supporting depositions, too, and boxes containing dusty bundles of personal letters and photos. From suburban Kew, I was transported to the slums of Málaga and the stately homes of England, the convent schools of Paris and the music halls of London, the South African veldt and the diplomatic world of late nineteenth-century Washington.

I am also grateful to the staffs of the London Library and the British Library, particularly the keepers of the newspaper archive at Colindale; to Christopher Whittick of the East Sussex Record Office in Lewes; and to the Lilly Library at Indiana University, Bloomington, where the diaries of the turbulent Victoria, Lady Sackville, found a peaceful, final resting place.

The internet has transformed research into the lives of those ordinary people, whose stories cannot be found on the shelves of libraries, but who can be traced, for example, on the General Register Office site (for records of births, marriages and deaths); on Gallica, the digital library of the Bibliothèque Nationale de France, for access to over a hundred years of French newspapers; and on any number of genealogical sites.

After all these virtual encounters, it has been a great pleasure to meet and correspond with real people. Françoise Cottin stayed in the Villa Pepa for a month in the summer of 1963, sleeping in Pepita's room as she cared for a convalescent son. The villa had been in her husband's family since 1876, and the interior, including some of the furniture, had barely changed since Pepita's day. Françoise's husband had grown up in the Cottin family house in the Rue de Monceau in Paris, and as young boy attended the Cours St Louis at No. 17, on the site of the convent school where Pepita's daughter, Victoria, had been sent to board. The Cottins subsequently lived for fifty years in the Rue de Monceau. No wonder that Mme Cottin, having followed so literally in the footsteps of the family, felt such an affinity for Pepita. She has been a great source of information on life in Arcachon and Paris in the 1860s and 1870s.

The Sisters of St Joseph in Lyons shared with me the few surviving archives of the convent in the Rue de Monceau. Brigitte Petit Archambault went far beyond what could be expected from a friend – even one of my oldest friends – in chasing arcane requests for information from France. Jesus Rivera-Rosado, a Spanish balletomane, helped me acquire some letters of Flora's written over a hundred years ago; and Maxine Park returned some of Amalia's that had gone astray. Dr Judith Beniston, a lecturer in German at the University College of London and an authority on the history of German and Austrian theatre, gave me fascinating insights into Pepita's professional career. The Mooi River Farmers' Association in South Africa helped me to understand the world into which Max was dispatched; and Jenny Duckworth conducted research for me at the Pietermaritzburg Archives Repository.

Thanks, as ever, to Caroline Michel, my literary agent, for encouraging me to write this book and finding for it the perfect publisher. Michael Fishwick at Bloomsbury is an exceptional editor, combining an eye for both the broad sweep of a story and for the tiny, telling detail. Once again, I cannot think of a single suggestion he has made with which I have disagreed. His team, notably managing editor Anna Simpson, have handled the project at all stages with great good humour and efficiency.

The family in which I grew up is similar in structure to Victoria's. I am the oldest of five children, like Max (and born exactly a hundred years later), and am then followed by three sisters, with the youngest of us, like Henry, a boy. But there the similarities end. I am grateful to my parents for the loving and supportive environment in which they raised me and my siblings. And, above all, I thank my wife, Jane, and our three children, Freya, Arthur and Edie, who live at Knole, and share an inheritance that has troubled many previous generations, with such equanimity and grace. May they never feel disinherited.

Index

Page numbers in **bold** refer to illustrations.

Adams, Mrs Henry 70
Albolote 14–18
Anastasia, Grand Duchess 133–4
Anglo-Zulu War 56–7
Anton, Manuel 183
Arcachon
    Boulevard de la Plage 23–4, 37
    Casino 30
    English community 36–7
    Grand Hotel 27, 30
    health resort 26–9
    Henry visits 46–7
    inhabitants 30
    Pepita's final resting place 47
    Pepita's funeral 41
    Pepita's life in 30–3, 33–9
    the Railway Buffet 29
    railway line 25–6
    registration of children's births 34
    social exclusions 32
    town of 25–30, **27**
    Victoria visits 112
    Villa Pepa 23–5, **25**, 35, 45–6, 174
    Ville d'Eté 26
    Ville d'Hiver 27–9
Argentina 48–9
Arthur, Chester 72
Arthur, Sir Frederick 1
Astor, William Waldorf 207

Baccelli, Giovanna 12
Baden Baden 19–20
baptismal certificates 34
Bayern, Max in 18
Bedford, Elizabeth Sackville-West, Duchess
    of 42–3, 63–4, **64**, 105

Bedford, Francis, known as Hastings, 9th
    Duke of 42
Bedford, Herbrand, 11th Duke of 237–8
bedints 117
Bell, Maud 118
Béon, Count Henri de 8, **37**, 85, **146**
    and Lionel's relationship with Pepita 37
    relationship with Pepita 38
    and Pepita's funeral 40
    given charge of the children 41, 48,
        49–50
    and ownership of Villa Pepa 45–6
    Victoria visits 53
    death of mother 58
    Victoria's letters to 60, 70, 104
    relationship with Max 77
    and Flora's wedding 86–7
    wedding present to Victoria 110–11
    compensation claim 123–4
    and the legitimacy claim 146–8, 148–9
    blames Victoria 147–8
    financial support for Henry 179–80
    Max blames 203
Berlin 19
Bigham, Right Hon. Sir John 210, 216–17,
    218
Bildt, Baron Carl 72–3
birth certificates 34
Blaine, Mrs 69–70
Blakiston, Georgiana 63–4
Boer War 80, 252
Bond, Marjory 221
Bordeaux 24
Boscawen, Miss 109
Bothnia, RMS 68
Brain, John 136, 158, 159, 182

Buckhurst Park 3, 132
Buenos Aires 42, 44–5, 48–9
Bulletin de Naissance, Amalia 213
Bulwer, Sir Henry 56
Butt, Alfred 244

Camara, Petra 13
Cameron, Elizabeth 71, 73
Campbell, Kenneth 142–3
Cancela, Pedro 177
Cannes 95–6, 143, 145–6, 150
Casa Blanca 14–17
Caseria Buena Vista 17–18, 20–1
Cerutti, Teresa 244
Cetewayo 56–7
Charing Cross Hotel, London 157, 162–3
Cheston, Maria Stockton 67, 98
Clarke, Sir Edward 211–13, 216
Clay, Violet Spender 136
Cleveland, Grover 88
Clifford, Lady Anne 99
Collins, Wilkie, *No Name* 95
Convent of the Sacred Heart, London 60,
    63–5
Copenhagen 13
Cornwallis-West, Maie [Mary] 150
Craven, Mr 116

Daily Mail 195
Daily Mirror **185**, **205**, 243
Darwin, Charles 104
Day & Russell 137, 144
De La Warr, Constance, Lady 77, 105–6
De La Warr, George West, 5th Earl 3
De La Warr, Gilbert, 8th Earl 132–3, 135–7,
    237
de Lisle, Lizzie 268
Denbigh Street, Pimlico 65
Denuncia proceedings 172–8, 183
Derby, Earl of 42, 45, 45–6, 56, 63
Derby, Mary Sackville-West, Lady 42–5,
    45–6, 103
  breaks news of children's status 60
  advises children's names be changed
    60–1
  relationship with children 63
  arranges for Victoria to go to
    Washington 66–7
  settlement on Max 80
  and Flora's engagement 85
  and Victoria's engagement to Young
    Lionel 105
  and Victoria's wedding 111–12

response to circular 134–5
  Amalia's letters to 149–50
  and Henry's reconciliation attempt
    157–8
Derby House 63–4
Derbyshire, Renishaw Hall 241–2
Desombre, Auguste 24–5, 38, 39, 152
Dignac, Louisa 37, 152
Dios Gonzalez, Juan de 151
Dorremocea, Ricardo 177, 184, 186
Dover, Lord Warden Hotel 241
Druce case, the 193–4
Duran, Catalina 4, 14–18, 19, 20–1, 22
Duran, Diego 4
Duran, Josefa (Pepita)
  appearance 1–2, **2**, 10–12, **11**, 16, 17, 30, **31**
  family background 3–4, 14–15
  dancing lessons 4
  marriage 4–5
  children 6
  family myths about 6
  dancing career 9–12, 20
  relationship with Lionel 1, 2–3, 6, 9–10,
    24, 32–3, 33–9
  portraits **11**, 11–12
  visits to Spain 12–13
  wealth 12–13
  jewellery 13, 15, 16–17
  visits to Albolote 14–18
  birth of Max 17–18
  in Heidelberg 18
  birth of Victoria 19
  separation from Lionel 19–20
  miscarriage 20
  relationship with Oliva 21–2, 178–9,
    214–15
  question of marriage to Lionel 23, 33–4,
    35, 40, 179, 212–13, 218–19
  life in Arcachon 30–3, 33–9
  relations with servants 31–2
  social exclusions 32
  as Countess West 33
  birth of children in Arcachon 34
  registration of children's births 34
  notoriety 35–6
  reputation in Arcachon 36–7
  relationship with Béon 38
  death 39–40
  funeral 40, 41
  estate 46
  exhumation 47
  final resting place 47
  reburial 47

marriage certificate found 137
validity of marriage questioned 172–8
marriage to Olivia proved 175–8
marriage by reputation evidence 206–7,
  211–12, 213–14
Duran, Pedro 3

Edward, Prince of Wales 96, 99, 109, 130,
  154
Elveden Hall 129–30
Ephrussi, Charles 51
Essenhigh Corke, Charles 99, **100**
Estevenet, L'Abbé 180–1
Evans, Effie Mackenzie 165–6
Exposition Universelle, Paris, 1899 168–9

Faduilhe, Charles-N. 29
family photos 8–9
Fay, André 38
Fellowes, Mr 196–7
Finlay, Sir Robert 213–15, 216–17, 218
First World War 235–6, 239, 249–50, **250**
Fitzgerald, Percy Hetherington 65–6
Folkestone 279–80
Frere, Sir Bartle 56–7

Gainsborough, Thomas 12
Gerard, Father John 66
Gibraltar 150–1
Grahame, Sir George 240
Granada 14, 21
Granville, Lord 67
Grasslands, Balcombe, Sussex 59–60
Greene, Edward 252–4
Greenwich, Umvoti 55
Grier, Mrs 255
Guerrero y Casares, Manuel 13

Hakenfelde 19
Hall, Marshall 135, 137
Hameau, Dr Gustave 27–8, 35, 40, 47, 152
Hameau, Dr Jean 26–9
Hardinge, Charles 72
Hare, Augustus 130
Harrison, Alfred 151, 178, 182, 217
Heard, Amy 86
Heidelberg 18
Hicks-Beach, Sir Michael 114
High Court hearing
  opens 210
  Victoria and 210–11
  and marriage by reputation 211–12,
    213–14

Henry's case 211–13
Holst's testimony 212
marriage evidence 212–13
Bulletin de Naissance, Amalia 213
Sackville case 213–15
Sackville witnesses 214
character evidence 215
Vita attends 215–16
adjournment application 216–17
Sackville witnesses' evidence 217
second adjournment application 217–18
Finlay presents his case 218
Henry retires petition 218
summary 218–19
and the Marriage Book Register 219
Petition dismissed 219
victory celebrations 219–22, **220**, **222**
Hillier, Miss 65
Holst, Colonel Fritz 40, 212
Hôtel Britannique, Cannes 143, 145–6
Hutton, E. M. 150–1
Hythe 279

illigitimacy revealed 65, 75–9, 83–9, 94–5,
  127
Imparcial (newspaper) 173–4
Irish Question, the 70
Isandlwana, battle of 57
Italy 19
Iveagh, Lord 129–30
Iveagh Bequest, the 130

Jackson, Stanley 117
James, Henry 68–9
Johnston, Harry Scott 35, 152, 214

Kenwood House 130
Keppel, Alice 194
Keppel, Violet 195, 206, 266
Kirstein, Edward 213
Knoblock, Edward 260
Knole 3, 12, 22, **108**
  Amalia's position at 139–43
  barn fire, 1887 **93**, 93
  Christmas, 1890 114
  condition 91–2
  estates 90
  family leaves 198–9
  flower show 154
  housekeeper 98
  land rents 90
  life at 187–9
  Lionel inherits 89

Lionel Salanson visits 120–1
park 92
picture sale accusations 120
power of 7
Prince of Wales visits 154, **154**
servants 99–100
succession 61–3, 132
Victoria and 97–101, 102, 211, 264–5
Victoria leaves 262–3
Victoria's offer to rent 269–70
Knox, Mrs 98, 99, 115

Laguna, Señor 175–6
Lanquine, Camille 177, 181, 183, 186
Lastres, Señor 176, 178
Lee, Dr Edwin 26, 29
legal costs 189
legitimacy claim. *See also* High Court
      hearing
   Henry learns registered as legitimate son
      127
   requests confirmation of legitimacy from
      Lionel 130–2
   letter to Gilbert, Earl De La Warr 132–3
   circulars 133
   response to circulars 134–9
   supporters 135, 137
   Sackville family law firm 136
   Max's response to 137–9
   relationship with Victoria 138–9
   threat to Knole 143
   Béon and 146–8, 148–9
   perpetuating testimony statements
      150–2
   Spanish witness statements 151
   French witness statements 151–2
   Sackville statements 152
   examination of witnesses 152–4, 160
   Henry continues investigations 178–9
   relaunched 179
   financial backing 179–81, 201
   Max and 202
   appointment of official receiver
      requested 204, **205**, 206
   marriage by reputation evidence 206–7
   delays 207–8
   Letters of Request 207–9
   the High Court hearing 210–19
   notoriety 222–3
   re-hearing motion 223
Legitimacy Declaration Act, 1858 193
Lemaire, Madeleine 51
Lens, Albert 175, 181

Leo XIII, Pope 119
Les Landes 26
Lesnier, Joseph Goring 148–9, 180
Lisbon 241
Littlechild, John 136
London 116
   Convent of the Sacred Heart 60, 63–5
   Marble Arch House 247
   the Palladium 246
Lopez, Lola 15
Lopez, Manuel 4, 14–15, 17, 20–1
Louet, Eugénie 64–5
Löys Chandieu, Marquis de (L. C.) 96–7,
      98, 101–3, 149
Ludwig, King of Bavaria 12
Lutyens, Sir Edwin 263, 267
Lyons, Lord 39

Macdonald, Ramsay 241
Madrid 4, 13, 22, 172, 175, 184
Maisonneuve, Max 186, 227
Málaga 3, 22
Marriage Book Register 175–7, 181–3,
      183–7, 219
Martin, William 239–41
Maximilian Joseph, Duke 18
Meynell & Pemberton 136, 151, 178
Molina, Micaela Gonzalez 15–16
Monte Carlo 149, 228
Montez, Lola 12
Mooi River Farmers' Association 80
Mooi River, Natal 79–81
Mulhall, Marion 9, **59**
   impressions of Buenos Aires 48–9
   Between the Amazon and the Andes 58
   engaged to help with children 58
   breaks news of children's status 59–60
   and Victoria's wedding 110
Murchison Affair, the 87–8, 106

name change 61
Napoleon III, Emperor 26
Natal 56
New York Times 73, 227, 246
Nicholson, William 274
Nicolson, Adam 257
Nicolson, Ben 276
Nicolson, Harold 239, 240, 269, 270–1,
      276–7
Nicolson, Nigel 276–7
   Portrait of a Marriage 7
Nobody's Children 95
Nocker, Phine de 247–8

North British Insurance Company 44
Northcliffe, Lord 237–8
Norton, Captain 78–9
Norton, John 129
Nourse, Cracroft 252–4
Nussey & Fellowes 201–4, 208–9, 213

Oliva, Juan Antonio de 4–5, **5**, 21–2, 46,
    53, 137, 139, 172–8, 214–15
Osborn & Osborn 178

Paraguay 58
Paredes, Señor 177–8, 183, 187
Paris 1, 19, 32–3, 49–50, 163, 171, 240
    Boulevard Suchet 228–9
    Exposition Universelle, 1899 168–9
    Rue de Monceau 50–3, 58, 229
Paulus, Matias 181, 186
Pégat, Jean 122
Pemberton, Percy Leigh 196, 200–1, 202,
    208–9, 235, 278
Pepita. *see* Duran, Josefa (Pepita)
Pereire, Emile 28
Phillips, Charles 264
Phillips, Lushington 78–9, 80–1
Pichon, Stephen 240
Pinel, Rafaela Moreno 20–1
Plank, George 269
Ponce de Leon, Francisco 217
pretenders 133–4
Pretoria Pit explosion, Lancashire, 1910
    244
Proust, Marcel 51

Radcliff, Samuel 35, 36–7, 152, 214
Ramirez Galan, Francisco 16
Ramirez Galan, José 16
Régnauld, Paul 30
Renishaw Hall, Derbyshire 241–2
Rhind, Cecil 277
Rodin, Auguste 234–5
Rojas, Muñoz 3
Rophon Ortega, Enrique 174–6, 181, 181–3
    trial of 183–7, **185**
Royal Courts of Justice 152–4
Rubens, Olive 235, 240, 260, 261–3, 267
Rubens, Walter 261–2
Ruiz, Antonio 4

Sackville, Edeline 77
Sackville, John Frederick, 3rd Duke of
    Dorset 12
Sackville, Thomas, Earl of Dorset 92

Sackville West, Amalia 7, **55**, **83**, 119, **142**
    birth of 34
    parentage 37
    reburial of Pepita 47
    childhood letters 54
    education 58, 60
    in Washington 73–4
    and Flora's engagement 85–6
    in Cannes 95–6, 143, 145–6, 150
    Victoria's protectiveness 97
    and Victoria's engagement to Young
        Lionel 107
    life at Knole 113–16
    relationship with Victoria 113–18,
        139–46, 149–50
    allowance 115, 199–200
    extravagance 115, 117
    search for a husband 116–18
    maintenance payments 122
    and Henry's legitimacy claim 137
    position at Knole 139–43
    lies 140, 155
    debts 144–5
    returns family jewels 145
    Lionel's settlement on 145–6, 149
    letters to Lady Derby 149–50
    rapprochement attempt with Victoria
        154–5
    lifestyle 167–8
    Lionel's funeral 197
    legitimacy affidavits 206
    compromise suggestion 209
    Bulletin de Naissance 213
    psychology 224
    and Henry's death 227
    allowance stopped 237
    financial situation 237–8
    later relationship with Victoria 237–43
    Savoy Hotel fancy-dress ball, 1911 238–9
    marriage 239–41
    relationship with Max 242–3
    resentments 242–3
    threatened stage career 244
    letter to Vita 278–9
    death 279–80
Sackville West, Carmen 255–7
Sackville West, Cecil 257–8
Sackville West, Flora 7, **55**
    birth of 34
    education 58, 60, 64–5
    name change 61
    coming-out ball 73
    in Washington 73–4

appearance 84
engagement 84–6
marriage to Gabriel Salanson 86–7
and Victoria's engagement to Lionel
    107–9
and Victoria's wedding 110
search for a husband for Amalia 117
relationship with Victoria 118–23, 168–71
allowance increased 122
second child 123
and Henry's legitimacy claim 137
debts 144, 156
Mardi Gras dinner 1897 148
divorce 155–7, 164–7
alimony 156
relationship with Henry 156, 170,
    199–200
infidelity accusation 165
slander action 166–7
courtesan lifestyle 167, 170
threatens to come to England 168–9
allowance 169–70, 199–200
and Lionel's death 197–8
decline 209
support for Henry 209
psychology 224
death 243, 248
stage career 243–8, **245, 247, 249**
resentments 244, 245
English stage debut 246–7
disappearance from record 248
Sackville West, Frédéric 39
Sackville West, Guy 254–8, **255**
Sackville West, Henry 7, **55**, 130
    birth 34
    birth certificate 34
    parentage 37
    visit to Arcachon 46–7
    childhood letters 53–4
    education 53–4, 65–6, 80
    learns of illegitimacy 65
    sent to South Africa 74, 80–3
    purchases farm 82–3
    and Victoria's engagement to Young
        Lionel 106–7
    and Victoria's wedding 110
    financial difficulties 125–8
    relationship with Victoria 126–8, 160–1,
        170–1
    visit to Europe 126–8
    learns registered as legitimate son 127
    claim to be recognised as Lord Sackville's
        heir 128

requests confirmation of legitimacy from
    father 130–2
response to circulars 134–9
supporters 135
creditors 144
and Béon 146–8
Mardi Gras dinner 1897 148
relationship with Flora 156, 170,
    199–200
suicide threat 157
reconciliation attempt with father 157–9
situation, 1898 160–3
debts 161
allowance settlement 162–3
life in Paris 163
engagement 170–1
relationship with father 171
Denuncia proceedings 172–8
alters Marriage Book Register 175–8
allowance stopped 178
continues investigations into legitimacy
    178–9
relaunches legitimacy claim 179
financial backing 179–81, 201
relationship with Max 183
reopens *Denuncia* proceedings 183
and Rophon's trial 186
files petition under Legitimacy
    Declaration Act, 1858 193
wife 194
father's funeral 196–7
requests appointment of official receiver
    204, **205**, 206
legitimacy affidavits 206
marriage by reputation evidence 206–7
case delays 207–8
Letters of Request 207–9
Flora's support for 209
and the High Court hearing 210–19
retires petition 218
income claim dismissed 223
re-hearing motion 223
psychology 223–4
death 226–30, 234, 235
decline 228–9
funeral 229
Sackville West, Mary (née Norton) 75–81,
    82, 107
Sackville West, Max 7, **37**
    birth 17–18
    father 18, 37, 139, 204
    education 48
    kidnap threat 53

father's visits 54
in South Africa 54–7, 75–81
relationship with father 57
learns of illegitimacy 75–9
engagement to Mary 75–81
visits London 76
marriage settlement 78–9, 80
purchase of Dartington 79–80
Henry sent to join 80–1
and Victoria's engagement to Young
    Lionel 106, 107
and Victoria's wedding 110
financial difficulties 124–5
relationship with Victoria 124–5, 224–5
and Henry's legitimacy claim 137–9
lack of trust in Béon 148–9
bankruptcy 163–4, 252
death of son 163–4
relationship with Henry 183
support for Victoria 201–4
and the legitimacy claim 202
blames Béon 203
and Henry's depositions 203–4
visit to England 224–5
relationship with Amalia 242–3
later life 251–4, **252**
Camden Hotel investment 252–4
death 279
Sackville West, Reginald 257–8
Sackville West, Vivian 224–5
Sackville West, Zelda 255–6
Sackville-West, Anne 269, 278
Sackville-West, Bertrand 194
Sackville-West, Cecilie 106
Sackville-West, Charles 62, 118, 239, 260,
    269–70, 278
Sackville-West, Eddy 136, 188–9, 260, 269
Sackville-West, Eva 194
Sackville-West, Lionel, 2nd Lord
    Sackville **9**
  family background 3
  introduced to Pepita 1
  relationship with Pepita 2–3, 6, 9–10,
      18–20, 24, 32–3, 33–9
  diplomatic career 3, 9, 19, 24, 32–3, 39,
      42, 48–9, 70–1
  possible father of Max 18
  separation from Pepita 19–20
  question of marriage to Pepita 23, 33–4,
      35, 40, 179, 212–13, 218–19
  purchase of Villa Pepa 24
  visits to Arcachon 30–1
  registration of children's births 34

and Pepita's death 39–40
Pepita's funeral 41
William Edward's loan 41–2
financial affairs 41–5, 75
debts 43–4, 50, 94
life in Buenos Aires 44–5
arrival in Argentina 49
relationship with Victoria 49, 53, 115,
    198
arrangements for children 49–50
visits to children 54, 58–9
relationship with Max 57
engages Mrs Mulhall 58
succession memorandum 61
heir to the title and to Knole 62
appointed British Minister to the
    United States 66
Victoria joins in Washington 66–7
in Washington 68, **69**
professional style 70–1
tells Victoria of illegitimacy 76
settlement on Max 78–9, 80
sends Henry to South Africa 80
and children's illegitimacy 83
and Flora's engagement 84–5
and Flora's marriage 86–7
the Murchison Affair 87–8, 106
recalled from Washington 87–9, 90
inherits Knole and title 89
and Mortimer's will 91
and Knole 93–4
in Cannes 95–6
and Victoria's engagement to Young
    Lionel 103–4
appearance 114, 136
preoccupation with money 115
increases Flora's allowance 122
Béon claims compensation from 123–4
loans to Henry 125–8
and Henry's visit to Europe 126–7
Henry requests confirmation of
    legitimacy 130–2
response to circular 135–7
settlement on Amalia 145–6, 149
and Béon's support of Henry 146–8
perpetuating testimony statement 152
deposition 153–4, 160
and Flora's divorce 156–7
Henry's reconciliation attempt 157–9
paternity doubts 160
and Henry's debts 161
Flora's allowance 169–70
relationship with Henry 171

Imparcial's account of meeting with
     Pepita 173–4
   Vita on 188
   health decline 188–9, 190–1, 192–4
   prostate cancer 192
   death 194
   funeral arrangements 194–5
   funeral 196–7, **197**
   estate 198, 199
   legacy 204
   marriage by reputation evidence 206–7,
     211–12, 213–14
Sackville-West, Lionel, 3rd Lord Sackville
     76–7, **144**, **261**
   first meets Victoria 98
   engagement to Victoria 100–9, **105**
   objections to marriage to Victoria 104
   wedding 109–12
   honeymoon 112
   wedded passion 113
   relationship with Amalia 114, 114–15
   London residence 116
   marriage blessed 119
   visit to Elveden Hall 129–30
   and Max 202–3
   victory celebrations 219–22, **222**
   and the Scott case **233**
   mistress 235, 240, 260, 261–3
   stops Amalia's allowance 237
   Savoy Hotel fancy-dress ball, 1911 238–9
   breakdown of relationship with Victoria
     259–65
   Victoria refuses to divorce 267
   appearance 268
   death 268–9
   funeral 271
Sackville-West, Mortimer 63, 75, 89, 90,
     92–3
Sackville-West, Reginald 62–3
Sackville-West, Victoria 6, **31**, **83**, **144**
   siblings 7
   birth 19
   life in Arcachon 30–3, 35
   parentage 37
   and Pepita's death 39–40
   relationship with father 49, 53, 115, 198
   education 50–3, 58, 60, 63–5
   First Communion 52
   social exclusions 52–3, 83–4
   status 52–3
   childhood family role 53
   father's visits 54
   learns of status 59–60

   name change 60–1
   shiftless existence 62
   tells Henry of illegitimacy 65
   joins father in Washington 66–7
   illegitimacy accepted in Washington 67
   voyage to Washington 68
   in Washington 68–75
   role in Washington 69–70, 71
   appearance 71, **72**, 136, 266
   'Book of Happy Reminiscences for My
     Old Age' 72, 265
   Washington suitors 72–3
   and marriage 73
   and finance 75
   and the succession 75
   father tells of illegitimacy 76
   and Henry in South Africa 82
   visiting cards 83
   return to London 83–4
   and Flora's engagement 84–5, 85–6
   and Flora's marriage 86–7
   leaves Washington 87–9
   return from Washington 90
   worries about status 94–5
   in Cannes 95–6
   and the Prince of Wales 95–6, 99, **154**,
     154
   engagement to L. C. 96–7
   and Amalia 97
   settles into Knole 97–100
   end of relationship with L. C. 98, 101–3
   first meets Lionel, later 3rd Lord
     Sackville 98
   Essenhigh Corke photographs 99, **100**
   and Knole 100–1, 102
   engagement to Lionel, later 3rd Lord
     Sackville 100–9, **105**
   benefits of marriage to Lionel 103
   objections to marriage to Lionel 104
   wedding 109–12
   honeymoon 112
   visits Arcachon 112
   wedded passion 113
   relationship with Amalia 113–18, 139–46,
     149–50
   London residence 116
   search for a husband for Amalia 116–18
   relationship with Flora 118–23, 168–71
   relationship with Gabriel Salanson
     118–23
   birth of Vita **119**, 119
   marriage blessed 119
   picture sale accusations 120

loans to Gabriel Salanson 121–2
and Béon's compensation claims 123–4
relationship with Max 124–5, 138–9,
   224–5
relationship with Henry 126–8, 160–1,
   170–1
visit to Elveden Hall 129–30
response to circular 135–7
Béon blames 147–8
warned of blackmail plot 149
perpetuating testimony statement 152
deposition 153
rapprochement attempt with Amalia
   154–5
and Flora's divorce 156, 164–7
and Henry's reconciliation attempt 157–9
in motor car **161**
visit to Exposition Universelle 168–9
visits Spain 172
anonymous letter, 1901 180
and Rophon's acquittal 187
money worries 189–90
relationship with Sir John Murray Scott
   189–90, 193
and Lionel's health 191, 192
sense of ingratitude 192–3
and father's death 194, 194–5
father's funeral 196, 197
leaves Knole 198–9, 262–3
draft letter to Henry 200–1
Max's support for 201–4
marriage by reputation evidence 206–7
supporters 207
and the High Court hearing 210–11
and illegitimacy 210–11
attachment to Knole 211
victory celebrations **220**, 220–2, **222**
Max visits 224–5
visit to Henry's grave 229
Scott inheritance 230, 232–4
and Henry's death 234, 235–6
visits Rodin 234–5
pays off Henry's debts 235
nervous breakdown 235–6
sisters' slanders 237–8
later relationship with Amalia 237–43
Savoy Hotel fancy-dress ball, 1911 238–9
and Amalia's marriage 240
and Lionel's affairs 240
and Flora's English stage debut 247
depression 259
breakdown of relationship with Lionel
   259–65

resentments 260
late visits to Knole 263–4
relationship with Knole 264–5
houses 266–7
refuses Lionel a divorce 267
and Lionel's death 268–70
offer to rent Knole 269–70
breakdown of relationship with Vita
   271–2
reconciliation with Vita 272–3
health decline 273
eccentricities 273–4
final years 273–6, **276**
Roof of Friendship Fund 274
sense of time 274
death 276
ashes scattered 277
memorial stone 277–8
Sackville-West, Vita **144**, **272**
   on Pepita's birthplace 3
   Pepita 6–7, 11–12, 22, 39–40, 65, 94–5,
      188, 210, 230, 232
   and the disinherited 22
   Knole and the Sackvilles 61–2
   birth of **119**, 119
   and Lionel Salanson 120–1
   in motor car **161**
   life at Knole 187–8
   on grandfather 188
   The King's Secret 193
   and grandfather's death 195–6
   attends High Court hearing 215–16
   victory celebrations **220**, 220, 222, **222**
   on the Scott inheritance 230, 232
   pet bear **231**
   Savoy Hotel fancy-dress ball, 1911 238–9
   and Amalia's marriage 240
   parenting skill 257
   relationship with Knole 265
   exile from Knole 270–1
   breakdown of relationship with Victoria
      271–2
   reconciliation with Victoria 272–3
   and Victoria's later years 274–5, 274–6
   and Victoria's death 276–7
   letter from Amalia 278–9
Sackville-West, William Edward 1, **144**
   loan to Lionel 41–2
   and Lionel's debts 43, 44
   and the succession memorandum 61
   tells Max of illegitimacy 76
   and Victoria's engagement to Young
      Lionel 103–4

St Petersburg 155
Salanson, Charles 85
Salanson, Gabriel 46–7, **121**, 243, 249
  Flora's engagement to 84–6
  and the illegitimacy 85
  marriage to Flora 86–7
  and Victoria's engagement to Young
    Lionel 107–9
  relationship with Victoria 118–23
  picture sale accusations 120
  financial affairs 121–2
  Victoria's loans to 121–2
  debts 144
  Mardi Gras dinner, 1897 148
  denies knowledge of Flora's illegitimacy
    153
  at the examination of witnesses 153
  infidelity 155, 165
  divorce 155–6, 165
  Max blames 203
  and the High Court hearing 215
  learns of Henry's death 226
Salanson, Lionel 120–1, 156, 169, 248–51,
  250, 251
Salanson, Louis 85
Salisbury, Marquis of 42
Sanchez, José 182–3, 183–7, **185**
Sandringham Estate 130
Saumarez, Baron 32–3
Saurin, Dudley 19
Savoy Hotel, fancy-dress ball, 1911 238–9
Saxe-Coburg, Duke of 24
Scott Case, the 232–3, **233**
Scott, Sir John Murray 168, 171, 189–90,
  190, 193, 195–6, 230, 232–4
Seligmann, Jacques 232–3
Sevenoaks, victory celebrations **220**,
  220–2, **222**
Singh, Prince Duleep 129–30
Sisters of St Joseph de Belley 50–3, 58
Sitwell, Osbert 260
Sitwell, Sir Sacheverell 241–2
social exclusions 52–3
Société Immobilière d'Arcachon 28
Société Pégat 121–2

South Africa 54–7, 75–81, 80–3, 251–8
Spain
  Denuncia proceedings 172–8
  marriage law 172–3
  Victoria visits 172
Speall's 75
Spring-Rice, Cecil 72, 84, 101, 110
Stonyhurst 65–6, 80
Streatham 267
Stubbs, Dorothy 221
Sturgis, John 68
Sturgis, Mary 68
succession memorandum 61

Teatro del Principe 4
Teatro Real 13
Thiers, Adolphe 42
Tichborne Claimant, the 134, 193
The Times 223–4, 247
Tobin, Mr 118
Tozer, Basil 246
Tregan, Georges 39
Turin 19, 19–20

Varty, Nourse 82
Versailles, Treaty of 239–40
Victoria, Queen 67, 91, 104
Vidal, Monsieur 244, 245
Vienna 13
Vigier, Madame 152
Villa Pepa, Arcachon 23–5, **25**, 30–3, 35,
  45–6, 50, 174
visiting cards 83

Walker, Hugh 116–17
Wallace Collection, the 230, 232, 235
Warbeck, Perkin 133
Washington DC 66–7, 68–75, 87–9
Weardale, Lord 207, 217
Wildernesse 93–4
Woods, Dr 235–6
Woolf, Virginia 268, 270, 276
Wyndham, Sir Hugh 207

Youssoup, Prince 10

After studying History at Oxford University, Robert Sackville-West worked in publishing, founding Toucan Books in 1985, which creates illustrated non-fiction books for an international market. He now combines that role with chairing Knole Estates, the property and investment company which runs the Sackville family's interests at Knole. In 2008, he and his wife and three children moved into the house, which has been occupied by the Sackville family for 400 years. His history of Knole and the Sackville family, *Inheritance*, was published by Bloomsbury in 2010.